THE KNOWING

BY

Gary Bonnell

Richman Rose Publishing, NA

THE *KNOWING*

Richman Rose Publishing, NA
Canada and The United States

ISBN: 1-879604-22-1
Library of Congress Control Number: 2004097151

This book presents nutrition and physical exercise information as well as transformative spiritual and psychological information, which may or may not be suitable for you. In view of the complex, individual and specific nature of health, fitness and psychological problems, this book is not intended to replace professional medical advice. Every individual is different. Get your medical provider's approval before starting any diet or exercise program, or changing an existing physical or psychological health regime. The Publisher and author expressly disclaim any responsibility for any loss, risk or injury incurred as a consequence of the application of the contents of this book.

The Knowing by Gary Bonnell
Editor: Linda Sousek

First Edition

**Published September, 2004 in the Japanese language by
Tokuma Shoten Publishing, Tokyo**

Printed in the United States of America.

Dedication

To my wonderful and lovely wife, Linda.
With you as my guide, I truly know love.

This work is dedicated to the tirelessly bold,
the compassionately courageous and all those
who so lightly hold The Knowing Way
in all its splendid forms.
Salute!

Acknowledgments

**Every work has its inspirations and angels
through which all is brought to bear.
A very special thanks to:**

My long time friend and colleague, Yuriko Ohno, whose work is most excellent in all ways. Her family has made my times in Japan whole and complete. To my friend and fellow essayist, Banana Yoshimoto. Her talent and great ease with words have given me joy and inspiration. To Chris Liaguno and John Walker, mighty companions, fellow followers and unravelers of things wholly misunderstood. To Lori DiGardi, Jack & Kaylee Mattingly and Othene Munson for their insights and provoking words as they ploughed through the first drafts of this "very easy" read. To my dear friends, Moko & Koichi Sakamoto, for their excellent intuition, connectedness, kindness and their son, Ken, for his wonderful music. Each of your life demonstrations are wonderful examples of community.

A very special thanks to Diane Jacobs for crossing all the "Ts" and dotting all the "Is" as she proofread the manuscript. Having a fine wordsmith makes all the difference. Thank you.

Other books by Gary Bonnell

ASCENSION The Original Teachings of Christ Awareness

YOUR BOOK of LIFE Accessing the Akashic Records

THE TWELVE DAYS of LIGHT

Table of Contents

THE *KNOWING*

Foreword

By Banana Yoshimoto

I wonder when Gary came into my life...

It was eight years ago when I first had a private Akashic reading session with Gary. That was the moment when I clearly understood the basic model of my life. It was so natural how we became friends. I don't remember the exact details of how it happened over time, but it was primarily through the kindness of Ms. Yuriko Ohno, our mutual friend and Gary's translator. We would have lunch or a cup of tea together each time he would visit Japan.

Concerning my personal private life: Gary told me that as I had had so many lifetimes as a male (yes, I understand this part well), so much so, that I had completed my masculinity. But the problem is, because I completed my male side, I can see weak points in any man. As for my work, my purpose in this life is to keep writing novels for the younger generation in the world, especially for those, who have insecurity or self-esteem issues.

Fortunately, I seldom forget my life purpose as a writer. Yet at times, when I am tired or when things get overly ambiguous; when I am overwhelmed by circumstances or when some peculiar ambition pushes me to write a novel, forcing me to set aside my family life until it is done or when I feel as though I might be cracking up…When these things happen, I always remember that Akashic reading session and in a way I can come back to my own framework. Not a framework that limits, but the framework of fundamental energy I chose before I came into this life. Remembering the reading always has the same affect: I feel recharged and I start walking my life path with renewed feelings and uplifted liveliness.

I was entering my thirties and in my thirties, my life was full of turbulence: I divorced, married, moved to a new place, ruined my health and recovered from it, had a baby… many things happened. During the period when these events were happening, we would visit with each other over lunch and enjoyable conversation. I always felt sort of secured and relaxed during our meetings and did not think about things too seriously. I have met too many people, so, I usually do not trust people easily. When I first met Gary, I simply thought,

"Well, a nice gentleman. Looks like Robin Williams; and besides he is psychic." But his warmth swept all my distrust. There is calmness and true love in his warm smile. Also under his quick direct words, there is something you cannot call other than love. Sometimes in his workshops, participants get angry when they are told things so directly with such pointed words. But please think about this: even if he is psychic, or a being beyond common reality, he is a human being with a physical body. He lives a comfortably affluent life with his family and the time when he had to work to make his living had finished long ago. Then why does he come all the way from America to Japan to spend time listening to strangers' problems while staying in a very small hotel room? I think it is because he loves his fellow human beings. His straight words are always given through his smile, and push people out from the darkness with the directness of the truth. Above all, I am just so happy that I could show my life and my growth to Gary.

When he seems sad, I feel sad and when he seems happy, I feel happy. This is all I want from our friendship. I never had expectations for an Akashic reading or wanted him to spiritually guide me. He does not have such desire himself. He does not want people to do something for him, nor does he have any expectations from others. Actually, you can seldom, if ever, find such a person like that. Gary gives his attained wisdom completely without any hesitation. To live his life means to share what he knows. Not because he wants to become a guru, but just to share. Each time I meet Gary, I think "I feel so happy that I could see him today." Both Gary and his pretty wife Linda have wonderfully bright smiles. Just looking at Gary and Linda smiling makes me happy. Such a cute couple they are! No restrictions, no secret intentions exist between the two. They are softly caring for each other.

When Gary's mother passed away, I gave him condolence. "This experience will come to all human beings," he said. But his eyes were sad and that made my heart ache. I felt love for his being a human. Such a being who knows so much, he still is a human being with emotions just as we are. This is an example that through great knowing and human frailty, we have unlimited possibilities. The possibility to know beyond what we have learned and to feel all we know.

This book is very difficult to read, but the information – the knowing we can feel deep within – is clearly written. As you read, you can feel the information coming to you with power. It is like a modern version of Swedenborg. I think the most critical point is that this book is written for "us who are living now in this present world." Up to now, there are so many people trying to give us information of ancient wisdom through books. I have been eagerly studying Carlos Castaneda. In his book, Don Juan said, "Our assemblage point is the same, so we humans share the same reality. But if we move that point with intention, we have possibility to live a different reality." His idea has the same meaning as Gary's knowing, though the way of expressing it is different. Yet, we are not ancient Mexicans or an old Native American Indian whose parents were killed through racial discrimination or hopeless poverty. Those expressions of wisdom backed with the teachings of a severe life, do not fit us in this modern world.

We now have many new problems. The environment of Earth is suffering like never before. Yes, most of the population has the basics, such as food. However, war exists because there is too much food in one place and hardly any in another. There is a growing gap among ideas of different generations and cultures. It is so hard for us to shift our thoughts to unity because of this widening gap. Because there is an excess of information, our over intellectualization is creating people to be less grounded in their bodies and relationships. We are taught to live and survive in contemporary societies, but the stressful issue of money diminishes our quality of life. We created time and its defined flow, which now seems to be collapsing to the point that we cannot deal with it emotionally. Before we know it, we are pushed to a premature death we did not choose.

These new anguishes are particular to the people living in the present day, and yet, this Knowing book of ancient wisdom will give you answers to these and other current issues. What is written in this book is firmly corresponding to us today and due to Gary's own rich experience of manifestation, the information takes a more sophisticated form.

Gary wrote that it takes understanding the contents to practice the immediate solutions outlined in this book. Actually, he planted this kind of knowing device here and there in the book. It is stressed that you need to understand the teaching and that you cannot attain the ability of manifestation unless you understand the basic teachings. If you physically use your body to just practice the techniques, you will be on a different path, but in order to move forward in the process "understanding" is indispensable. He also states, if you can achieve the state where your body integrates the teaching, then everything written in this book will come true in your reality.

"To move the assemblage point", "to go beyond one's framework" or in this book, "to go beyond consensual reality" is to know the Beginning Moment of your Soul: to know who you are, and to use your words and intention to manifest your reality in the moment. Then, ultimately you will be able to even live without eating. Of course, I have not reached this state, yet. I vaguely understand how the creation works and feel it with my physical body. Sometimes I am successful a little with manifesting my own reality. This is my current level. Still I am on my way, but this book will be my great support for me, as well as, Gary himself. This pathway is not only for one person. Other people have been on this path before. This is the pathway of eternity existing beyond the flow of time. When Castaneda dropped on his knees looking at God in the bright light, Don Juan professed calmly that it was only a template of a human being. Gary has this same calmness.

The most important thing is Gary's eyes, looking at the truth without any fear. He writes about Souls and about the purpose of life with a clear and precise explanation of reincarnation. He writes about the history of the Earth and humankind and the purpose of life all from a different point of view. He writes about manifestation as one's ultimate creation not from greed but from joy. Gary describes these concepts thoroughly in detail with his unruffled calmness. It must have been tempting for him to use simple phrases when explaining these ideas, but he did not and instead goes to the last inch in explaining the concepts. Unless you are really willing to understand them, this book might seem difficult in some aspects. That is why this book has the emanation of wisdom and love. I think this is a very beautiful book. Gary puts unattainable information into sentences of high level and creates a book to give to anybody who wants it. This is Gary's commitment and I really feel great joy deep from my heart because of his decision.

After a long break, I had Gary's private session again in Spring of 2002. In that session, Gary said to me through his smile, " There is a little soul flying around you. And it is trying to get in. You went to Egypt recently" he asked. "I think you liked one of the temples very much, the temple of Isis. Many lives ago you were standing there with that little soul together hand in hand. You were a mother and that child was a girl." I was a bit shocked, since I really liked only one temple in Egypt. That temple was discovered under water, and moved to a little island. It is called, "The Temple of Love." The first time I saw it, it appeared to me as though it were surrounded by a warm pink light. The temple felt so familiar and safe. Without any reason, I almost cried.

When Gary told me that I said to him, "Well…right now I am too busy and it is impossible to have a baby in this life…! I have no intention to have one!" and I laughed. One month after the session, all of sudden I found myself pregnant. I don't know the exact conception date. I keep seeing Gary while I was pregnant and after the delivery…as usual. The person to whom my child first waved his hand was Gary. When Gary waved his hand to my baby who had just turned one year old, without hesitation, the baby waved back to him smiling. Gary advised, "Wave to him emanating your true inner light." (You know this is not so easy!) So I tried to wave to him with that in my mind, but my baby did not wave back. Gary is such a mysterious man…

I wonder when Gary entered my life? Maybe he came into my life eons ago. We must have been friends in several lifetimes. This idea naturally came into my mind. We could have killed each other, hated each other, loved each other and did things together….we did these things sometime, somewhere….That is why we are naturally together now. And as long as I am staying in this body as this soul, I will keep respecting and having love towards Gary.

Fall of 2004
Banana Yoshimoto

~ *About Banana Yoshimoto* ~

With her first work, *Kitchen,* Ms. Yoshimoto won the 6th Kaien Newcomer Writers Prize in November of 1987 and then the 16th Izumi Kyoka Literary Prize in January, 1988.

She was also awarded the 39th edition, Best Newcomer Artists Recommended by the Minister of Education in August 1988 with *Kitchen* and *Utakata/Sankuchuari.*

In March 1989 *GoodbyeTsugumi* was awarded the 2nd Yamamoto Shugoro Literary Prize.

In November,1995 *Amurita* won the 5th Murasaki-shikibu Prize named after the authoress of the Story of Genji. *Amurita* was awarded prizes in Italy; Literary Prize Scanno in June, 1993 and Fendissime Literary Prize in March,1996 and Literary Prize Maschera d' argento in November, 1999.

In October of 2000 *Furin to Nanbei* was awarded the 10th edition Bunkamura Duet Magot Literary Prize.

Her collection of short stories available in English through Grove Press include – Kitchen, Lizard, N.P., Amrita, Goodbye Tsugumi, and Asleep.

Orientation

~ *The Knowing Way* ~

This work is concerned with the spiritual knowing of humanity and not with organized religion. While the rhetoric herein is clearly against corporate religion, it does hold with extremely high regard those individuals who, for brief moments in time, demonstrated for all to witness, the brilliance of each Soul's natural radiance. The names alone of such wonderful human expressions could fill volumes. Individuals such as Archimedes, Babaji, Buddha, Confucius, Jesus the Nazarene, Kuthumi, Leonardo de Vinci, Mary of Sepphoris, Mary Magdalene, Mohammad, Moses, Oshoka, Patanjali, Paramahansa Yogananda, Quan Yin, Saint Bernadette (Bernadette Soubirous), Saint Catherine (Catherine Laboure), Saint Nicholas of Bari, Sananda, Serapis Bey, Socrates, Thoth, etc., and all those whose lives have gone unrecorded or whose mention has been obliterated through conquests and plunder, are the real focus of this presentation. Organized religion has reached its zenith with the advent of the jihad period through which we now collectively find ourselves sluggishly wading. This does not mean that the wonderful purity central to those organizations is to be lost. To the contrary, people will soon begin to awaken to the greater truth, the mysticism found at the center of all religions.

Before the present millennium, spiritual organizations and religious collectives were essential to Western humanity's relief from the slavery of the crippling superstitions that became horribly exaggerated during the feudalism of the Dark Ages of Medieval Europe. It is true that the three major Western religions of the last five hundred years, Judaism, Christianity, and Islam, have given a dynamic cohesion to their faithful through a pronounced hope for a better afterlife. It is also true that humankind has been held back by the hardened dogmatic beliefs fostered by competing gods, their lawgiver (Moses), messiah (Jesus) and last prophet of God (Mohammad) respectively. It took Christianity from its legalization in AD313 through the fall of the Roman Empire, up until 1000 CE to integrate the local religious customs of the peoples of Europe and the Mediterranean into a singular cohesive religion that worked as governance for most of the civilizing cultures. Once established, the Church ruled across kingdoms and countries with a mighty hand through the systematic devastation of rival religions such as the Church-declared heretical Cathari (Gnostics) and Waldenses or non-Catholic Christians and through such atrocities as Pope Gregory IX's papal inquisition. What of the crusades? While Christianity drove its stake through the heart of competing ideologies by incorporating the fabric of their indigenous offerings into its only-son-of-god doctrine, Islam was busy replacing Mithraicism, with its harsh eye-for-an-eye dictates from the only true god, Allah's, "last" prophet, Mohammed. At the same time isolated medieval Hebrew communities devoted to pious study of the law were giving way to the more materialistically motivated modern Judaic movement whose primary focus was to secure a place in the world through financial dominance, while socially isolating itself through rigid adherence to Judaic Law. Thomas Jefferson put it succinctly in 1782 when he noted for posterity: "Millions of innocent men, women and children, since the introduction of Christianity, have been burnt, tortured, fined and imprisoned; yet we have not advanced one inch towards uniformity." If we replace "Christianity" with "organized religion", we can take sole responsibility off Christianity alone and more realistically understand the dogmatic dynamics that have brought us to the jihad we now face.

While it is true that each of the World's major religions carries within its core the truth of our unique place in creation, it is also true that all the World's religions have become self-interested and self-serving corporations that are more focused on cultivating blindly following members than sharing the greater knowing they have to offer. The three Abrahamic religions – Judaism, Christianity and Islam – representing almost half of the World's population, see this present age as a time for the conversion of Souls into each of their respective paths as assurance for their salvation. Each of these religions believes they must fill their ranks with the conversion of Souls; if not the conversion, then the complete annihilation, each of the other, through a holy war that will ultimately end with the one true religion's World dominance: all this waste and suffering just to prove the victor's religion as the one true way, or in the old vernacular, might equals right. Perhaps a more accurate definition of hell would be more aptly expressed as being forced to live for eternity in another's version of heaven.

All religions, no matter how widely accepted or integrated into a given culture, begin as cults and practice cult-like techniques to enlist and manage their faithful. As they grow, these organizations develop dogmatic guidelines, first as a way of controlling groups of individuals, then as a means of governing the masses. We are at the beginning of an age when we will once again experience the phenomenon of a unified creation free of the survival and deliverance filters that have so imaginatively distorted our pure awareness of Creator God. We are now at a time in our collective journey toward liberation when blindly following a religious order or the spiritual dictates of those individuals who proclaim to know the "only" way to salvation is counterproductive to complete emancipation from human suffering. Without universal, unrestrained revelation leading to self-realization, illumination, enlightenment and finally liberation, we will not collectively experience our release from the limitations imposed by our Souls incarnating into Dyadic matter.

With the recent (the last hundred years or so) advent of our right to pursue heretical, or non-church related paths to more fully understanding the nature of our cosmic predicament, we, as a collective gathering of Souls, have allowed the former knowledge of creation from a past civilization and epoch to once again present itself. This is The Knowing Way from the later Lemurian and Atlatian periods.

The Knowing Way material offered through this work is put forward as a guide to understanding how it is that we have come to be here in this physical dimension and how it is that we can best utilize our time here as observers of creation. This is meant as a reminder of our unique place within the great creative template; of how we were derived and how it is we can best serve ourselves and then other Souls as they gain a more expansive understanding of themselves through the revelation of creation's order. This is not a religion, nor is it a cult of exclusivity that allows in only those who are willing to subjugate their wills to superstitiously based doctrines or harshly legislated dogmas of a priestly class. This work is a message of life that has survived the ages and is once again relevant to collective humanity's endeavors toward knowing its unique place in creation.

~ How to get the most out of this book ~

Read all the chapters without practicing the lifestyle suggestions, then go back and reread each chapter incorporating as much of the practice section, reflective thoughts, invocations and lifestyle suggestions as is practical for your current circumstances. It is important that you feel at home with the material being offered before fully integrating the concepts into your daily life. Chapters one through five are broken into four sections: the main subject, a chapter practice section, chapter thoughts and a chapter lifestyles suggestion; chapters six through eleven each have five sections by adding an additional invocation section to the existing sections. Each section within the chapter is meant to work with the chapter subject except when one of the subsequent sections is reviewed in the next chapter as a continuation of that teaching.

The content of the main subject of each chapter is comprised of material taken from The Knowing Way text material as it has been updated, then verified and supplemented through information contained in the Akashic Records. The main subject of each chapter is meant to challenge long held beliefs concerning humanity's place within the creative schematic. Rereading the main subject several times will allow the reader time to integrate the more subtle offerings. Challenge the information being offered by asking how the information will allow you a more expansive view of creation and a greater volume of joy. The material of the main subject will be of little value if the reader remains wholly the same after being exposed to its message.

Each chapter practice section is offered as a method for unlocking conflicts that keep intuitive perceptions minimal. The effects of regularly using the practice sections will be to shift your conscious awareness away from just using your intellect to decipher the content of the mystical knowing contained in each chapter. Some practice sections will be very familiar and easy to implement while others will seem all at once foreign and perhaps even repelling. For the most expedient results, it is best if the student sticks with the section as it is written. Taking the more enjoyable pieces from one section to blend with the offerings of another might seem creative, but will offer less impressive results.

The chapter thoughts are meant to act as internal affirmations and mantras. These "thoughts" are meant to stimulate your own mental processes regarding the material being offered. Journal your own thoughts as you begin remembering your birthright, then share them with others as a means of solidifying them in your body, mind and Spirit. Jesus the Nazarene stated, "You are the Truth and the Light." Choose thoughts that reflect that truth and you will begin to operate as the Christ you are.

Because you are a Soul, a First State Being, every word you speak into the ethers of planet Earth is a sacred vow. This is the most important aspect of this work. Invocations are vocal commands that become directly manifest within our experience as "called" substance from the subtle body of Earth. Every word you speak eventually manifests in some form or another and has its primary reality at the level it manifests. Taking direct command over the eventuality of your words becoming manifest is important if you are to, "Be in the World and not of the World." You will no longer rely exclusively on the gross energies of Earth to fulfill your purposeful needs once you begin "calling" thoughts directly into form.

The lifestyles suggestion section is comprised of information taken from various health disciplines, cultural ideologies from around the world and directly from the Akashic Records. This section is devoted to how mammalian bodies acquire, assimilate and dispel lifeforce energy referred to in ancient texts as chi, prana, ki or ka. This section is presented in three areas of interest: meditation, diet and exercise. Meditation is listed first because it is through meditation and the conscious control of breath that the physical human body most effectively utilizes lifeforce energy. As for diet: from very early on we are told we must eat to be strong, so we do. The average individual never questions this, so they continue eating, more out of physical habit or emotional need than to be strong. Exercise is of the utmost importance to mental clarity and physical longevity. We need only get thirty minutes a day of sustained aerobic activity to feel fully present in our bodies. Body sculpting through extreme exercise programs is of little value and may cause considerable damage that will lessen your day-to-day quality of life as your body ages. The saying, "No pain, no gain," is quietly being replaced with, "No strain, no pain." Remember to incorporate a warm-up and cooling-off period before and after any exercise program to avoid injury.

It is true that we are better in body, mind and Spirit when we are fully present in life, unfettered by the 'what-if' and 'if-only' intrusions of our ever-rehearsing mind. Using the practical exercises and meditation techniques offered through this book will dramatically shift your awareness, if conscientiously applied. This shift in conscious awareness will give you a greater frame of reference with which to observe life. These shifts can sometimes mask or euphorically override chronic issues that relate to your physical health or mental well-being. It is well documented that a sudden shift in perceptions can ease physical, mental or emotional pain and this is not a cure or even a true indication that a chronic condition is actually changing. This new-lease-on-life exhilaration is important to the dynamics of change but can be deadly under the wrong circumstances. Be careful in making life-altering decisions. It is important to consult a qualified licensed health care professional before dramatically changing any diet or exercise programs, especially if you have any chronic conditions that would make any significant alterations in lifestyle dangerous to your overall health. It is highly recommended that you consult a physician before prolonged fasting, liver or colon cleansing or altering the intake of carbohydrates by dramatically reducing the fat to carbohydrate ratio, especially if you are more than twenty percent above the ideal weight for your body type. In short, be very responsible to your body. It is your most important relationship. It is impossible to completely command the body if you lack an intimate relationship with the body.

Gary Bonnell
Naples, Florida
Fall of 2004

"Thought manifests
as the word;
The word manifests
as the deed;
The deed develops
into habit;
And habit hardens
into character;
So watch the thought
and its ways
with care,
And let it spring
from love born out
of concern for all
beings....
As the shadow follows
the body,
As we think, so we become."

—. *Siddhartha Buddha*

Introduction

~ The Atlatian Knowing Way ~

The subject of this work is the nature of our presence in creation as known from the Akashic Records and from the spiritual traditions of the global civilizations of Lemuria (now China) and Atlatia or Atlantis as it was referred to in Plato's dialogues, *Timaeus* and *Critias,* around 370 BCE. Plato estimated the destruction of Atlatia to be ten thousand years before his birth in 427 BCE and placed the continent of Atlantis just off the Isle of Gibraltar in the Atlantic Ocean. The Akashic Records show the Atlatian civilization as a global civilization whose geographical center was in the valley called Os Sira (from the Akashic Records) in what is now known as the Mediterranean Sea, existing there for approximately thirteen thousand years during the approximate period between twenty-six to thirteen thousand years Gregorian. The Atlantic Ocean was kept from filling the valley by a natural dam, running from North Africa at Morocco to southern Spain, that was some thirty kilometers (over eighteen miles) thick. At the other end of Os Sira, the Nile River flowed out into the valley floor creating a freshwater inland sea that covered an oval-shaped area from what is now the coast of Italy at the Ionian Sea south to the Gulf of Sirte at Libya. The Nile continued north through a series of closely linked lakes and cascading waterfalls, to finally form a large lake situated slightly north off the Sardinian coast extending its banks northward to the coast of what is now Spain. The lesser of the two bodies of water was, for the most part, relatively shallow with a spongy peat bog-like bottom and was used for growing a now extinct form of reed. This reed was one of the only naturally occurring material objects used by the Atlatians in their daily lives, being used primarily for the creation of containers for storing water.

In the center of the larger lake were a series of loosely formed concentric islands that were created when an ancient volcano had erupted toward the end of the Jurassic period. Knowing the volcano to be extinct, the Atlatians used these islands as the ceremonial capital of their society creating them to be eternal cities built of special metals and extremely hard stone.[1] While there were wilderness outposts, the furthest being in Peru, through which the Atlatians observed the more slowly evolving primitive peoples, this exceedingly sophisticated civilization thrived in the fertile areas along the Nile and around the banks of the two great lakes. They created city centers and villages founded on the ideals of unified personal interaction, with every community member being a valued resource and an individuated point of communion with the Divine. Because of their expanded empathic and telepathic abilities, all Atlatians were in constant harmonic attunement to nature and each other. This allowed them vast insights into the evolutionary desires of the varied life forms on Earth, giving them a wonderful sense of cooperation between all species. Because of the surrounding cold arid regions to the north, much of the warm Nile water was channeled into expanded population areas throughout the valley floor where many different forms of non-consumptive agriculture were practiced, giving rise to many new species of plants as seed-bearing hybrids. The only evidence of how the Atlatians used the water of the Nile to keep a productive climate within the valley floor is found in how the Incans used water to extend their growing seasons well beyond the first snowfalls of the winter season. The life-giving waters of the Nile expertly channeled through Os Sira, kept the valley in a perpetual paradisiacal state during the encroachment of ice fields of the last Ice Age. There is a mass of archaeological evidence indicating some two hundred cities on the Mediterranean seabed corresponding to the natural flow of the Nile as it meanders away from the African continent. Scientists will only privately speculate as to the reason for these seabed sites for fear that any public speculation will bring censure and ridicule from colleagues and those funding their projects.

It has been speculated that the inhabitants of Atlatia were highly advanced with abilities beyond our present technology. The Akashic Records do not show the types of advancement we would want to associate with a highly mechanized culture, but instead indicate profound achievements in areas very unfamiliar to us. This is so primarily because their technological advancements were not hinged on our scientific models of substance endurance and energy transmission velocities. The Atlatian advancements were generated through the manifestation of thought forms from within the etheric body of the planet projecting into actualized matter within a single moment as a whole expression. The vast times needed to generate the different Earth substances were sidestepped through this manifestation of thought into form. There were no production lines, parts factories or assembly plants in Atlatia. Unlike rapidly degenerating Earth matter, Atlatian manifest forms held their integrity without having any effect on or being at the influence of their rapidly changing environment. The Atlatians were acutely aware of any influences their manifest forms had on nature, making sure to limit the life of all actualized forms to the apparent need of the originator. The only manifest forms that endured beyond the collective Atlatian culture were certain metallic-like substances they generated for their ceremonial centers, such as those found at Delphi and Tiahuanaco. The Atlatians did create the odd temple or two from Earth's substances, such as the Sphinx and pyramid complex at Giza and the temples at Delphi, but sadly, little remains of their self-generated forms.

One of the most profound differences between our modern world and theirs was the harnessing of thought energy as a raw power. In several burial tombs in Egypt, a particular glyph is drawn showing individuals placing their heads up against a transparent eggplant shaped tube that is attached at one end to a square box. The Akashic Records show these structures to be thought amplification modules. Certain genetic groups within the Atlatian culture were trained to generate very specific bands of thought energy. These bands of energy were stored at varying magnitudes, and then later amplified for use by everyone as an adjunct to their own etheric energy. It is because of this power base that most of the Atlatian system of technology was not grounded in the lower vibrational frequencies of Earth, but existed more as holographic-like forms operating within the etheric body of the planet, just outside the laws of our known physics. Those individuals who introduced new forms of technology into actualized matter always considered the implications their advancement would have on nature before lowering the substance form of the technology into the energy fields of the physical body of the planet.

During a thirteen thousand year cycle of unity,[2] such as the one enjoyed by the Atlatians, the currency of exchange was pure unadulterated creativity. In this state, there is no real concern for wealth because each individual is more than aware of his or her intrinsic value to the whole and does not find a personal valuation in material possessions. Because of this, the achievements of the Atlatians seem more pure or more advanced to the casual Akashic observer. Faced with the cycle of separation and duality we have lived within for the last thirteen thousand years, we, as a whole, have advanced in areas unknown to the Atlatians or even the Lemurians before them. In this sense, we might seem more advanced to them if they were to look our way along the time continuum.

The most lasting and still perplexing artifact of the pre-epochal Atlatian culture creations was the pyramid.[3] This is so because the Atlatians understood the natural influence of pure geometric shapes on human consciousness with square shapes locking in mental vibrational fields; circles dispersing unfocused emotional energy; cones magnifying mental acuity and triangles amplifying pure intention and corresponding etheric fields. The four-sided cone shape of the pyramid brings two of the influences together – magnified mental acuity and pure intention amplified through analogous etheric fields. When the Atlatians needed to move mountains, they did it with pyramidal shapes. All human intention is placed within the etheric body of the planet on the voice. Pyramidal shapes lend authority to the human voice by amplifying the etheric fields within the modulations of the voice harmonics bringing the full intention to bear on the object or subject. The Atlatians harnessed this energy to move heavy objects within the influence of known physics by gathering the energy of the voice around the object to be displaced, moving the gathered etheric energy instead of the object. In this sense, the pyramidal shape itself built the great pyramids of Giza. They used pyramids in every aspect of their daily culture in that they built temples to withstand the ages. They even introduced the geometric technologies to the uninitiated humans living outside the influences of the unity wave that they encountered at their outposts in the wilderness areas of what is now North, Central and South America. One gentleman of modern times knew the secret of this dynamic and publicly demonstrated it by constructing the

The primary city centers of Atlatia were destroyed when the land bridge connecting the continents of Africa and Europe was breached during a natural disaster. This cataclysm was generated as the top third of the African continent dropped as much as forty meters (131 feet) on its uppermost northern and northwestern boundaries, flooding the valley for roughly forty days and nights as is told in the historical document, the Hebrew Bible or Old Testament. This event also created what is now the Red Sea, and through a series of subsequent minor events, later formed the Black and Caspian Seas. Because of their advance knowing of the coming disaster, the Elders of Atlatia arranged to have most of their important artifacts sent to temple complexes high above the valley floor in what are now the coastal areas of the Mediterranean Sea. The one thing the general population of Atlatia did not know was that the natural disaster reshaping every aspect of their existence also directly coincided with the new thirteen thousand-year cycle of energy that shifted the collective human consciousness on and in the etheric body of the planet into the present age of separation. The bulk of those Atlatians who escaped the floods first formed the Sumerian culture, then later the Minoan, early Greek, Roman and Egyptian cultures, while a smaller group traveled to what is now the greater island chains of the Caribbean and later to North America. What had worked for the Atlatians during their thirteen thousand years in Os Sira no longer applied to the experience unfolding before them in the new cycle of separation and duality. They were completely unprepared for the experience of duality that pushed them into forming tribes and clans and kingdoms. They were jarred by the overwhelming fears of having to survive in a world without empathic and telepathic communication. They found it increasingly difficult to comprehend the new focus of complex emotional and mental energies overwhelming their Souls' consciousness. Their bodies began to hurt from having to use more and more muscle tissue. The vast majority of Atlatians seemed to immediately forget the purity of the past age and became focused on manipulation to gain, especially in areas of sexuality and greed.

A small group of Elders held the complete knowing of the previous collective experience during the age of unity. They had quietly known about the coming shift back to duality and separation from the Lemurian texts that had survived the cyclical shift from separation and duality into unity. This small group was responsible for the building of the Giza complex one thousand years before the shift as a future place to store the ancient texts that recorded and predicted all the ages of humankind's journey upon Earth from that time forward. With a silica or crystalline-based technology for storing records, they had preserved a chronicle of the Earth's history, giving a complete accounting for the Lemurian and Atlatian cycles. They did this knowing that in thirteen thousand years humanity would have the technology to extract the information and hopefully the spiritual maturity to move into the coming cycle of unity with the knowledge of what had gone before.

The Akashic Records give startlingly similar progressions between the Lemurians and our present global civilization, so much so that in most ways we are the same in our desire to control the elements of nature through the manipulation of our environment with one small difference: the Lemurians valued harmony and balance above their individual existence. If the important details of their thirteen thousand-year journey that ended twenty-six thousand years ago were illustrated in text, the reader would think it was an account of the past nine thousand years of history. Many Lemurians actively refused to make the transition to unity at the end of the last period of separation and duality, just as there are those now who would kill and be killed to hold onto the beliefs of separation as we enter this new cycle of unity now upon us. In the last hundred years of their duality cycle, most Lemurians failed to realize the "Kingdom of God" within themselves and perished in a global conflict that pitted differing belief-based cultures against one another in a fight for world domination. Those individuals who did survive had already made the shift in consciousness before the wars began. As a result, they were led to be at the right place at the right time, suffering little or no pains of the global conflict. This will again be the case with humanity: some will struggle against unity; others will find it natural to their existence.

~ The History of The Knowing Way ~

Before we get to the heart of the material of The Knowing Way, it seems important to cover some history of how the information survived the natural disasters and karmic calamities of humanity since the shift into separation at the end of the Atlatian period thirteen thousand years ago.

As was stated, approximately thirteen thousand years ago the collective consciousness of humanity shifted from one of unity into the duality of separation. Before this shift everything and everyone was honored and acknowledged by all other forms of consciousness as integral facets within the whole of creation. After the shift, duality clouded intuitive awareness and telepathic expression, plunging a suddenly vulnerable humanity into suspicion and intolerance for anything different from itself. Before the shift, collective humanity stood as the highest pinnacle of evolution on Earth. Then, as if overnight, the human herd became the most divisive form of life on the planet. It was as though everything they knew to be true would not work. Families and extended families clung to one another trying as best they could to communicate their overwhelming experience through gestures and unintelligible utterances. It took a significant block of time for the collective mind to develop an effective means of communicating its remembrance of what had taken place during the shift to separation. Because of this, much of the history of life on the planet prior to the shift was lost to the inadequacies of the new languages used to recount the events, as humanity came forward in time from the period when all was known through telepathic expression, empathic impression and manifest holographic thought projection. A small number of Atlatians remained fully conscious at the apex of the shift,[4] retaining all the abilities afforded through unity of body, mind and Spirit. They had been ritually preparing for the new cycle based upon the information presented in the Lemurian scrolls. This group also knew that an expansiveness of body, mind and Spirit in a new unity period would once again cycle through humanity in the distant future. That group makes up a portion of the circle of Dyadic Bodhisattva and awakened Triadic Souls that watches, inspires and encourages all of present day humanity to a greater knowing of life beyond the separation of duality.

Apart from the Earth-derived Souls of the Bodhisattva, there was a group of individuals, The Brothers of Light,[5] who dedicated themselves to preserving The Knowing Way, a global understanding of creation and humanity's place within the great schematic of life. The Lemurians[6] had first pieced together the knowing of our Soul's role in Creation. They had openly shared this with the Atlatians just before a sequence of conflicts nearly destroyed their entire civilization some twenty-six thousand years ago, which, coincidentally, happened right at the point when humanity was entering the thirteen thousand year Atlatian period of unity. The Atlatians used this Knowing Way to build their civilization into a gathering of humanity that lived in perfect balance with nature. The Lemurians consumed the resources of the Earth; the Atlatians brought substance into physical form by verbally commanding its existence from out of the Earth's subtle etheric body. The cycle of unity that overtook the Atlatians allowed for this expanded ability, whereas the Lemurians, holding onto their long-held traditions and beliefs, still struggled under the idea that they had to use the physical body of the Earth to manifest their needs. A good number of those Lemurians who did understand, awakened to the new cycle of unity, knew and demonstrated the expanded abilities, but instead of leaving their Soul gathering, chose to stay and guide the stubbornly willful Lemurians who did not consciously make the transition from duality to unity. These knowing Lemurians could have joined the Atlatians or they could have gone off on their own, but chose instead to stay with their community to help those who would spontaneously awaken during the next several centuries after the shift. These few spiritually awakened leaders took the Lemurian remnant into seclusion, away from the conflict that would be created if those who had not awakened witnessed the effortless Atlatian way of life. This isolation was also necessary if the new Atlatian experiment was to begin on an even footing without the threat of those Lemurians who would not allow unity within their experience and sought to eradicate this new effortlessness through the waging of wars.

During this five hundred-year transition, the few Lemurians who became knowingly unified in body, mind and Spirit retreated into what is present-day central China, and began to systematically hide their technological treasures and prized artifacts by burying them en masse. Whole temples along with everything from statuary to the pebbles that paved the walkways were transported to areas known to be safe from natural disasters. They even buried seven astrological pyramids, identical to the one attributed to Cheops (Kofu), that were a gift from the Atlatians as a tribute for the sharing of The Knowing Way. They did this because of the future visions showing that one day, in the not-so-distant future, they would be overrun and conquered by primitive Northern invaders. In essence, the Lemurians systematically buried everything of any real importance and took up lifestyles of simple farmers. Because their civilization existed before the Atlatian shift into unity, the Lemurians had developed a written language and it is because of this written history,[7] later stored by the Atlatians, that the modern world will soon fully understand humanity's complete journey on Earth. Many astounding artifacts will be found buried in perfectly preserved tombs that will tell of Lemurian history and their interaction with the Atlatians as they moved into the new thirteen thousand-year cycle twenty-six thousand years ago.

For several generations The Brothers of Light (also known as the White Brotherhood) was comprised only of direct descendants of the Atlatians. It was believed that the Atlatian bloodline was as important as The Knowing Way material itself because it contained a direct experience of unity within its cellular structures. In a sense, this ideation of bloodline significance was the beginning of royalty and priestly classes, such as the ones that flourished in Egypt immediately after the last shift and that continue today through all of the World's religions.

The Brothers of Light, who saw to it that The Knowing Way artifacts and materials were kept for future generations, moved with great stealth among common humanity after the Atlatian period of unity ended. Because they retained their expanded abilities from the Atlatian unity cycle they oftentimes hid in plain view from their enemies, those who would kill them for being so effortless amongst so much toil and sorrow. After a period, some of these individuals deliberately began to use their abilities to confuse enemies by projecting images of themselves in stone statuary or shape shifting[8] into fierce hybrid forms, such as griffins or harpies, to scare off would-be attackers. These types of events occurred with greater regularity as populations began to spread into the areas where the Order maintained its temples. Many of the lesser gods described in Greek and Roman myths have their origins in the actions of those Atlatians who remained fully conscious after the shift and by necessity commingled with spiritually unconscious humans. Some of the original Atlatian Elders are still with us, keeping their vigil until we enter this next wave of unity. The name of this group has changed from time to time and has been centered in alternating cultures around the globe, and, the function of this group has remained the same to guard The Knowing Way information until it is once again acceptable to collective humanity.

The Knowing Way teachings of Atlatia came into the possession of the pre-Amun priest cult of Egypt through Thoth, some 10,500 years[9] BCE. The Egyptian priestly class, along with Pharaoh's family, was initiated into The Knowing Way during the period of Thoth. Thoth was to Egyptian culture what Patanjali was to the Hindus culture; both were the givers of knowledge and The Knowing Way; both gave the teachings in such as manner as to make it practical for the peoples of their regions and both were deified by their cultures as a result of their efforts. Somewhere around 8,500 BCE, other portions of The Knowing Way material came into the countries of the Middle East from the Lemurian remnant in the Far East. The Knowing Way became known in present epoch China as The Tao, and only resembles the original teachings of the Lemurian and the Atlatian unity period in that its message to humanity emphasizes simplicity in all things through non-judgment. This direct Lemurian teaching from the Far East was slightly different from the Mediterranean version in that it did not focus on the Solar Deity[10] as was the case in Egypt. The Eastern approach stressed the hierarchal structure of Soul Beings (First State Beings) as they relate to the phenomenon of human consciousness on Earth. This teaching also went on to acknowledge the Soul Beings of several other planets in this solar system, who are involved in the hierarchal structure of this solar system but do not include themselves in matters concerning humanity.

The Knowing Way material passed into the Persian culture and hid there for a few thousand years, later to surface in Greece and Turkey. In the Israelite tribes of around 1,000 BCE, it was the son of David, King Solomon, 970-928 BCE who understood The Knowing and how to manifest thought into matter, as was The Knowing in Atlatia. He is thought to have had superhuman wisdom and the ability to see directly into the hearts of his subjects and visiting foreigners. Some historical accounts report Solomon as building the Temple to the God of Israel on the summit of Mount Moriah without the benefit of hammer, saw, or labor of any kind. The Akashic Records show Solomon's feats as the only public demonstrations of The Knowing or more simply, The Way, by a leader of a nation. The Knowing Way finally made it to Rome about 290 BCE where it was used to guide the leaders in their bid to rule the world with a democratic form of government. The purity and manifest power of the

Atlatian way of life eventually fell into the hands of those in Rome who wished to be acknowledged as gods. This was the true fall of Rome when those in power raised themselves above others as gods to be worshiped in temples.

The Akashic Records show that Joseph of Arimathea held The Knowing Way teachings as a gift to the long prophesied Christ child that was to be born to his niece, Mary, daughter of Joachim and Ann of the city of Sepphoris, during her fifteenth year in 7BCE. In this sense, Joseph of Arimathea passed forward in time The Knowing Way to Jesus through the bestowal group in Judea called The Elders of Solomon. Mary and Joseph of Nazareth went into Egypt shortly after Jesus' birth and stayed there for three and a half years. It was during this time that Jesus was initiated into The Knowing.[11] The family then traveled to Ethiopia to study with those who held the teachings of the Twice Born[12] at the Monastery of the Rose, The Brothers of Light. Jesus then returned to Egypt to study with the priesthood before going on to a Knowing Way gathering place in Srinigar, India where he perfected the art of manifesting etheric thought energy into immediate form through "calling" in the tradition of the Atlatians. Beyond the teachings of The Knowing, Jesus the Nazarene (or "Nazarite," which comes from the word "Netzerim," meaning "Keepers of Secrets") could also transform existing matter into modified forms, such as water to wine. This had been considered by the Atlatians, but was always dismissed because of their common concern for not disrupting the evolutionary currents of nature.

Because of his unique place in the long story of Soul consciousness manifesting in flesh, it was thought that Jesus the Nazarene would be the one individual who would be able to be humankind's collective shift back to The Knowing. The disciples of Jesus initiated as many worthy individuals as they could find into the ways of Atlatia, but to no avail. Those wishing to control the new sect routinely altered the teachings to fit their immediate needs and to accommodate the expansion of the Church beyond Rome.

Somewhere between 1,800 and 1,850 years ago The Knowing Way material fell into the hands of a group studying the Alexandrian Basilides, Egyptian Hermeticism, Oriental occultism, Chaldean astrology, Persian philosophy, Mystic Christianity, and ancient Celtic pagan mysteries. That group went by the name Cultus Abraxas. The members of Cultus Abraxas were into the high magic of transmuting existing matter into other desired states. Jesus the Nazarene had been the only individual to give a public demonstration of this type of high magic, but he had left no formulas, or so they thought. Even though the members of this group were known to be ruthless in obtaining secret formulas from whatever sources they could, they were unconvinced of the utterance methods used by Jesus even with the overwhelming evidence of the miracles he had publicly preformed such as verbally commanding the dead to rise from their tombs. The "calling" or commanding of thought energy into existence from out of Earth's subtle body or planetary ethers was held as a very dubious proposition by most of the cult's elite members. As such, The Knowing Way traditions were not immediately what the leading members of the Cultus Abraxas cult had hoped for in their search for "real" power, so The Knowing Way teachings quickly fell out of favor. However, a small group within Cultus Abraxas kept deciphering the codes contained in The Knowing Way material in hopes that something would be revealed – it was. Shortly after their discovery, this small group vanished from sight, later to resurface in Ethiopia at a location near the ancient Monastery of the Rose, hidden high in the cliffs above the lake where it is still rumored that the Holy relics of the Hebrews are kept. In these dated accounts they are once again referred to as the Brothers of Light, or the Golden Ones, or Light Elders. Very little is historically known of them except to say that they have been in the area off and on for some sixteen hundred years. It appears they went into hiding to protect The Knowing Way material from the power-hungry elders of the Cultus Abraxas. It is thought in some conspiracy theorists' circles that the Elders of the Cultus Abraxas Order exist now as the ruling families of the Illuminati and have been the real ruling elite of the world. There is no real substantiation to fully support this notion, although there is some rather compelling evidence to suggest that a generation of this ruling elite attempted to reestablish the Cultus Abraxas through the Fascist movement in Germany from 1908 until just before World War II.

Since the time of Jesus the Nazarene, several sacred orders, most of them secret in nature, have doggedly preserved the mystical knowing at the heart of Western religious dogma. The members of these orders did so at great personal expense, giving every breath of their life, reincarnating repeatedly to directly oversee the preservation of the Greater Truth that survived the destruction of the Lemurian and Atlatian cultures. They have demonstrated selfless deeds as Guardians (Watchers) of The Way or The Knowing. The most recent historically visible of these orders was The Most Sacred Order of Knights Templar, a group consciously formed in the 1100s, then quickly branded by the Church as heretics. By 1314, the publicly known members of the Knights

Templar had been systematically hunted and summarily executed. This drove the remaining loyalists to the preservation of the Lemurian/Atlatian knowledge underground where they protected The Knowing or The Way material from The Church. This group held the core knowledge of the inner circle of Jesus the Nazarene, Mary Magdalene and Mary of Sepphoris in a form that is as close to the original teachings as is currently known. This particular form of The Knowing (The Way) is referred to as the Holy Grail, whereas, the Grail bloodline refers to the descendants born of the union between Jesus of Sepphoris and Mary of Magdala. It is this underground secret Order that ensured the advancement of the teachings of The Knowing forward in time so that we, in a world free of superstition, may know the true creative schematic (Holy Template) and be liberated from Earth-bound limitations imposed by the present duality-driven collective human consciousness. The body of study contained within the Holy Grail line of teaching is the focus of this work and will be referenced as The Knowing as was the case at the time of Jesus the Nazarene. Interestingly, early Christianity was openly called, The Way, and had as its symbol a five-pointed star that served a reminder of the five points of agreement each early Christian vowed to keep: simplicity, gratitude, compassion, generosity and integrity.

The pure Lemurian line of teaching, that is to say, The Knowing without the Atlatian influence, comes forward in time to us through the Tibetan people and their traditions. This is the most sacred of all the Lemurian understandings of creation and the Soul's journey in the realms of desire. In a small temple situated in the center of the Tibetan culture, there is within its foundation a sealed chamber containing a complete version of the Lemurian Way teachings. This is the greatest of all the treasures of the Lemurian culture, far exceeding any monetary value or the technological wonder of the seven astrological pyramids buried beneath mounds of dirt dotting the Chinese countryside. When this chamber in Tibet and the Chinese pyramids are discovered, it will change the world, as we know it, by illuminating the history of humanity beyond the sketchy historical accounts of ancient storytellers and the fumbling of modern archeologists.

~ *Creator God vs. God Almighty* ~

Every post-Atlatian culture, no matter how remote or far flung, has a version of our beginning here on Earth. Some have us arriving from the sky, others emerging out of the Earth, or from consecrated swirls of fire and sacred pools of water, while still others tell of paradisiacal origins in which we communed with the God of our creation. Each set of stories carries a defining moment for humanity when Creator God separated from Its creation, leaving a bewildered humanity to faithfully journey toward understanding its unique place within creation. Most modern religions are still variations on those very distant (8,500 BCE) beginning themes, with the exception that modern Western religions have instilled the fear of God and the promise of "hereafter" paradise as a means of controlling the masses they wish to govern – religion has become the leading form of government on the planet. When the serious seeker deepens the search for the great truth, he or she comes to understand that all of the Creator God themes share one common core directive: the single commandment to "Know thy Self." This proclamation is simple but becomes a profoundly difficult task if we labor under false impressions of Creator God as a God Almighty that has to be approached through Its "only Son" or the "final Prophet" or be one of Its chosen people. All over the globe, in every culture, we have labored under the contracted beliefs of conjured culturalized images of gods and demons, to the point that we no longer remember who we are and why we are here. If we fail to know Creator God as our singular First Moment of liberated creation, we will fail to know our purpose in relationship to the all of creation.

This attempt to write down the nature of Creator God represents a conveyance of ideas going back to the very beginning of our incarnations here on our adopted home, Earth. Human consciousness, at all levels of sophistication, has thought itself to be the center of creation, with all the stars, including the sun, revolving around an observation platform that mysteriously exists in an otherwise dark void. Up until very recently (the last five hundred years or so), for most of the World's civilized cultures any idea to the contrary was grounds for imprisonment and even death. The Jewish Bible, as the Christian source of all information concerning humanity's relationship with its Creator, was not available to the masses until approximately fifteen hundred years after the death of Jesus the Nazarene, around whose life and actual teachings a portion of the New Testament is formed. Except for the interested wealthy, or the spiritually entrusted upper levels of church society, almost everyone suffered from the crippling superstitions and antiquated beliefs meant to enslave followers to blindly support the God Almighty form of government – The Church – that replaced the successive Caesarian rule of Rome. The illiterate masses needed a governing spiritual force; if it had not been the teachings of Christianity, it would have been the spiritual ideations centered on Mithraism. Furthermore, religion could govern with immunity as it extended itself across country borders by winning the loyalty of the people. Then came the reformer Martin Luther (1483-1546) and the excommunicated Henry VIII (1491-1547). Both men sought to restructure Christianity to their own purposes.

Luther began the Protestant Reformation when he nailed his Ninety-Five Theses to the door of the Wittenberg Church, a document directly attacking papal abuses, primarily the sale of "Peter's indulgences" by church officials as a form of absolution from sins. His parishioners were no longer bothering with confession as a result. Luther believed himself responsible for the salvation of his parish members and sought to refocus the masses toward personal salvation through humility not with the purchase of indulgences. Luther saw the Reformation as something far more important than a revolt against ecclesiastical abuses. He believed it was a fight for the core teachings of the gospel. At the heart of the gospel, in Luther's estimation, was the doctrine of justification by faith – the teaching that Christ's own righteousness is imputed to those who believe, and on that ground alone, God accepts them.

Henry VIII of England, on the other hand, needed a divorce and Rome would not grant him such an indulgence, no matter how much he paid. The only solution left was the king was a complete break for The Church. The Anglican Order, or The Church of England as it is called today, reformed Christianity in England and portions of France placing Henry at the head of the new church. Henry took this very seriously and began several sweeping changes to bring the truth of the gospel to the masses. By the time Henry had commissioned the first English language Christian Bible, the apostles Paul and Peter, several ruthless popes, several ecumenical councils and some rather insistently self-deified emperors had already edited any material that disagreed with their desired vision of creation. Christianity, to make its dogmas more palatable to such a wide variety of peoples, had integrated most of the localized Pagan, Celtic and Nature practices of Europe, along with the Mithraic ideas of the Persian culture and the stories and practices of the Egyptian Isis/Horus cult. The modern Christian Bible was then greatly flawed by the translation out of Latin and Greek into English by Miles Coverdale. Coverdale, a gentleman who was raised by and later joined the Augustine monks in Cambridge, offered the new English rendition to the King. As recorded history reports, Coverdale sent copies of the first English translation of the Bible to England from Europe for review by the King; Henry, in kind, turned them over to various bishops for comment. When they replied that the translation contained many reprehensible errors, Henry asked, "Well, but are any heresies maintained thereby?" They answered, "There are no heresies." Henry thereupon ordered, "Then, if there be no heresies, in God's name let it go abroad among the people." When the Bible was finally made public, it was allowed to be read only by the upper class, with women only reading it in private with little or no tutoring. Unfortunately, with all the contextual abbreviations and theological edits, The Knowing truths held within Jesus' teachings were damaged to a large extent, creating an even more confused group of revelation-seeking Souls who were unconsciously wanting to prepare for the coming shift back to unity.

During the same time period individuals in the Orient were free to pursue a daily life filled with spiritual awareness. Everything was tied together by a simple set of cyclical laws that everyone was bound to experience through the wheel of birth, death and rebirth. While the priestly class performed rituals and acted on behalf of a family, the family was never intentionally enslaved by mysterious, unexplainable concepts that only the priest could possibly comprehend. Everyone was actively connected to the all of existence by the mere fact that they were alive. Those who wished to pursue a life of contemplation were honored and respected by the whole of society, because the priests saw themselves as servants to the whole of creation instead of agents for the conversion of non believers into their dogma. The spiritual ideals by which these priests lived were active principles found in nature. Yes, there were atrocities committed by the ruling classes of these cultures and those atrocities were carried out in the name of greed and personal power. They were not hidden under the banner of Almighty God. There was never any confusion with the average person as to how creation operated, with an all-powerful god working in mysterious ways. There was never a war fought over the idea that my god is bigger and more powerful than your god. No matter who won, the people still knew how creation was ordered. Because of this, there was little spiritual confusion in the Orient. The spread of Islam into the Far East is changing that certainty as it forces conversion on the indigenous peoples. For these newcomers to the war of the Abrahamic titans, there is a right way to believe. For those who will not convert to Islam or for those who are simply nonbelievers, the wrong way to believe is punishable by death.

The Eastern teachings and traditions of The Tao, Buddhism and Shintoism have maintained a general overall feel for the early concepts of creation that were central to the everyday spiritual lives of Lemurian and Atlatian cultures. The Eastern way of unified peace within all aspects of life will prevail on Earth with the next global spiritual movement. The Tao with its non-judgmental middle path: neither this nor that; Buddhism with its eight principals of intention, i.e., Right View, Right Thought, Right Speech, Right Action, Right Livelihood, Right Effort, Right Remembrance, Right Contemplation, combined with the four affirmations of Shintoism: Tradition and the Family, Love of Nature, Physical Cleanliness and "Matsuri",[13] will combine to be the next global religion. Off-world, almighty Deity worship will not have a place in the unity that is coming for collective humanity. The future human will live life in a Knowing of how creation is ordered and how humankind is to live in balance with the natural forces that shape the circumstances of this World.

~ *Holy Conundrum* ~

This brings us to the mystery at hand. How do we integrate the common Western religious ideas and persistent spiritual superstitions of the current age with The Knowing brought forward out of time from the Lemurian and Atlatian periods? Every story of our beginnings here in creation has a thread of truth concealed within them – no one way is the greater path. With humanity, it is really more about willingness, about how willing we are to allow ourselves a non-judging beginning moment, empowered by a savior-free knowing of how creation is ordered and exacted. As long as we willingly assign our "redemption" or "salvation" from conflict to someone else, we will be forever unaware of our collective place in the great schematic. What does it matter if an individual's connection to their Soul is through the anticipation of a messiah yet to come as in Judaism, the gentle words uttered by a carpenter's son held to be the savior of humankind as in Christianity, or the verbatim recitation of the Divine Presence by an illiterately illumined prophet as in Islam? After all, all roads lead to Rome, right? While on Earth, what a Soul believes is true is dominant to what is true. Being lost in dogma or doctrine is a choice as opposed to a knowing. To become illumined and then liberated a Soul must relinquish the illusion. As is stated in The Tao, "What is isn't and what isn't is."

All god-based religions ultimately must convert those whose ideas run contrary to their doctrine. These religions are based on the need to be right above all other concerns. Look at the history of the Catholic Church regarding its refusal to keep pace with sociological reforms. We as a collective gathering of

Souls are now at a time when such blatant stubbornness will no longer be tolerated. Moreover, we have very little to say about the timing of this shift. The transition from one thirteen thousand-year energy cycle to the next is about one thousand years in duration owing its length of time to the width of the wave as it moves through our sector of Creation. The energy of this wave is what forces a shift in our perceptions of reality and conversely alters our consciousness from the previous cycle. The current wave from the center of Creation began to overtake us some five hundred years ago. With the leading edge of the transition, our consciousness began to radically shift from separation to unity creating the renaissance of thoughtful exploration that has led us to the Twenty-first Century. We are near the 2011[14] apex point of the transition. This new cycle of unity will allow each of us to again know our Soul's place within the greater schematic. For those wishing to be complete with duality, it will be very important to collectively know who we are in the greater scheme and why we are here manifestly captured in space traveling through time. If only a few hundred thousand Souls awaken, there will be profound amounts of confusion and a long period of purging the inner conflicts that want to keep separation alive. The Akashic Records indicate a collective shift to unity in 2026 for those still on Earth. The period between 2001 and 2011 will be a weighty period of collective purification of the general misunderstandings and judgment-generated conflict stored within our collective being for the past thirteen thousand-year cycle. The period between 2012 and 2026 will be extremely difficult for those who wish to hang onto the old beliefs of illusory power and manipulative control and the need for external validation. Those who are not willing to consciously awaken to the unification of body, mind and Spirit will either be awakened into other dimensions to live out those ideas or they will be allowed to toil on Earth alongside those who are living effortlessly through the unity of this new cycle.

The unfortunate aspect of this purging of our collective conflict is humankind's tendency toward war. Several of the prophecies concerning this age are rife with the bloodletting of the innocent as several religious factions try their hands at World domination. The more awakened we are to The Knowing (the Way) the less we will be affected by those wishing to continue the manipulative powers of the previous age. To those fully awakened through knowing, bullets will pass through what appears to be their solid forms. They will be in the World and not of the World.

~ *Introduction Footnotes* ~

1 Some remnants of these materials can be found in odd relics housed in the Cairo Museum's room of curiosities, in metallic pillars in Delphi and in Peru at Tiahuanaco, the other capitals of the Atlatian culture.

2 Every thirteen thousand years a thousand-year-thick wave from the center of Creation has collective human consciousness shifting in alternating patterns from duality to unity, back to duality and then back to Unity.

3 The pyramids and Sphinx of Giza were built by the Atlatians just before the floods as a calendar marking the millenniums until the next collective shift brought humanity back into unified understanding. The pyramid attributed to Kufu also contains clear round disk-like memory crystals, much like our compact discs and DVDs, that are to be found in a small chamber above what is thought to be the king's chamber.

4 At the exact center of the thousand-year-thick wave, those individuals who remain fully conscious, not holding onto the old belief patterns of the previous cycle, become cosmically aware.

5 Men and women dedicated to The Knowing who incarnated only to guard and bring forward in time the ideals of unity. They were referred to as the Sons of Light in the Hebrew texts.

6 The Oriental race is the oldest civilization and the remnant of the Lemurian global community.

7 There will also be several discoveries in Egypt that will give a full account of the four global civilizations that have experimented on Earth prior to our global community. Modern science and religion will want to discredit all these discoveries, lest they be discredited.

8 Shape shifters have the ability to consciously and willfully take on any form they need, animate or inanimate.

9 It is somewhat difficult to give accurate times because the cultures of long ago had their own idea of marking time. Usually time is indicated in the Akasha by a phase, such as, "In the forth year of the reign of…" or "In the tenth year after the fall of…" which then has to be connected to known historical dates within Gregorian time.

10 There is a Solar Consciousness emanating from our sun that governs this system, as there is with all similar systems in Creation. This Solar Being is without the type of conscious awareness we Souls have and exists as a balance to a stationary dark star which will soon be discovered by Hubble about a one and a half billion light years away.

11 The Knowing Way was called The Knowing during this time and later was referred to by the early Christian cult as The Way. To be an early Christian you first had to become a Jew, then you had to initiate into The Way. The symbol for The Knowing was a five-pointed star; the symbol for The Way was a fish.

12 The term Twice Born referred to those who would undergo the initiation of The Knowing. During this initiation, the devotees are consciously taken out of their physical bodies and escorted into the Akashic Records where all their past and future incarnations are revealed. When they returned to their bodies they are said to be reborn in the same body, or Twice Born.

13 The spiritual feelings experienced at the center of a festival or group celebration.

14 In his book, *The Twelve Days of Light*, Gary Bonnell gives a time frame window and a sequence of events concerning the thousand-year-cycle that precede each thirteen thousand-year period.

*"Science
without religion
is lame;
religion
without science
is blind."*

—. *Albert Einstein*

THE *KNOWING*

Chapter I

~ In The Beginning ~

Usually a course of study begins with the least difficult material, then continues to build in complexity as the course unravels its intended gifts. Because of the nature of The Knowing Way tradition it will be necessary to begin with the most significant and inherently most difficult material. This is due to the certainty that very little can be conveyed concerning the exact nature of humanity unless there is a liberated knowing concerning the true nature of Creator God as the First Moment – The Moment.

The term, Creator God, as it is applied in The Knowing Way tradition is a substitute term used for the vast self-conscious energy source that has given rise to all of what is currently known to our intellects and all that is beyond our ability to fully comprehend. While the term Creator God itself implies a singular source of conscious creation, what is shown in the Akashic Records is a complete vision of actualities held within a framework of consciousness and energy that was released into manifestation within a single moment. This first vision within the First Moment is the template through which all evolutionary substance (Dyadic matter) is brought into primary evolutionary states. It is the purpose of Dyadic matter to fulfill the possibilities within the original vision of the First Moment through self-selecting a course of evolution simpatico with its harmonics. In the beginning moment there was another type of energy brought into existence as primary forms that were complete as First State Beings. These complete forms were created in the exact likeness of the source of that single First Moment, the singular point referred to in this study as Creator God. In that cosmologically defining moment was energy as Dyadic matter and within one envelope, one form: consciousness, energy and the urge as a Soul – Triadic First State Beings. The former has its existence through evolution, the later through completeness. This was the beginning: the light and the dark, the one and the other.

There have been many different attempts at summing up the Original Moment or Creator God, primarily because it is very difficult for the human intellect to comprehend the Grand Oxymoron – the ever-morphing extremes of complexity within simplistic manifest creation. So many books have been offered in Western cultures since the advent of civilization that attempt to gather enough simplicity as to fully engage the reader while conveying the complexity of Creator God's singular momentary vision of All That Is. One need only explore this physical realm to intimately know the nature of how Dyadic substance is fulfilling the visions within the First Moment, at least here on Earth. Life is so simple and profoundly complex in its apparent details, which are only multiplied by the intricately interlaced, constantly conjoining contradictory terms – creation and destruction. And, if that were not enough, once a full investigation of physical creation has been exercised through the five senses, our consciousness must also contend with the many adjacent parallel expressions of creation viewed through the more subtle, non physical aspects of each of the five senses – each sense also being multi layered. Outside the normal constraints of our animal senses, we can gain an expanded view of the singular momentary vision by being aware of the layers of energy that form all of creation. The complete vision is comprised of multi layered, multi dimensionally intersecting planes of corresponding conscious existence, each operating in accord with the next along harmonically formed waves of pure primary energy. To fully comprehend creation from our singular vantage point experienced through the five senses seems at first daunting, and yet, the full knowing of All That Is, is completely attainable with a little nudge in that direction.

In the Akashic Records, The Knowing Way directives begin with: *Before all, Creator God Was.1* The symbols used to convey this message are all emphatically exclaimed and richly detailed to convey the magnitude of the forces existing before our state. The opening statement ends with, *Creator God fashioned all in one moment leaving nothing without* (lacking) *beginning form. In that moment was all that will be – The Divine Darkness and the Divine Light.* This is the only reference to a beginning of any kind. Later the verse turns to symbols used for what can only be a first vibration – *The Motion* – and a resulting sound – *The Word* – as coming from the First Moment and existing in a perpetually impartial relationship to each other throughout eternity along harmonically attuned waves of pure energy.

Interpreting and verifying the symbols used in the simple four line statements that make up The Knowing Way material is simple enough when the context can be applied to known concepts such as those found in the existing documents of the Old and New Testaments of the Holy Bible, Dead Sea, Naghammadi scrolls or Gnostic Gospels. When the symbols move into new territory of thought, the variations on symbolic interpretation can be easily misread. Because of this, great care is given to each line or stroke placement of the cuneiform-type symbolic forms. Unfortunately, the results can be abrupt sound-bite-like sentences that seem more like commands than narratives of how all Creation came to be and our role within the grand design or great schematic held in the First Vision. Where it is practical, the interpretation is augmented with a more casual language to enhance its readability. The Knowing Way textual information is divided into two distinctive books: the first focusing on causation, the second on manifestation. Toward the end of the first book, the information turns exclusively to our role as creators of god myths and spiritual hierarchical structures in an attempt to be one in consciousness with our Creator. The limitation of this is our projection onto Creator God of those human qualities that reflect our most harmonious state or our highest human ideals. This was most evident when early mythology was formed in an attempt to explain our place within the template of creation. Perhaps the original sin was our movement out of our simplistic union with Creator God when we first attempted to explain Creator God's nature in relationship to our inherent predicament – Our Souls as First State Beings inexplicably entangled with the evolving elemental Dyadic substance of this dimensional realm.

The Knowing text continues: *Creator God is without concern in creation* and *Creator God is in each moment of our concern within creation. Creator God is without specific form and Creator God is all known and unknown form. Creator God is without limitation and Creator God is alive within the power of the limitations It imposes on Itself through the details of Its Creation. Creator God is All that is Known and Creator God is joyfully unaware of* the specifics *of Its knowable creation.*

This one singular core belief is important in forming an active understanding of Creator God as it is determined in The Knowing Way material: *We are aware of Creator God as our beginning source and Creator God is consciously unaware of us as individual forms of creation.*

The notion that Creator God is unaware of us as Its creation will strike many as being completely and wholly wrong. Why would the Bible and other Holy books indicate otherwise? After all, if not God, then who is looking out for us? Who will know if we have been morally right or pious in our day-to-day dealings with life? Who will judge and punish those who have not been as compassionate, just and fair in their relationships with others as we have been? Who will decide who goes to heaven and who goes to hell? We could fill a sizeable volume of work with just the list of concerns and questions relating to this one singular thought.

The notion that Creator God is consciously unaware of us does not leave us alone here in Creation. There are those beings who, through dedicated incarnations, have come to fully understand the commandment to "Know thy Self" and in fulfilling the commandment, have themselves become guardians of the human journey. They are Bodhisattva, Avatars, the Eternal Ones and the Ascended Masters. They are both physically embodied and fully conscious in the realms of Spirit, serving humankind from both sides of the consciousness rift simultaneously. They move among us as physical beings inspiring us to expanded levels of knowing and action. We could be sitting next to one on the bus or train or at our workstation during the day; we could be in a nurturing friendship with one; we could encounter one as a peer, teacher or mentor. In light of this, how we treat each other becomes even more important.

Without them, whether we are unconscious of the concept of their existence or actively aware of them as mentors, our lives would instantly seem hopeless and profoundly lacking in light and we would dwell in a constant state of despair. They are the true emissaries of Creator God – First Vision – brilliantly unassuming in every manner, yet powerful beyond the intellect's ability to comprehend true power. We encounter them in historical accounts brought forward in time through myths, fairytales and folklore. They visit us in images of Angels filled with the benevolence of knowing, through firsthand experience, what it means to be encased in physical form. Many have incarnated as our greatest minds and leaders, our prophets and holy men and women. These Watchers of our way are of untold numbers and of many forms, observing our every move, hearing our every word and witnessing our every intention. They are of this world's substance and know its most minute details. These mighty companions of humanity seek to elevate us to liberated knowing, free from the blinding superstitions rooted in the separation experience of this present cycle. These judgeless, Dyadically formed Souls lovingly, watch over us as the Divine agency of the Earth Spirit and the Logos while we incarnate in this dimension. When we pray, they are the agency that answers our requests; when we directly manifest thought to form to fulfill our purposeful needs, they fulfill our command by manifesting our spoken thoughts into time and space.

~ *The Language of The Knowing* ~

There are several ways to read spiritual text with the two most common being that of the common layperson, who attempts through verse to understand the mysterious contradictions of life. The other is that of the initiate who is shown how the contradictions within the text are precisely placed, juxtaposed cryptograms. In this system, the layperson is deliberately confused and spiritual progress is slowed, while the initiate is hastened along and further illumined. With this in place, it is impossible to take the ancient texts literally, word for word. These texts were written to stimulate consciousness into expanded knowing through practically woven metaphors and symbolically articulated allegories. These documents were to be read aloud with a certain cadence to induce a Divinely altered state of otherworldly awareness. To read these documents as though stating fact was never the intention of those compiling the stories. Once the books were made public, without the benefit of an initiate's instructions, the dogmatic reality of modern religion dawned upon the collective human experience further guaranteeing a spiritually drudging lower class within the Church.

There has always been an inner circle of experts who decide how much the average individual is allowed to know, whether secular or sacred. After all, it is believed that knowledge is power. Because of this, the spiritual texts that are made available to the general public differ greatly from the core texts studied by those who have been initiated into the numinous teachings at the heart of a religion, such as those sacred traditions centered on Mystic Christianity or the Gnostic Gospels. The layperson or uninitiated is asked to follow certain peripheral spiritual beliefs while the initiate is allowed to know a more expanded view of his or her relationship to Creation. The common lay language of the Bible toils in the god-blamed request for blind faith, while the initiate is allowed to know certain spiritual exactitudes about the kingdom of God within. The layperson plugs away at the mysterious nature of God Almighty in heaven, while the initiated student of scripture and verse gains a certain grace-filled knowing through reading beyond the contradictions of blind faith. The initiate can read the common language with knowing; the average individual has great difficulty seeing beyond the semantics-cluttered verse into the mysteries contained within the simple language codes of the Hebrew Testaments.

Example: In the common language of the Bible, God Almighty (the Judeo/

Christian term for Creator God) is explained to be a trinity – Father, Son and Holy Spirit. In the initiate language Creator God is Consciousness, Energy and the Command, or in some translations, Consciousness, Energy and the Urge. The Judeo-Christian Father, Son and Holy Spirit is meant to personalize the relationship to a local hierarchy of learning child to knowing parent. The common language leaves so much to personalized, emotionally-charged intellectual interpretation, and that is the point: common language is always up for debate. This keeps the seeker seeking and those who know the greater meaning in control of the core spiritual truths.

The language of the initiate is precise - Consciousness, Energy and the Urge - albeit, to those unknowing, impersonal. The true initiate, one who has taken vows of devotion, takes nothing personally and lives above the concerns of life's contradictions. Spiritual studies offered in the common language keeps the spiritual seeker personalizing every aspect of life, including his or her relationship with Creation. It is impossible to "Know thy Self" if the seeker is squabbling with life's seeming complexity, all the while questioning how it is that God, as a father, allows certain things to happen and not others. In this case, the "blind faith" aspect of organized religion demanded by the language of the Bible seems the least of average spiritual seekers' concerns. For the most part, life on Earth is easier for the average individual if he or she will not see and follows blindly on "faith" without questioning – ignorance is the average individual's chosen form of bliss. Unfortunately, blind faith creates blinded followers that are at the mercy of circumstances not easily explained by those who act as intermediaries to God, claiming to know the God personalized in the common text of those spiritual books allowed the general public. The Knowing Way information herein will always be presented in a language that is direct and liberating.

More from The Knowing: *Creator God shaped Souls in Its image* that they would be able *to* (immediately) *Know thy Self* (from our First Moment). This is *the true nature of Creator God – Liberation.* At the moment we were created, we were completely liberated by wholeness, immediately aware of our unique place in creation. *Creator God is* (witness) *to Its creation through us, as US. Creator God has no concern after US* (for) *we are created in ITS template* (image).

The last display of this knowing awareness of Creator God was with the prophet and master teacher, Jesus the Nazarene. It was he who first declared, *"I and*

My (The) Father are One."[2] He also made an assertion for those who would come to know this relationship for themselves when referring to the miracles, *"These things I do, you will do and more."*[3]

The problem is this: if we are unfamiliar with the nature of Creator God – the First Moment – then we cannot fulfill the command from Creator God – "Know thy Self."

In the common language, if we project human qualities, such as judgment and revenge, onto a deified Creator God, we cannot know Creator God because we are making Creator God in our conflicted image. If we cannot know Creator God, we will not "Know thy Self" because WE are of ITS image. This is the Holy Conundrum. Why do average seekers take life so personally? The average religiously superstitious individual dwells in the darkness of projections, assigning good and evil values to everything in life. The average individual projects a "good versus evil" process to be right in the eyes of their man-created God Almighty. We are not creators or even co-creator with the First Moment – Creator God. We are in Its image and as such are able to manifest our purposeful needs out of the substances It has made manifest. We are observers of creation. Just as Creator God projects us out from within Its being as a complete vision, we project inner standards onto the world to assign valuation. The difference between Creator God and ourselves – Creator God liberates as it Creates; we possess as we evaluate.

The initiate knows his or her place in the trinity as observer (consciousness) and is able to know the proper value of things material. Once the uninitiated drops the habit of projecting value judgments outward, Spiritual epiphany swarms body, mind and Spirit allowing the individual to self-initiate to a more expansive knowing. Once the initiate fully "Knows thy Self" through inspired observation, he or she becomes the voice or command, such as with the example of Jesus – then Creator God becomes the clay out of which all material substance is reformed and purposefully manifested. Creator God no longer has to be the voice or word made whole (manifest); the initiate has taken that rightful place to complete the relationship of Creator to Created.

Practice:

Set aside twenty minutes in the morning and evening to just observe your surroundings. Use all your senses to survey your environment by beginning with sight. Watch how light and shadows help to form your visual priorities. Notice if you are drawn to certain shapes or specific colors. Be aware of any thoughts you might immediately associate with visual impressions. Then close your eyes and catch any odors lingering in the air. Be mindful of any emotions associated with smells. Next, become conscious of the temperature of the air on your skin or any variations of skin comfort. Notice any memories the textures of your clothing elicit. Lift your tongue to the top of your mouth and become aware of any tastes that want to be known. Then gently focus on your breath. Naturally, notice the still moment when the inhalation becomes the exhalation, when the exhalation becomes the inhalation – the slight moment just before one part of the breath becomes the other. Allow the breath to be natural in its rhythm. Do not force a pattern while looking for the point of transition between the in and outflow of gases and chi.

Once you are naturally observing the breath, be quiet and allow life to be different than you might expect it to be. Suspend expectation. Just let the space around you be itself without any sensory expectation on your part. Let your senses take on their own priorities as you become more comfortable with observing the in and outflow of your breath. Let whichever of your senses that wants to dominate come forward. Notice how your senses are different when they are not about the business of fulfilling your expectations. There is clarity in colors and images, sounds, smells, tastes and textures when you are in the natural moment.

When you have connected with the transition point between the breaths, expand that awareness outward by taking a conscious walk, or just by sitting quietly with an animal friend, or simply be quietly engaged in common activity with others. Remain the observer of the transition point of each breath. Notice any desire or attempt to bring past comparative observations of life into the present moment. Be aware of any desire to project past expectations of how things should be onto yourself or others in the present moment. Notice any past details you have memorized and are using to define your present moment; notice where you assign present values based on past judgments. Do this without judging yourself in the process.

During the day watch your expectations and avoid projecting value judgments out onto life. Suspend the habit of taking life personally by giving up expectations. Keep your opinions of others to yourself even if directly asked; stop gossiping. Be tactful and respectful of every situation when refusing to engage in behaviors others have come to know as part of your personality. Watch how powerful the conscious consideration of life can be in each new moment. Stop judging. Become aware of your inner conflicts about life. As you stop fulfilling expectations, you will think in patterns that add energy to life.

Thoughts:

My response to life reveals my true nature in all my relationships.

In all ways, I will always be willing to know beyond current beliefs and disbeliefs.

I know myself through my relationships: I know what I accept about myself through my areas of acceptance with others, just as I know what I will not accept about myself through my intolerances.

Lifestyle Suggestions:

This first lifestyle suggestion section is very basic and offers what might seem like very common or fundamental knowledge regarding meditation, diet and exercise. Each chapter will strive to build in depth and intensity toward greater levels of awareness concerning these activities.

Take Notes: Make it a point to write for a determined amount of time each day or have a special day each week. Writing every day is very cathartic and a lot easier on the pocket book than a formal therapist. If you reach a point of impasse with your thoughts and feelings, seek trained help. Do not edit, grammatically correct or intentionally go back over your thoughts in an attempt to organize them. The more liberating approach is to write in free flowing streams of thoughts and feelings. Remember conversations and write them as dialog complete with gestures, body language and overall descriptions of circumstances. Get it all out. Once you are clear of the past you can begin to form your clear observations of life. At some point along your journey to 'Know thy Self', or self-realization and enlightenment, you will begin to put thoughts about your revelation process on paper or in a computer file. This is important in that others will be able to benefit from your spiritual journal once you are willing to share at that level of intimacy.

Meditation: As a beginning it would be enough for those new to meditation to follow the conscious breathing technique offered in the Practice section on page 38. Just watching the still transition point between the breaths is truly enough to develop the concentration needed for meditation. There are dynamic meditation techniques specifically designed to energize your body, mind and Spirit that will be covered in the next several chapters. For those readers already involved with a specific meditation technique, please continue without variation. If you can incorporate the still point breathing technique into your present meditation program, so much the better. In subsequent chapters, we will cover very specific meditation techniques that experienced mediators will find familiar and may want to incorporate into their existing programs. The important thing with all spiritually based techniques is that they fit into your life without creating stress in your routine.

Diet: Very little need be added to the overabundance of information and in some cases, misinformation that is being pushed by modern-day diet experts. There are sure to be more trends in diet and health regimes yet to come. It is big business. Most diet and health trends will not address some very important essentials. First, just like all animal species, our specific mammalian bodies are designed for certain foods and certain activities that correspond directly to the geographical regions of our genetic origins. In other words, we need to be aware of the foods and activities of our ancestral regions. It can take twenty generations just to shift minor regional food and activity behaviors. This migration effect lessens as genetic lines intermingle and it is still experienced in base blood and body types. If you are from a family with mixed regional genetics, you will more than likely take after one side of the family more than the other. Identifying this genetic skew can be very important to how and what you eat as the base foods that make up your general diet. Second, it is also important to understand how the seasons determined what foods were eaten by the people in your region of genetic origin. Today it is possible to eat any type of food all year round, no matter where you live. We are the only animals within this ecosystem that can alter our environment to that degree. This seems like a lot to know in addition to all the other programs being touted as the answer to proper height to weight ratios, and it is, if we consider how much work is demanded of us in our daily lives. Stress is another health factor that will be covered in detail.

There are some simple actions we can employ to overcome the problems generated by our ability to migrate out of our natural genetic habitats. All physical vitality and health begin with the stomach. Some very basic steps can be taken to ensure the health of your stomach:

1. Accept in extreme cases and under very rare conditions, it is impossible for the human body to become sick if its overall ph is alkaline. Each genetic predisposition will eventually surface as a health crisis if the body's ph is acidic. It is believed that foods contribute most to the ph of a body; however, negative thoughts and emotions play more of a role than science suggests. Inner conflicts that create stress combined with bad eating habits are a killer.

2. To maintain a proper balance in weight to body type: eat less, chew more.

3. Digestion begins in the mouth with adequate mastication. Do not drink fluids while eating, unless it is red wine and then only sip the wine between mouthfuls.

4. Be conscious while eating. This does not mean sitting alone in silence being fully aware of each chew, although that might be nice for an occasional change in habit. It does mean being consciously aware of the food chain and cycles of life that have brought the sustenance you are ingesting to the table. Something has given its primary form of life to fulfill your nourishment. Being conscious of this fact honors that relationship. Eat with a feeling of gratitude.

5. Eat well-prepared foods with as few added ingredients as is possible. Packaged foods are of little value to our bodies because they take more energy to digest than they give in return.

6. Avoid preserved or pickled foods. The herbs and vinegars used in pickling stay in the colon for years and the chemicals used as preservatives promote illness by taxing the immune system.

7. Cook foods with olive oil or ghee.

8. Limit the use of refined sugars and grains.

9. Eat dark green leafy vegetables as often as possible.

10. Eat less animal fat and increase fish oils.

11. Reduce your overall intake of dairy products. Every human is allergic to cow's milk to some degree.

12. Eat organically raised meats. As is commonly known, most commercial beef and chicken growers use antibiotics and hormones to quickly bring their meat products from birth to market. It is widely known that our bodies actively retain these antibiotic and hormonal ingredients. It is less widely known that we also retain the natural chemicals released into the tissue of animals at the time of their death. This is true of how we mass slaughter mammals, particularly cattle and pigs. While cooking or curing helps release most of the stress secretions, we are still impacted at more subtle levels by the residual emotional anxiety generated at the time of death. At some point in your journey toward knowing, you will eat less flesh – particularly meat and poultry. It is important to allow the habit of eating meat to fall away in its own time. Suddenly giving up meat will not hasten your progress toward knowing and might instead create a greater conflict at the emotional level through the sudden dietary change.

13. Drink as much water as is practical without over doing it. A minimum of eight, eight ounce glasses per day is needed for the basics – lubricating joints, building new blood cells and lymphatic fluids, maintaining eyes, nose and sinus fluids, moistening inner ear membranes, body openings and maintaining the body's electrical field. Drink small amounts at a time, about five ounces an hour. Prolonged excessive water intake will deplete the body of much-needed salts. Do not drink late in the day: never past nine o'clock. Remember, we also get fluids from some foods, such as raw fruits and vegetables. Becoming aware of other resource of hydration can be very helpful in getting the proper amounts of fluids. If you have sporting events, such as a foot or bike race, that will require more than normal intake of fluids, begin hy-

drating a few days before the event by slowly increasing your hourly intake. We lose a lot of minerals and trace elements through exaggerated sweating. Make sure you take in replacement levels of salt immediately after a major physical event. If you are a coffee or black tea drinker you will need a little more water than normal – twelve more ounces of water per eight-ounce cup of coffee or tea.

If you are moderately overweight and want to lose a few pounds, be reasonable in your approach to dieting by first decreasing the total amount of carbohydrates and processed foods. Do not snack between meals! Become aware of the emotions that drive your eating habits. Eating smaller portions at each meal will, over time, give you the desired affect. Do not have a target date for weight loss. Trying to get into the latest fashion for the next clothing period is not being kind to your body. If you are overweight by twenty pounds or more, remember that you got that way over time, so take time losing. Eating five smaller meals instead of three larger meals is also a good plan. Exercise is particularly good at increasing weight loss, but only after you have already begun to lose fat. Wait for a good month before augmenting your diet program with exercise. Remember, stay off the weight scales for at least three months from the onset of any weight loss program. For the average person it is important to know that you will gain weight and lose inches with the proper exercise program. Muscle tissue weighs more than fat cells; muscle tissue burns calories, fat cells do not.

Exercise: All exercise programs should be designed to better your relationship with your body. It has been scientifically proven that a regular exercise program is essential for longevity and quality of life. Any well thought out exercise program will include a warm-up phase of stretching and flexing, a phase of anaerobic and aerobic workout and a cool-down phase. One aspect of exercise that was common to most of us when we were children was rolling and tumbling. This cannot be stressed enough – get upside-down for at least twenty minutes three times each week. Hatha yoga inversions work very well for this physical activity. Inversion tables or giant inflatable workout balls are very effective in getting the most out of inversions. It is important to know that each yoga asana (posture) begins with the spinal column and expands outward in all directions through the body out into the extremities.
In all "new" physical programs, be active in a manner that supports your current lifestyle. As you gain in flexibility and endurance, you will naturally change your approach to life. Be conscious and get into the "Zen" of every activity.

Any form of chi exercise, such as Tai Chi Chuan or Chi Gong is worth pursuing. The meditative state combined with exercise is very dynamic. Check the six Tibetan rites instructed and illustrated at the back of this book. Remember to always be kind to major joints – hips, knees and ankles. Strengthen your abdominal muscles to give your back some much-needed relief. The adage, "No pain, no gain" is for people in their twenties who believe themselves immortal. If you are creating pain now when you exercise, you will pay for it later when age slows you down. Pain is an indication of damage. "No strain, no pain" is for those who are knowledgeable about exercise. Damaged tissue is less strong and far less resilient after it heals. Getting a lactic acid burn is no indication that your program is working and might instead be a warning to slow down.

~ Chapter I Footnotes ~

1 In the first few chapters of this work italicized words or phrases are taken directly from The Knowing Way material as taken from the Akashic Records and the Atlatian Codes. Bracketed words have been added to help give clearer understanding to the text.
2 From the Akashic Records on the declaration of Jesus the Nazarene as fully aware of his place within the Great Template of the First Vision.
3 From the Akashic Records on the promise Jesus the Nazarene made of their individual abilities to those who could hear.

*"Nothing is
more dangerous
than an idea,
when it's
the only one
we have."*

—. Emile Auguste Chartier

THE *KNOWING*

Chapter II

~ *We as Frames of Reference Within the First Vision* ~

As was previously stated, Souls are uniquely created as individuated expressions of conscious energy from out of the substance of Creator God, imbued with the Divine Urge to completely observe the all-encompassing template. In this sense, we (Souls) are forged in Its likeness, being given all of Its innate qualities. Conscious knowledge of this concept is critical to living a fully knowing and exacting life. If we are unaware of our origin and how we were derived, we will remain unaware of how creation is ordered. For many, this unawareness generates a feeling of uncertainty as to purpose or life meaning, while for others it is a sense of aloneness. And, it is this lack of knowing that is the fuel of despair and longing.

Analogy: Each of our Souls[1] is like a single piece of glass in a very large mosaic window like the ones found in cathedrals and temples. Our Souls, like the pieces of glass in a stained glass window, are formed of varying sizes, shapes, hues and opacities; individuated by the ubiquitous awareness of the Grand Artist, imbued with unalterable characteristics, then placed without conscious intention in precise accordance within the framework of a greater rendering.

The only difference between this analogy and the truth of our Soul's interlacing within the Grand Design is that the stained glass window analogized above has its primary residence in the five dimensions of this realm and is held in place by the limitations of physics. Our physical bodies are the focus of our conscious awareness because they are the observation platforms, so to speak, for this particular point in Creation. As incarnate Souls, we are constantly in seven parallel bodies simultaneously: the physical, Etheric, Astral, Causal, Mental, Celestial and Christ[2] bodies. Imagine seven stained glass windows, each with a uniquely different pattern, one standing in front of the other. As the Initial Light passes through the first window it is altered by the characteristics of the sizes, shapes, hues and opacities of each of the pieces of glass making up its pattern. The next window then changes the spectrums of Initial Light available to the next, and so on. Our personality consciousness, held in time and space through our physical bodies, is the product of such an arrangement, except, imagine those same windows each as a multi dimensional construct projecting out in all directions simultaneously, each one more expansive than the previous and each altering the light density and luminosity of the Initial Light through the distinctiveness of its projection.

We are indeed enormous beings – literally. This might sound rather simplistic but imagine as an analogy one thousand kilograms of light stuffed into a one-gram container. The brilliance of our Souls is beyond our physical senses just as the thousand kilos of light is far beyond the one-gram container's volume. Yet, here we are, crammed into these rather limited and, when compared to our Souls, overly restricted bodies. Our point of insertion into Creator God's overall cosmic composition is more chaotic, intuitive art than thoughtfully organized science, and once generated we are without replication and cannot be uncreated, even by Creator God. We are created and entirely liberated into the Grand Design from our First Moment. The overall picture of creation, in relationship to us, can and has changed from time to time, although the significance of this is outside the realm of our complete understanding even by those Souls of great expanse and knowing.

This is important: It can be knowingly stated that we are vast beings *unequal in our presence* within the mosaic of creation while inexplicably linked in eternal significance to the inclusive eternal expression of the First Moment. We are related through Creator God's opus as one tonal variation within a symphony of tones to the complete harmonics of the overture. We are not equal in any way except to say we are First State Soul Beings existing multi dimensionally as observers of creation. In that reality, we are wholly unique in creation, each observing creation through a singular frame of reference to the First Moment. We are unequaled in every way.

The one known aspect of our collective existence, the one thing we all have in common as First State Beings: unlike the carefully selected and shaped pieces of an artist-labored stained glass window, we were all created in exactly the same moment out of an Urge within the First Moment (Creator God) to Know Itself as Itself through Us, or that aspect of Its creation that is of Its own image.

Looking back through Greek and Roman mythology, we observe that all the gods were not equal in their expressed abilities, purposefulness and usefulness to each other, or even to us humans for that matter. Each had a vastly important role to play out within the context of other worldly realms, as well as in the cyclical concerns of humankind. These myths demonstrated that even the lesser gods knew their rightful places within the overall scheme and only created conflict when they stepped outside their assigned duties and officiating locales. Each god was unique even though it might share similar characteristics with other gods.

Does this imply that some of us are more adept at life here in this particular realm? A qualified yes. Some of us have abilities and talents that others will never develop, more out of interest and willingness than ability. Some interests developed in other systems might translate directly to needed abilities in this system, while others might not. If we are unequally formed, do some of us have a greater ability to know The First Moment (Creator God) than others? An emphatic no. We are each an individuated piece within the framework of Creation, and each piece, like a holographic image, carries within it the whole image (Vision) of the First Moment.

Creator God's relationship with us is unconsciously constant. Our relationship with Creator God is consciously situational.

The Knowing Way text: Judging and intolerance stops when we know we are all unequally formed. Judging is the act of comparing items to a given standard. *No One is as the Other; All being formed regardless of the Other.* In *the First Moment was the Vision* (Creator God), which *exists as All.* We are unequal yet unique frames of reference within the All that Is. There is no one singular defining template creating All that is to be held as a standard, nor is there a state of perfection to attain that would have us in just the right size, shape, hue and opacity. *We are* just *as First Moment* (Creator God) *intended – Unique* and *without replication.*

With the dominant belief-driven condition of humanity, our relationship to Creator God becomes situational due to the varied beliefs influencing our awareness of Creation. Primitive core beliefs that we acquire over lifetimes of incarnations act as additional filters that alter the Initial Light of the Seven Bodies, refracting it as it moves out through us into the relationships of our current experience. The refracted Light of our projections shines back to us through the further influences of the animate and inanimate objects we are observing. In addition, there is the awareness that survives the death of a body that is at once peculiar to that body and partially derived from the previous bodies it helped form. In other words: each human form has a reincarnating instinctual awareness and incarnating Soul consciousness that work together to organize the inquiry of that life. Then there are the dense filters of circumstantial and social conditions that color the observation of a given bestowal.

~ *Caste System & Racial Divides* ~

Example: The analogy of the stained glass window could also be used to represent this dimensional realm's varied global beliefs as they relate to the seven bodies that comprise an incarnate Soul. An attempt at this was never so apparent than in the Hindus culture of Asia Minor with its four distinct castes. The caste system of India attempted to delineate out into this world the characteristics of the seven simultaneous bodies previously mentioned.

Interestingly, the term "caste" is a Portuguese word, used as an equivalent to "varna," a Sanskrit word, which means 'color'. Each of the Seven Bodies that comprise an incarnate Soul is observable as being a distinctly different color with the lighter hues within the spectrum of a given Soul being associated with the Christ, Celestial and Mental/Casual bodies, or higher bodies. The lighter-skinned Brahman caste, the highest caste, is the social representation of the upper bodies, in that, our Earthly life is a dispensation of the Christ, Celestial and Mental/Casual bodies; much the way the lower castes owe the benevolence of their existence to the Brahman Caste in the Hindu culture. The darker skins of the lower castes represent the more refracted hues of the Astral, Etheric and physical bodies. This type of otherworldly representation has been going on since the beginning of social consciousness and continues in all the World's cultures.

These refracting beliefs can be subtle even among people who collectively share a similar vision of liberation. In the Black communities of North America, color, as in the lightness of skin, is used to designate a similar largely unspoken "caste" system. This system is unlike the Hindu, in that, this newer version of caste designation is more about privileges associated with credibility within the African-American subculture of the United States. In the Hindu culture individuals are bound by caste from birth to death, and are subject to social regulation and tradition of the caste over which they have no control. In the Black community, if not so privileged by birth, individuals can gain control of their circumstances by moving up the socio-economic ladder from the stifling ache of scarcity to a life of opportunities derived from abundance.

They will, however, still be subject to the designated privileges of their color – for the most part, the darker the skin color the less significance will be given to their contribution. In the city of New Orleans, before the Civil War, lighter-skinned blacks owned darker-skinned slaves at a per capita ownership rate six times higher than the per capita national average of 5%.

This tendency to subconsciously designate good as being light and bad as being dark is bound up in our unconscious desire to replicate the spectrum delineations of our more expansive bodies over our more contracted physical forms. This is one of the refracting filters that are core to our Earthly experience. Unfortunately, this "As above, so below" mentality has been horribly misguided by greed and power.

The resolve: When we Know that our place within the Cosmic Composition is unlike any other, we begin our active journey toward self-realization regardless of our mammalian characteristics. Self-realization allows us to observe Creation as it is without refracting or bending the rays of Initial Light through the myriad of generalized social bias and religious belief filters. Knowing we are not just different but are in fact, wholly unique allows us to get beyond the pettiness of social consciousness, which in turn allows us our authentic self.

Authenticity comes as we observe our unparalleled uniqueness. This state of awareness allows each of us to directly command the Initial Light through clear thoughts, direct words and compassion-driven selfless deeds. Through the trinity of focused thought, word and deed, our true colors shine forth into the World untainted by the distortion of everyone having to be equal to some notion of exactness, whether exoteric or esoteric. We, just as all that is, are unequaled in Creation. We must know this to expand our individuated conscious awareness.

Practice:

Begin each day motivated toward knowing. Try using a statement of intention, such as the following:

"Everything I experience through my senses is completely unique. No one thing is equal to another, just as no one moment is equal to the past or

the next. Each day is a unique birth into new realms of knowing. Today I allow myself to know the uniqueness of everything I encounter."

In addition, look for the unique qualities of each encounter as you move along through the moments of each day, sincerely acknowledging in thought, or more powerfully through a whisper, that everything is incomparable.

Example: When smelling a rose, think or state clearly, "The fragrance of this flower is unique, unlike any other flower, within any other moment. I celebrate life through my observation of its distinctiveness."

Thoughts:

In all ways, I am always available to enlightenment.

I am willing and able to allow complete knowing to be experienced in all my relationships, in everything I think, say and do. This ability and willingness is my unique gift that I freely give without attachment or expectation.

My response to life reveals my authenticity.

Lifestyle Suggestions:

Meditation: Still Point Breathing Pattern: Continue following the conscious breathing technique offered on page 38 in chapter one. Doing this technique for twenty minutes each sitting will give you the greatest amount of impact. Each moment of selfless reflection is meditation. When we loosen our frantic grip on life, we move our awareness into levels of knowing that include the intuitive. Intuitive reflection is without concern for the outcome, being more enthralled with the journey than destination. Allow your imagination to playfully consider a problem you are trying to solve in your daily life. Imagination is the dynamic force that brought us out of caves.

Diet: Eat less, chew more. Compatible food combinations help with all digestive disorders (turn to the food combining information and chart beginning on page 275). If it is unreasonable to consciously combine foods, then look into taking a natural digestive enzyme. Watching the amount of dairy products and complex carbohydrates ingested is also good for the digestive process. If you suffer from gastric reflux, reducing the amount of flour and sugar will immediately eliminate any torn or herniated esophagus symptoms. Bovine milk products produce mucus in most humans. If you use tobacco products, especially cigarettes, avoid all forms of milk products. The mucus the body produces in response to the presence of dairy products will keep the carcinogens in the lungs for longer periods. Drink more water between meals, not at meal times.

Exercise: Make a verbal, sincere commitment to effectively enhance your relationship with your physical body. Observe the three phases of all exercise: warm up, exercise and cool down.

Find an illustrated book on Hatha yoga postures. The B. K. S. Iyengar books and publications are most complete because they show the use of yoga props for beginning students. Iyengar's approach to yoga is excellent because it stresses precise posturing. Use the different body postures as a way of energizing your body. Always be aware that each yoga posture begins with the spinal column. Hold each of the basic standing postures for one minute, then the next day hold the same pose for two minutes, etc., until you are holding each basic standing pose for a minimum of five minutes. Then go on to the other postures (asanas) until you have a full yoga program. The reference section of this book provides several suggestions for books on yoga. If you just feel yoga is not your cup of tea, try the first five of the Six Tibetan Rites instructed and illustrated at the back of this book.

There is also the study of Pranayama, the study of breath, to get things off to a good start. Many beginning students find this the best place to initiate an exercise regime. Again, the B. K. S. Iyengar teachings are most complete on this subject. Pay particular care as to the positioning of hands on the alternate nostril breathing techniques. A variation on this will be included in this work in later chapters.

Some other forms of dynamic meditation, such as unstructured dance or spontaneous movement can be of great benefit. Simply listen to a series of songs for thirty minutes while moving your body in an unstructured manner. At the end of thirty minutes drop to the floor and rest motionless for ten minutes. Be aware of the streams of energy moving through your body.

Weight training might be experienced as dynamic meditation as long as you are in the Zen of it – you know, lose yourself to the process. Be mindful of your body and always avoid injuries to the soft connective tissue by starting slowly and building to a rigorous program over a period of time. Continue to watch for improvements in your form and endurance as you progress with your program. Even though it is important to challenge yourself, it is more important to listen to your body's changing limitations. Over-strengthening one area of the body will create weaknesses in other areas. Whatever exercise program you choose make it a balanced one.

~ *Chapter II Footnotes* ~

1 The term Soul applies to three types of Beings: 1) First State Triadic Souls 2) Dyadically derived Souls and 3) Souls spontaneously Created by Celestial and Solar Deities. Most all humans are First State Triadic Souls.
2 The term Christ body is a designation of the highest level of Conscious, Energy and the Urge and does not refer to the emanation given off when two Triadic Souls enjoin prior to incarnating.

*"If you want
something you've
never had,
you must be
willing to
do something
you've
never done."*

—. Anonymous

Chapter III

~ Souls Enjoining with Matter ~

We, as Souls, are uniquely created as individual expressions of conscious awareness in the likeness of the First Moment (Creator God). Through our complete liberation in the moment of our Creation, the First Moment (Creator God) is consciously unaware of our existence as individuated realities and unconsciously experiences Itself as Itself as Us. We are vast Soul beings, all created in the same moment, unique, unalterable and unequalled in the entirety of Creation's mosaic while inexplicably linked in eternal significance to the inclusive expression of the First Moment (Creator God) as the singular source of our existence.

We feel a void within our consciousness when we are ignorant of the knowing that Creator God is consciously unaware of us. This void is a result of the invalidation of our greater eternal knowing that we are completely liberated Beings, free to uncover and discover ourselves as ourselves within the All That Is. The invalidation is the force behind our continuous search for our connection to our source or the First Moment. Our troubling search stops when we finally know that we are irrevocably liberated through Creator God's conscious unawareness of us as being anything other than an integral facet of that First Moment's vision of all that is possible and probable. To know this about our relationship with the originating First Moment is to be liberated from the quest to find our Creator God. Once we know this, we are self-validating and the void is filled with Divine significance freeing us to express ourselves as ourselves. If we are not liberated in the moment of our Creation, then Creator God is not a liberated force upon which we can command life. In knowing our relationship, we are unfettered by the superstitious beliefs and archaic dogmas that keep the wounds of cosmic invalidation salted. We are not bound to the First Moment (Creator God) through some form of obligation to our Creation. Our complete liberation guarantees our eternal relationship of Creator to Created. This knowing will set you free.

As was stated in the previous chapter, all judgments and comparisons stop when we know we are unequal in abilities and willingness at the time of our Creation, whether in this dimensional realm or some other aspect of Creation.

Judgment within this realm, as experienced through our personalities, is the opaquely woven veil of self-centeredness that clouds our ability to truly sense dimensional and multi dimensional reality in all its authenticity. Through knowingly releasing judgment and conflict, we are free to liberate all our repressed abilities toward their ultimate expression. The entire range of life is then available to our knowing through the intuitive aspect of our physical senses, as we allow our latent abilities to capture the subtlety of Creation's multi dimensional construct.

~ The Two Basic Elements from the First Moment ~

Everything in the All That Is, is unalterable from its original form as it projects multi dimensionally from the First Moment (Creator God); everything, even the most minute particle in Creation holds the entire formula for the all of creation for all eternity. Infinite probabilities, beyond intellectual comprehension, exist from the first vision of possibilities held within the First Moment (Creator God). Even with all the possible combinations, the basic nature of Creation is dual, in that, there are two fundamental distinctions of form in physical and non physical Creation.

Non physical: Primary First State Beings called Triads are complete and unalterable from conception. The Akashic Records refer to these forms as Souls expressing as pure consciousness, pure energy and pure Divine urge. From the micro-frame of reference of human consciousness, these types of Souls are often just referred to as an individual's Spirit or conscious awareness.

Physical: Each particle of primary evolutionary matter, referred to in the Akashic Records as Dyadic beings, is intelligently aware, making the all of creation actively responsive to the probabilities envisioned within the First Moment. In our Earth circumstances, our complex multi-functional physical human bodies are observable as energy-based matter that has developed an etheric awareness as it has evolved from the basic, subatomic Dyadic particle beings into molecules and finally cellular animal form.

All Primary First State Beings or Triads (Souls) are whole and complete from the first moment of their formation and therefore do not evolve into higher forms. All primary evolutionary beings called Dyads combine together with other Dyadic forms as a means of completely fulfilling the vision of possibilities contained within the First Moment (Creator God). This combining of Dyadic forms into molecules brings non-sentient awareness into existence as the Dyadic substance evolves in the void from the First Moment. Once Dyadic forms achieve a cellular mass state they begin to form an "expanded awareness" energy that survives the deterioration and final destruction of that particular cellular mass. This expanded awareness is contained within an ether and plasma field of electro-energy that is able to disassociate with matter and exist on its own as a field of thought forms. In the early stages of formation, this continuing expanded awareness exists for a limited time beyond the cellular mass that created it and must immediately reincarnate to maintain its form. Because of this, the continuing expanded awareness seeks to recreate and occupy a similar cellular mass as part of the developing cycles of life. Once it becomes insistent on preservation, the non-sentient awareness (that was originally created by the cellular mass) replicates its former material structure and evolves that form through a series of strategies that ensure its continued existence. The unconscious, or pre-conscious "want" to survive tends to generate multi-functional cellular forms, which in turn give an even more expanded awareness that survives the Dyadic form after it has ceased to exist. Multi dimensional awareness is a byproduct of the multi-functional combining of evolutionary Dyadic elemental beings. Just as Souls can enjoin to share their unique characteristics, as Dyadic elements combine they enhance each other as they form the new evolutionary structures. Each of the minuscule original Dyads created in the First Moment remains unaltered from its original form even though it is the base substance for the complex molecular formation it creates to fulfill the possibilities held within the First Moment. These minute First Moment forms retain a completely individuated awareness of the combined forms they helped to create even after those forms cease to exist. In this sense, with each combining, or series of similar life form manifestations, Dyadic forms become greater non-sentient awareness as they reach for a final manifest form. The final form can be any type of manifestation – animate or inanimate – because all matter is aware and responsive to the First Moment. The most advanced final form in Earth's ecosystem is self-aware mammalian life – Humans.

In our primate forms, we are Souls (Triads) enfleshed in physical matter as multi-functional Dyadic structures of consciousness, energy and the Divine urge. The physical human body is made up of trillions of Dyads (primary evolutionary beings) that concentrate on creating certain specialized forms designed to all work in harmony as one larger form. Each one of the "certain forms" (cellular structures) is made up of the exact same Dyadic substance. In fact, everything within substance, i.e., minerals, gases, human organs, complex synthetic chemicals, all matter is the same at the base level. In humans, the basic Dyadic forms are called primary cell formations or "stem cells" and it is from stem cells that all other cells of the body are created into specialized structures.

One of the fundamental properties of a stem cell is that it does not have any tissue-specific structures that allow it to perform specialized functions. In other words, a stem cell cannot work with its neighbors to pump blood through the body like a heart muscle cell; it cannot carry molecules of oxygen through the bloodstream like a red blood cell; and it cannot fire electrochemical signals to other cells that allow the body to move or speak like a nerve cell. However, unspecialized stem cells can give rise to specialized cells, including heart muscle cells, blood cells, or nerve cells. When unspecialized stem cells give rise to specialized cells, the process is called differentiation. This evolutionary step is taken when multi-functionality is necessary for the physical form to survive in its environment. Scientists are just beginning to understand the internal and external signals that trigger stem cell differentiation. The internal signals are controlled by a cell's genes, which are interspersed across long strands of DNA, and carry coded instructions for all the structures and functions of a cell. The external signals for cell differentiation include chemicals given off by other cells, physical contact with neighboring cells, and certain molecules in the microenvironment of the overall manifest form.

What nonphysical (metaphysical) factors have a stem cell deciding to become one of the billions of cells that make up the spinal cord, for example? Self-selection begins with the continuing, expanded after-death awareness retained from previous manifestations. Does this mean, once a calf muscles always a calf muscle, once an anklebone always an anklebone? No, it simply means the continuing awareness of a given Dyadic mass that survives the life cycle of that Dyadic mass will tend to select future manifestations similar to the immediately previous Dyadic mass. Evolutionary leaps take place when the overall harmonics of the cell is shifted through "retained memory" and by surrounding micro environmental influences. This minute retention of expanded awareness changes their harmonics giving them new ranges of attraction that begins the self-selection process in stem cells that leads to multi-functionality and multi dimensional awareness.

~ *The One and Only Universal Law* ~

Triads (Souls) consciously and willfully join to experience another Soul's frame of reference; Dyads combine through the only Universal Law that affects all evolutionary elements in exactly the same manner, always – The Universal Law of Attraction. This one law does not influence Souls, or Triadic First State Beings, except to a minor degree when a Soul is enfleshed in Dyadic forms. This is our unparalleled presence – we were amalgamated consciousness, energy and urge as Triadic multi dimensionalities from First Moment. We do not have to combine with other First States Triads to achieve multi dimensionality; we have multi dimensional awareness from our very first moment. While the more elemental primary evolutionary Dyadic substance within creation is subject to this one defining Universality of Attraction as a means of unconsciously achieving multi dimensionality, we Triads willfully enjoin with Dyads and other Triads to increase or expand our ability to observe creation across adjoining layers of dimensionality. As Dyads gain in multi-functionality and multi dimensional awareness, they gain a permanent etheric body that houses the expanded awareness that survives each manifest form. The conditions or circumstances needed to form this new etheric structure are not clearly shown in the Akashic Records and it appears that once the combining of the base cells reaches a certain mass, an etheric body is naturally generated. This generation might also be triggered by the desire of the Dyadic mass to survive its ever-changing physical circumstances by retaining fields of thought that related to past awareness's. There is also this truth: when a Dyadic mass generates an etheric envelope to ensure the survival of that awareness beyond its manifest form, a new form of consciousness is born – Dyadic perception. This surviving awareness retains all the memories of its previous manifestation and actively seeks new opportunities to inhabit a similar form as the one it left and usually incarnates repeatedly into a given bloodline. At this point Dyadic evolution has generated a combined state of consciousness and energy. This expanded manifest form is now a willful state of existence gainfully intent on fulfilling the vision of the First Moment. As we enjoin with the Dyad (our physical human bodies) we gain an immediate understanding of manifest creation through the awareness (Dyadic perception) held within the etheric envelope of the physical body. We combine that awareness with the memories of previous incarnations in human form held within our Soul's etheric body, thereby rapidly expanding our ability to observe creation from both frames of reference – evolving Dyadic and First State Triadic.

~ *Consciousness, Energy and the Divine Urge* ~

Triads, or Souls, are one of the few First State Creations that exist naturally as uncombined forms and, as such, are not influenced by the Universal Law of Attraction. Souls, in the image (vision) of Creator God (The First Moment), are forever constant, in a static state as combined consciousness, energy and urge. Souls may, however, willfully join with other Souls to form enjoined beings (when two Souls act as one) and composite beings (when three or more Souls act as One).[1] When this occurs, the enjoining Souls give up their singularly focused consciousness to the combination and partially imbue the combined expanded being with all their unique characteristics. It is important to know that each Soul keeps its original First State significance and uniqueness and can reverse the inclusion of an enjoining at will, without exception. When a Soul leaves an enjoining, it takes with it all the dual memory experience as well as its version of the unique awareness of the other Soul(s) of the enjoining. In this sense, we evolve our frame of reference and our ability to observe a greater number of dimensions of reality simultaneously when we enjoin, then enflesh. The Akashic Records indicate this as our grand mission, so to speak. Dyadic forms seek to manifest the many different dimensions and forms within the vision of the First Moment; Triads observe the Dyadic manifestations of the vision and through enfleshing within selected forms, give them a biased self-conscious view of their manifest efforts.

Analogy: The tree fully knows itself as a tree because we observe it as a tree. The tree's awareness is beyond our human awareness because it lacks the hard edge boundary of sense-driven comparative self-awareness. As such, it observes itself through us as our unique frame of reference of its existence. It cannot directly know itself. This type of relationship is true with all inanimate and non-sentient beings such as minerals, plants, insects, reptiles, fish and lower mammals. This type of knowing observation takes on a different set of references when we interact with other higher mammalian forms – land or sea. Because there are very few genetic differences between our DNA and other mammals, our intuitive genre link instantly validates the existence of the others, allowing us to share our mutual observations across all levels including comparative emotional valuations. This is particularly true with the mammals we have domesticated over the last ten millenniums.

~ *Christ Consciousness* ~

As was stated, Souls (Triads) enjoin with another Soul, or with several other Souls, to create composite Beings to further their expanse as they sojourn in multi dimensional realities such as that of Earth. Jesus the Nazarene stated in Matthew 18:20 of the New Testament, "For where three or more are gathered together, there I AM in the midst of them." Jesus was the personification of the collective characteristics of the consciousness that exists when two or more Souls enjoin. He was speaking of the Christ Consciousness, or I AM awareness that springs into creation when Souls enjoin for the expressed purpose of enfleshing in Dyadic (human) form. "For where three..." the number three refers to the two Souls acting through the one body. This Christ consciousness or "I AM" awareness is the emanating force of all enjoining Souls, much like the invisible fragrance is to the flower – The Soul being invisible to the body. Jesus the Nazarene was one of the few public teachers who openly taught this concept. For a Triad to enflesh within the structured boundaries of a Dyad, it must first and always be enjoined with another Triadic Soul. In this regard all humans (two Souls enjoined and enfleshed within a Dyadic form) emanate Christ Consciousness. Christ Consciousness, or I AM awareness is pure incorruptible energy and is always present when a Soul indwells in flesh. The social behaviors demonstrated by a human personality do not indicate the intrinsic nature of the two Souls who enjoined to enflesh within the physical, thus generating the emotional and mental boundaries of that particular human. There are no good or bad Souls. Each Soul is completely unique without any comparison. Christ consciousness is always present when a Soul is in human form. This Christ Consciousness emanation is an envelope that "protects" the Soul from corruption, thus ensuring our escape from an enfleshment.

Souls exist as six "bodies":[2] two as Consciousness (awareness observing itself), two as Pure Energy (unalterable radiance) and two as the Urge (inexorable stimulus). When Souls enflesh in a Dyadic structure (human form) they have seven bodies; the physical human form is the least real of all the bodies in that it is subject to the governing Dyadic influences that are characteristic of the dimension in which it has its form. And yet, enjoined Souls that incarnate into the Earth realm are not subject to time and space in the exact manner of their Dyadic forms. Souls can exist in multi dimensionality and are only slightly influenced by the collective conditions and circumstances of their Dyadic host forms. When a new human body is formed through sexual intercourse, an enjoined Soul is attracted to the new Dyadic form either through a karmic resolution to those humans who created the new body, or through a pre-incarnational agreement to inhabit the new human form to achieve a definite purpose in that particular form. The combined awareness of the enjoined Soul (two Souls acting as One) can be present in the one human form to experience a purpose or set of circumstances specific to that enjoined Soul and the other Souls with which it will interact, or one of the enjoined Souls can be dominant to complete very specific tasks that relate to Its sojourn.

There is another possibility with enjoined Souls: Enjoined Souls (two Souls) can both be enfleshed at the same time in different bodies. When this happens, each of the Souls retains the enjoining and is in constant communion with the other Soul even though they occupy separate bodies. This will happen more with identical twins or other multiple births, and it can happen with incarnations separated by great distance and/or cultures. Example: An enjoined Soul incarnates within the same period but in separate areas of the World. A female human is born in Russia at almost the same time a male child is born in North America. They are the same enjoined Soul taking separate Dyadic forms. From early on the child in Russia displays a fascination with everything that is North American, learning English and dressing in American styles of clothing; the child in North America studies Russian history and Slavic languages to the exclusion of other subjects. One day, while waiting in England's Heathrow International Airport to connect with flights that will take them to the countries of their fascination, they accidentally meet. They have been completely unaware of each other and in the instant they meet they feel a profound fullness and complete knowing of each other. They have been communicating at the Soul level where they are enjoined since the time of both births. This is the twin flame concept. As they trade stories, they find that they have had very similar circumstances and influences. They end up missing their respective flights and spend the rest of their vacation at the St. James Hotel where they bond within an intimacy that is very hard to explain to anyone who has not directly experienced it for themselves.

If the enjoined Soul takes two different, Dyadic forms as identical twins, even if they are separated at birth, and unless circumstances are overwhelming against it, they will eventually find each other. If an enjoined Soul takes two different Dyadic forms that are separated by space it is usually to work on certain karmic issues with other Souls or circumstances that do not pertain to the other half of the enjoining. They will resolve these separate issues before they join each other in a physical relationship. If they were to connect before resolving past issues, they will be more than a mutual distraction to that completion. Not all incarnations are this romantic, with some Twin Flame meetings being downright disastrous especially if the "personality" of one of the incarnations develops deep resentments at feeling so incomplete and alone for so long.

As was stated, each Soul is unique and complete from its first moment and exists without comparison to any other First State Being or Dyadically derived Soul. To observe creation from the Dyadic platform of a physical body, a sense of "completion" must be established to produce the desire for a Soul to sojourn within a physical dimension. This "completion desire" is generated at the moment just prior to the incarnation by a sense of separation or incompletion. We can easily observe how this "completion desire" works in the above example of the North American and Russian being drawn to each other from an early age. If an enjoined Soul incarnates with one half of the enjoining being dominant to the physical incarnation and the other half remaining fully focused on the non physical "other side," then, because of the limiting beliefs of religions, the half of the enjoining focused on Earth will always feel an unexplainable "aloneness." This is how the "completion desire" works in this case: early on in the incarnation, this aspect of the enjoining Souls will strive toward completeness by learning of things non-physical or Spiritual in nature. The "other-side" aspect of the enjoining is not mired by the limitations of physical senses and superstitious dogmatic beliefs and will always feel connected and complete. This is not to say that all feelings of aloneness are explained by the above example. There are any number of exoteric and esoteric reasons for feelings of incompleteness or aloneness. The above is a simple indication of general tendencies with regard to enjoinings of Souls.

Not all Soul enjoining results in physical (Dyadic) incarnations. Some Souls enjoin to take greater advantage of the different layers of consciousness held within the etheric body of the planet. These layers would be akin to the broadcasting layers of radio and television waves, except that they are comprised of thought wave formations. When a Triad awakens to knowing Its unique place within creation, It begins broadcasting thought energy. Before that, It was just "receiving" thoughts. Non-incarnated enjoined Souls are attracted to enlightened, "broadcasting" Triads and virtually hang around in the ethers to bask in the joy being generated through self-realization or spiritual illumination.

Just as in all human relationships, not all enjoinings are equal. Souls enjoin to experience the complete uniqueness of each other and to take away from each enjoining their version of those qualities that most interest them in the other Soul – Holy matrimony. This sounds similar to the attraction one human personality might have for another, with this exception: Souls freely and completely exchange their unique qualities for the pure joy of the immediate exchange; human personalities exchange as a form of control currency attached to a future moment of comparatively equaled value. Unless self-realized, illumined or enlightened, humans tend toward narcissism and this statement applies to everyone equally. With that in mind, it is true that most Souls enjoin just to be able to enflesh within the Earth realm, to get a chance at being seduced by the sensations of Dyadic enfleshment. In the realms of Spirit there is no seduction of sensuality nor is there a need for "completion," or manipulation toward fulfilled expectations. Because each Soul is utterly unique and unparalleled in creation, Soul enjoinings in Spirit are always a win-win exchange because there is no self-centered agenda aimed at a future that is based on the past. When three or more Souls, acting as one (composite Beings), embody in a single Dyadic form, it is usually to achieve a transformative ripple through the collective human experience as a redirection of consciousness to specific priorities. Usually such incarnations are observed historically as turning points for collective humanity. The threshold expression of these incarnations can result in canonization (sainthood) or deification, they can be great artists or scientists, and they can also be devastating to humanity in outward activities as world subjugators or harsh dictators.

In the First Moment (Creator God), there were other unique forms of First State non evolutionary Beings. It is impossible to fully comprehend the vastness of such Beings because they are without cognizable boundaries, dimensional clarification or the boundaries of their knowable influence. As a result, little else can be offered to fully emphasize the magnitude of such a State of Being. What is known of these tremendous Beings, First State Composite Souls, is that they are comprised of twelve First State Beings (Triads) from their First Moment. These First State Composite Souls are sometimes referred to in spiritual texts as "Celestial Beings" and of all known First State Beings, these First State Composite Souls most closely resemble the Originator of the First Moment (Creator God), primarily because of their vastness. As far as is indicated in the Akashic Records, there are no greater First State Composite Beings than these Celestial Beings. The First State Composite Soul (Celestial Being) that took up residence as the matrix of Earth formed a harmonic union with a

Logos (a composite Being) to create a dimension into which First State Beings – Triads (Souls) could enjoin, then enflesh into dimensional reality.

Unlike a Celestial Being with Its First State Composition of twelve Souls, a Logos is a composite Being made up of twelve individuated First State Beings – Triads that have come together to further the First Vision and all probabilities therein. The particular Logos that joined in harmonic unification with the Celestial Being of Earth is comprised of twelve Souls, each of which is from one of the Twelve Universes that have human-type embodiments of Triadic/Dyadic forms as detailed in the Akashic Records. There are only twelve Conscious Physical Universes acknowledged in the Akashic Records that offer such opportunities. Until recently there were only eleven.[3] Each of the Twelve Universes has a constant contingency of 144,000 Logos. Each of the twelve Souls that make up the Earth's Logos was previously an aspect of one of the Logos of the Twelve Universes. Because of this universal Logos influence, the originating Logos of Earth carries within it a direct influence of each of the Twelve Universes. It is indicated in the Akashic Records that this had never been done in the exact same manner before the Celestial/Logos union here on Earth.

This originating Logos expresses its "body" as a multi-directional and dimensional grid-like structure surrounding the Earth in an evenly delineated web. This "web" is perfectly symmetrical and harmonically balanced with the Celestial Being that generates the matrix of Earth. The Logos' "body" of intersecting waves of pure energy allows for the multi dimensional projections of enjoined and composite Souls into the etheric and physical dimensions of Earth. Each of the twelve Souls that help to make up the body of the Logos has its own tonal quality within the overall harmonics of the union between Logos and Celestial Being. Out of the twelve tonal variations, seven express as energetically harmonic layers through which enjoined and composite Souls incarnate. A unique signature ray[4] of pure energy is produced for each of the seven different harmonic variations as they pierce the etheric body of the Earth. Enjoined Souls wishing to incarnate will choose one of those rays through which to express a given incarnation. That particular incarnation will carry the characteristics[5] of that ray for the duration of the embodiment. Usually enjoined Souls will incarnate through the same ray influence even when they have different bodies within the same time. It is very seldom that an enjoined Soul or composite Being will have different bodies within the same period expressing along different rays. This is shown in the Akashic Records to have happened in the past when a composite Being is purposefully shifting the collective human experience toward a critical point and requires different attributes within each of its collectively driven individual incarnations. The exact details of the how the many harmonic ray variations influence each incarnation could take volumes to express in complete terms, so we will leave that to previously published works. It is important to know that while enfleshed, we Souls reside at the center of a great hourglass with the Celestial Being (Earth Spirit) form-ing one side of the mobius and the Logos forming the other, that the rays of energy offered as incarnational channels are set, with the only variations in effect being that of the unique qualities each Soul projects onto matter.

~ *The Ascension of Dyadic Substance* ~

The direct benefit to Dyadic forms for allowing a Triad (Soul) to inhabit its dimensional reality is the quickening of their ascension into pure energy from gross evolutionary matter. For a Triad to become enlightened, it must first drop all conflict. In this state, we emanate First Moment (Creator God) purity without any hesitation or distortion through us as us, out into the world for all to witness. The purity of complete First State presence within evolving matter shifts the harmonics of matter creating a threshold through which evolving matter may choose to become pure static energy and retire from the wheel of creation/destruction.

Human Consciousness[6] is the divide separating exclusively Triadic or Dyadic realms. On one side of Triadic/Dyadic union, or Human Consciousness, there is the Originating Logos[7] and planetary Celestial Being.[8] On the other side of Human Consciousness are the exclusively Dyadic[9] non-Soul realms of evolv-ing consciousness and energy expressing without the Urge. Dyads achieve sentient awareness when joined in ever increasingly complex forms for the express purpose of gaining multi dimensional understanding. Remember, al-though intelligent, Dyads did not have sentient awareness from First Moment (Creator God). The ultimate evolutionary expression of Dyadic forms within the Earth Realms is the ascension out of gross matter into pure energy. This state is achieved when a completely knowing, fully innocent[10] Triad joins with a fully innocent Dyad with the intention of shifting the primary energy of the Dyadic form into pure ecstatic energy. The ascension of a Dyadic structure is a cooperative expression that requires the full consciousness of both and is only achieved through the profound effortlessness present when both aspects are free of conflict. To achieve Dyadic ascension, knowing Triads will incarnate within the same bloodline multiple times with the expressed intention of purifying the genetics of that particular Dyadic evolutionary line. The quantum leap from the limitations of evolved sentient awareness to that of compete consciousness is a profound moment whose effects are felt backward and forward along the Dyadic genetic lines usually going back to the first preparatory incarnation and forward at least seven generations beyond the moment of ascension – that is, of course, if there are genetic successors. This is our "gift" to Dyadic awareness, and is available to them for the taking. This is the exchange. From the ascension point on, they are no longer Dyads but are referred to as a Soul Entities. Triadic Beings are complete from their First Moment as First State Beings; Soul Entities evolve through Dyadic substance to a final expression.

Once a Dyadic expression has ascended to pure energy, it is free to express in its evolutionary realm in any form by commanding the Dyadic forms of that realm to manifest to its purposeful needs. Each time a Dyad manifests a body subsequent to its ascension, it retains the full awareness allowed that Dyadic life form and incorporates that wisdom within its overall Soul Entity. There are far fewer Soul Entities than Triad Souls in Creation. When a Soul Entity is created, its growth toward a final state is extremely rapid. It is because of this that most Soul Entities are given guardianship over Triads when they enflesh within a dimensional reality. Triads, preferring the communion of other Souls, do not retain much of the innate wisdom held within matter. This being the case, it can take several lifetimes for Triads to retain the basic wisdoms offered when in union with Dyads. A noted teacher once declared, "It can take five consecutive lifetimes to get over a good post-secondary education." Evolved Dyadic Soul Entities assist us in all our endeavors as part of the exchange; we open the door for them to ascend out of the limitations imposed by gross matter through ascension; they guard us while we are enfleshed and consequently at the overwhelming influence of Dyadic matter.

All Dyads are compelled to respond to our Soul's conflict-free, creatively clear intentions, just as we respond to the conflict-free inspired imaginings of the Logos and Celestial Being that give life to Earth. Soul Entities inspire and guide enfleshed Triadic Souls for the full course of an incarnation. You are never alone, ever. Triadic Souls give their Dyadic forms a glimpse of the First Moment (Creator God) at the exact moment of their joining through birth, through self-realization/illumination and during their separation from the Dyad at the exact moment of death.[11] Dyads allow Triads a glimpse of the evolving vision of the First Moment as the Triad progresses through an incarnation from birth to enlightenment. This relationship is bound and sacred and does not change. In short, while on Earth we command Dyadic forms just as the Logos and Earth Spirit command us through our will. New Souls, those incarnating for the first few times on Earth, tend to enflesh within pure bloodlines that have had human expression for thousands of millenniums. The last remaining pure bloodlines are those in Africa, Australia, China, Japan, North, Central and South Americas. Consequently, many of the new Souls attracted to Earth from other systems take human forms in these older bloodlines. Newly arriving Triadic Souls, those with fewer than five incarnations, retain the greatest amount of wisdom held within the etheric body of the Dyadic form after the incarnation. After they have gained enough Dyadic wisdom through successive incarnations, they can then incarnate into less pure bloodlines without being overwhelmed by the genetic chaos prevalent with such combining. The macro-reason is that older purer bloodlines carry the wisdom of survival of the fittest within each race; newer or less pure bloodlines offer survival through innovation. This strategy of incarnating first to survival then to innovation allows the human race to advance rapidly toward its conclusion – Ascension.

To ascend Triadic Souls must first be aware of who they are, why they are enfleshed and how they were originally derived. They must ceaselessly know this as the driving awareness that shapes their individual inquiry. The knowing that they are First State Beings enfleshed within the Dyadic substance of Earth must be present in their conscious awareness at all times. This correctly establishes the relationship of consciousness, energy and the Divine Urge to the energetic structures put into place by the Originating Logos and the Earth Spirit. We are honored guests to the host (Logos) and hostess (Earth Spirit) and gracefully and willingly assist in fulfilling their combined vision of probabilities as an aspect of the First Moment (Creator God). In our awakened, knowing, authentic state, we do this by celebrating all forms and cycles of life through our clear command over substance. While enfleshed, our Dyadic physical human forms are our honored retainers and are bound to carry out our purposefulness by fulfilling our expressed intent as it relates to the vision of probabilities of this realm. In exchange for their willingness to house our consciousness, our Dyadic forms evolve at ever-expanding rates toward evolutionary completion.

All conscious Beings and Entities are innately aware of their place within creation. Most often a host or hostess will appear as a servant to the guest, just as an honored guest will seem to joyously contribute to the fulfillment of those who effort toward the purposeful needs of the party. There is no fixed hierarchical structure of greater or less than Beings or Entities in Creation. All unions, enjoinings and completions are esteemed relationships that empower each other toward the ultimate moment, the joyous fulfillment of knowing an eternity within All That Is.

Practice:

Each of us comes into this world with agreements set into motion with our birth and released at our death. These agreements are with our Soul groups, our enjoined Souls, other Dyadic or Triadic Souls, Angelic Beings, other Dyads or Elemental Entities, such as those we call Gnomes, Sprites, Fairies, Brownies and Elves. We all work vigorously in cooperative unison to fulfill a mutual purposeful need toward the First Moment's vision of probabilities.

Before your feet reach the floor in the morning, take a moment to consciously gather around you those Beings and Entities who assist you in all your endeavors, great and small. You do not have to know their names or their designated realms. The act of simply acknowledging them is more than enough. Try using a statement of intention, such as the following:

"I acknowledge you who invited me to this realm, that in my coming, I might know a more expansive vision of Creation. I am sincerely grateful. I acknowledge you who agreed to assist me in my pursuit of knowing, and now call upon you to gather around me as my heart opens to joy and my eyes to clarity. Gather around me and straighten my path to fulfilling our mutual interests in all our relationships. I acknowledge that without you, my life on Earth would be impossible."

At the end of the day, just before going to sleep once again acknowledge their gifts to you. Using a statement of gratitude, such as the following, seals your work together:

"I rest in gratitude for the assistance, known and unknown, which was

given on my behalf today. I acknowledge and evoke the presence of those who energize and refresh my physical body while it sleeps. To them I am grateful. I acknowledge that without you, my life on Earth would be impossible."

Thoughts:

In all ways, I am always an ally to creation and Creator God.

All around me creation is unfolding itself to my greater knowing. I allow my physical senses to perceive everything in its purest form, and in so doing, vitalize my innocence.

My authentic response to life is evidence of my gratitude toward life.

Lifestyle Suggestions:

Meditation: Before we begin, take a moment to loosen your neck muscles. Do this by sitting comfortably in a straight-backed chair. First move your chin to your chest, hold it for a moment, and then bring you head back up in a natural face-forward position. Now move your head as far backward as possible, hold it for a moment, and then return it to a face-forward position. Now try to touch your right ear to your right shoulder. Hold for a moment and then return to the face-upright position. Try to touch your left ear to your left shoulder, hold and then bring your head to the face-upright position. Do this for about ten minutes. You might even want to include making large sweeping circles with your head by first starting with the chin to chest position and rotating back around to the back, then back down to the resting chin position. Do this slowly, especially if you have any chronic neck complaints.

Consciously working with the breath is vital to a sense of being grounded in your body. It also allows you to fully energize your body with life giving prana (life force energy, chi, ki or ka in other cultures). A rather simple means of consciously breathing is by counting each inhalation and exhalation while pausing for a single count at the transition points between the breaths. Sit comfortably with your spine lifted upward. This is achieved when you consciously put space between each of the vertebrae from your tailbone to the top of your neck. Notice that this is not about straightening the spine – this is about lifting or elongating the spine. Some spines cannot be straightened because of a genetic malformation or injury. Another way to do this is to imagine a cord tied to the top of your head at the crown. Imagine someone pulling that cord upward. Your head lifts as your chin drops slightly downward. It might be that you will have to just practice lifting your spine for a few days to become accustomed to the sensations of sitting in a lifted position.

Once you feel relaxed with your spine lifted, begin to count the inhalation for seven counts. It is important that the inhalation and exhalation be exactly the same in duration. The best way to achieve this is with a metronome. You can get a metronome from your local music store or online. Set the metronome tempo to one beat a second. Breathe in for a count of seven beats; hold one beat and release for seven beats; then hold for one beat and repeat. Do this for at least twenty minutes each day. Remember to check that your spine is remaining lifted. Just as every other function of the body, breathing begins with the spine. The more open and lifted your spine is the better you will breath.

Diet: Eat less, chew more. Begin to investigate how the digestive system functions. It is not enough to put food in one end, then eliminate the waste out the other end some eight to twelve hours later. It is important to have a working knowledge of how your body metabolizes the sustenance you ingest.

Exercise: Keep investigating dynamic types of exercise that allow you to meditate while being active. If you are fortunate to have access to a pool, swimming is one of the most complete forms of activity in that it uses almost all of the major muscles in the body. It is also beneficial to use the shallow end of the pool to create greater resistance while doing aerobic workouts. If you have chronic pain or your body is simply getting older, doing a scheduled workout in the shallow end will also lessen the impact of certain aerobic programs on the major joints. In all ways, be kind to your body.

~ *Chapter III Footnotes* ~

1 The Akashic Records indicate a limit to the number of Souls that can enjoin – twelve. It is shown that the magnitude and expansive intensity of Souls enjoining beyond this "magical" number would create beyond what is Known, becoming completely unknowable to Consciousness, Energy and Urge, and in essence, to Creator God. Because of this, there is no data in the Akashic Records to indicate that this has ever happened.
2 The six bodies of a Soul prior to enjoining and enfleshing break down in descending order as: Consciousness – the God Head or Christos and Celestial bodies; Energy – the Mental and Causal bodies; Urge – the Astral and Etheric bodies.
3 Ten years ago the Akashic Records showed the formation of another Conscious Physical Universe capable of supporting human type life.
4 The subject of ray projections is covered extensively in the works of Alice Bailey, Dione Fortune, Edgar Cayce and Manly P. Hall. Review the suggested reading list for select titles.
5 Several books listed in the suggested reading section cover the subject of ray characteristics.
6 For those looking in the Akashic Records for data concerning this, the human designation is Ah-Ney Ea/Ah-Na Ese. This expresses the dual nature of an enfleshment.
7 Indicated as YAH WEH El-uh-Heem in the Records.
8 There is no designation in the Records for the Celestial Being that generates the matrix of Earth. Information in the Akasha concerning Earth is sorted out to Its Dyadic self-selections.
9 Indicated as PAN-Au/GEH-HEN Auh in the Records.
10 This will be covered in detail later. For now the use of the term "innocent" would be defined as a human who is without conflict of any kind.
11 In Gnostic studies, it is taught that the single most important moment in a given life is a fully conscious death. With that, a Soul can be fully conscious at birth. This fulfills the Triadic/Dyadic relationship.

THE *KNOWING*

*"Live as if you
were to die
tomorrow.
Learn as if you
were to live
forever."*

—. Mahatma Gandhi

THE *KNOWING*

Chapter IV

~ *Knowing Our Birthright Within the First Vision* ~

In review of the previous three chapters: Each of us is a vast Being, unique, unalterable, unequalled and completely liberated in the first moment of our creation, all the while inexplicably linked in eternal significance to the inclusive expression of the First Moment - Creator God. We have our reality in multi-dimensional expressions of consciousness, energy and urge; we are First State Triadic purity and have grace-inspired dominion over all Dyadic and Elemental Beings that aid us in all pure, conflict-free intention-driven pursuits that expand our ability to knowingly observe creation.

Just as was in the very First Moment of our creation, at our individual moment of self-realization or illumination here in this realm, we once again become completely liberated Beings, free to uncover and discover creation at will. Once illumined, we are free of the initial primary conflict[1] (original sin) of Triadic consciousness enfleshed in Dyadic evolutionary form. As fully knowing or illumined beings, we are grace inspired to bring all purposeful needs into manifest form by generating and regenerating the substance of our purposeful needs from the Earth's etheric body through the energetic forces at play within dimensional reality. By providing for ourselves and each other in this manner, we are in the World and not of the World.

As we have come to know through this presentation, in our First Moment we were created as consciousness, energy and urge contained within what can only be described as an ethereally formed, electromagnetic plasma-like energy field that, when viewed is the shape of a large, encompassing upside down chicken's egg. It is unclear in the Akashic Records, and in all other familiar esoteric sources, whether this surrounding substance existed first as an initial space, whether it exists as a direct consequence of our fused Triadic First State or was generated in the exact same moment as an aspect of our overall uniqueness. What is known is that this non-cellular mass forms the expressive boundary for our consciousness, energy and the Divine urge. We call the total expression of this phenomenon our Soul and know it to be eternal to time and space.

The Earth Spirit (Earth's Soul or Celestial Being) is fashioned in much the same manner as our own with these exceptions: we are singular Souls expanding toward enjoined and composite forms. The Soul of Earth (Earth Spirit), while essentially the same in composition as our own, i.e., consciousness, energy and the urge, is held within an etherioplasmic matrix (etheric body), comprised of twelve Souls from Its First Moment. These twelve Souls are eternally enjoined as one singular First State Being. The Earth Soul's etheric body is suspended within the electromagnetic envelope of Earth for all time. It is not fully known whether the Earth's Spirit called substances together to form the planet (this is the primary esoteric attitude) or if the planet was formed in response to the existing Celestial forces already present in the beginning of the solar system. This event took place in the "time" before the Logos. As a result, not much is mentioned in the Akasha[2] regarding the true beginning of the Earth. Interestingly, we can exist here within the multi dimensional construct of Earth because we are micro to its macro – How we treat the Earth is a direct reflection of how we treat ourselves; how we treat ourselves is how we treat one another. Our primary relationship is to our physical bodies. Our physical bodies contain all the elements of the planet.

As stated in chapter three, Christ Consciousness, or I AM Awareness, is the energetic emanation experienced in physical realms when two or more Souls enjoin. Christ Consciousness is not experienced in the realms adjacent to physical dimensional realms of planet Earth, but is more a phenomenon within the dimensional and etheric realms of our planet. To enflesh, we must already be enjoined with another Soul; by virtue of this, we emanate Christ Consciousness as we incarnate. Christ Consciousness is a minor force when compared to the emanations of Celestial or Solar gatherings. To limited human awareness, these forces approach what can only be described as "Creator God" status. This attitude was most evident in primitive tribes but truly exists in the deep instinctual behavior patterns within all humans, no mattered how civilized or learned. In the "civilized" ancient cultures of Rome, Greece and Egypt, for example, these Celestial and Solar emanations, such as the radiance of the sun as Amun-Re,[3] or the nurturing Gaia[4] principles of Earth's biological manifestations, were deified as the very essence of life itself. These life-giving, life-taking forces inspired all religious ideations as a means for humankind to explain the cyclical ebb and flow of its existence.

The Akashic Records show the one defining moment in which the Universal Law of Attraction began to separate substances into gathering forces as was scripted from within the vision from the First Moment (Creator God). This indicates that through one singular event everything existed within a vision of probabilities, with substance (Dyadic matter) forming the circumstantial conditions and boundaries of the first vision, and Triadic Awareness observing the First Moment by infusing itself within the confines of Dyadic circumstantial conditions and boundaries. This is very important to this presentation: nothing in creation is of greater significance or singular importance than anything else. Everything in creation holds within it the seed of the whole, the first vision, even the smallest of all forms. Everything is incomparable. To know this is to drop all judgment and allow the one single thought of the First Moment to reside in dominion over creation – all is complete and liberated unto itself.

As we come to know our place in creation, we are infused with pure joy at simply being. We are not here to learn lessons by bouncing between the extremes of duality, nor are we here on Earth to be voluntarily exploited by Entities or Elementals that are more knowing of this system through their evolution out of its Dyadic matter. We are simply here to expansively inquire and observe the circumstantial boundaries of Dyadic realms.

~ *Subconscious and Conscious Minds* ~

The constantly evolving awareness of our Dyadic human forms is what science has labeled as the subconscious or unconscious mind. According to classical Freudian psychoanalysis, the subconscious mind is an aspect of the whole mind that stores repressed memories, most of which are too painful to allow into full conscious awareness. Freud postulated that these repressed memories surface through our unconscious behaviors forming the quirky wrinkles of our personalities or in extreme cases form the foundational dynamics of all psychosis or neurosis. Carl Jung and Charles T. Tart believed the subconscious mind to be a reservoir of transcendent truths spoken to us through the symbolic language of dream-realm preconscious thought. These divergent views touch on the complexity of our Dyadic/Triadic awareness, but fall short of actually naming it for what it is – pure Dyadic awareness. For fear of losing its perceived superiority, the intellect refuses to acknowledge the Dyadic awareness that survives the physical body as the vast creative powers of the subconscious mind.

With the advent of civilization, or more pointedly, socialization, our Dyadic awareness (the true subconscious mind) has become unconscious to the conscious mind (intellect) because we no longer rely on Dyadic awareness to guide our search for sustenance (now expressed as eternal validation) and survival (now expressed as material success). For the last five hundred years or so, humankind has learned to survive almost completely by intellectual reasoning. In the West, the one single reason for this is the prevailing dogma of the Abrahamic religions that dictate existence as one physical incarnation with an afterlife of heaven or hell. Freud was correct when giving a prognosis for those who live out a life filled with increasingly complex layers of denied thoughts and feelings; Jung was right when he gave us the symbolic language model used by our unconscious mind as a means of reestablishing the conscious union of Soul to form. As for the East, the one single cause for the overdevelopment of the intellect in Japan and China is the culturally perceived notion that the East is lagging behind the West. There is a growing pressure throughout Asia to make a quantum-like leap beyond the West's economic, scientific and spiritual capabilities as a means of reasserting its ancient Lemurian dominance while there is still time remaining in this present cycle of duality and separation. They will achieve this through expanding their presence in the global market place.

Whatever the forces, real or imagined, humanity reordered consciousness to satisfy an ever-increasing range of repetitive expectations based on repeating observations. Instead of relying on a blend of Dyadic, instinctually derived, intuitive impulses (full subconscious awareness) and analogously unbiased Triadic observations to guide us through life, we search for the formulated conditional expectations that our intellects have memorized as "necessary" for surviving a modern global society. Because our Dyadic precognitive intelligence (subconscious mind) is Earth based and our intellectual projections into the future seem off-world based, we associate the intellect with the Soul or Triad. We have deemed the conscious mind (Soul) as dominant over the subconscious mind (Dyad) and by doing so have created a conflict that fuels all other conflicts. The original conflict of Triadic consciousness enfleshed within Dyadic awareness is constantly revived through the split created within our whole field of conscious awareness when we solely operate from one aspect or the other. The Dyadic awareness associated with human physical forms can survive without the presence of Triadic infusion; however, the level of self-expression is experienced as very primitive with physical strength and aggressiveness being the dominant aspects of the survival selection process.

It is natural for our Triadically associated intellects to be reaching for the stars. Afterall, we Triads are from other Worlds. Our otherworldly skewed intellects will seek space-oriented solutions for humanity as we create Dyadic problems within our living environment. In this sense, the Dyadic awareness and intelligence that makes it possible for our presence on Earth feels betrayed. When we are aware of our unique place within Creation we seek harmonic attunement, then the Triadic dominance of our Dyadic form ends with the subconscious and conscious minds blending as harmonically balanced conscious awareness, as was the case in Atlatia. This completely conscious awareness is forever invulnerable in all the realms it observes because it is wholly precognitive as a continuous knowing.

~ *The Blending of the Minds* ~

Our Dyadic awareness (subconscious mind) is not limited by the linear time boundaries of dimensional awareness, nor is it confined to the superstitions or dogmatic beliefs of intellectual consideration. Time is an intellectual construct and is therefore not a limitation to Dyadic awareness unless the intellect completely dismisses that awareness through dogmatic denial. It can therefore draw from and reflect upon actualities outside consensual time and space because it holds within its continuing awareness the survival experiences of each of its previous Dyadic forms going back a distance of seven generations through each set of combining bloodlines. Attained abilities, such as artistic, computational, languages, or say, cooking or building skills, are usually retained for only one life, that is, the most recent past incarnation. This same continuing survival awareness is also cognizant along a forward progression for seven generations. In this sense, we can predict the future as well as we can know the past through either regressing or progressing Dyadic awareness through "time," especially when it concerns events of a threatening nature. When you mix this ability to know beyond consensual reality with a full awareness of First State uniqueness, the resulting effect is a human who is without social allegiance and belongs to the World as an expression of the World, such as is the case with the Dalai Lama or was the case with Mohandas Gandhi, Rudolph Steiner, etc. This complete blending of conscious awareness is rare with one enjoined Triad enfleshed within one Dyadic form, and becomes more common when a composite Soul enfleshes within a singular Dyad. Even though Triadic consciousness is dominant over Dyadic awareness, Dyadic awareness is equal and will seek to balance or harmonically attune to this greater knowing. The intellect-dominated conscious mind is said to be the tip of the iceberg called conscious human awareness, with the subconscious mind forming the much larger submerged base of the frozen form. This rather inaccurately colorful way of referring to our multi dimensional awareness is not so far from the truth, albeit fundamentally flawed. It can be diagramed in this fashion because of the intellect's tendency to isolate itself through the ego. Until a Triad (Soul) becomes consciously aware of itself, realizing its fundamental place within the greater experience of life as dominant to matter, Dyadic awareness will tend to shape most of its conscious experience through the five senses. In this sense Dyadic awareness is equal because the focus of the observation is primarily experienced through Dyadic sensory input.

Most of us are keenly aware that all human forms come into existence through the process of procreation within the species. The molecules that make up the trillions of cells in your body have evolved through time by specializing and joining in unity with other cells to generate the multi-functional bodies housing your Soul. The awareness generated by these combining structures continues after the death of the form they help to create. Each molecule of every cell has awareness; each cell of every tissue has its collective awareness; each tissue of every structure is a collective awareness of all the structures that come together to form its unique properties; all organs are a collective awareness of all the tissue, etc. Modern science has demonstrated that these specialized structures are all decided by the genetic code,[5] created in the moment of fertilization when the sperm of the male breaks through the lining of the female's egg, this being true of almost all biological life on Earth. The genetic code used by all known life on Earth displays a very large degree of similarity. Since there are many possible genetic codes that are thought to have similar utility to the one used by Earth life, the theory of evolution suggests that the genetic code was established very early in the history of life as a means of guiding life through changing systemic circumstances no matter where it might find itself.

We are First State, complete in our First Moment, consciousness, energy and the urge fused within one eternal form – this is our birthright. Evolving matter starts as a singular consciousness and energy signature whose "urge" is the gathering momentum of the Universal Law of Attraction. Each Dyadic signature, the smallest of all particles, is aware from its First Moment of the exact "final" form it will eventually manifest as its unique place within the vision of the First Moment. Triads know this "final" form from their First Moment, while Dyads continually build upon themselves through successive incarnations until they establish their rightful place within the first vision from the First Moment. Dyadic signatures are symbolized in the Akashic Records as multi dimensional spiral structures beginning as miniscule points in creation, culminating in a series of interlocking geometrical forms expressing a static state, or a completed form. In the Akasha, these Dyadic spiral signatures are observed as structural genres.[6] Once they attain this pre-encoded state, they only reincarnate to that type of form until released from Dyadic evolution by joining with an illumined Triad through the process of ascension. Once ascended, they are then known as an Entities. Through successive incarnations in its final form, Dyadic consciousness develops a profound knowing of all the limitations and boundaries that govern its final form. When a Triad enters a Dyad that has been manifesting exclusively as a human mammal for several millenniums, the Triad gains enormous wisdom through the linearly evolved Dyadic consciousness. Using the example of our physical bodies: if a human form is a Dyadic signature's final static expression of matter, the pre-encoded consciousness and energy will evolve matter to that state and then only incarnate as a human mammal. After tens of thousands of incarnations, the final static expression will have explored all the possibilities of its final state and longs to leap into the realms it has glimpsed through the Triad's birth and death-glimpses of the completeness of the Soul state. The Dyadic signature will then begin its search for a Triad capable of joining it in a conflict-free union for the express purpose of ascending out of the evolutionary path it has traveled to express its unique place within the first vision. Once a union of this type is formed, the exact same Triad and Dyad incarnate over and over again, releasing any minute conflict captured within each of their etheric bodies, bringing both to a harmonic balance of pure energy and consciousness. An excellent example of this is of the Soul, Kundon, His Holiness, The 14th Dalai Lama of Tibet. He has incarnated with the same Dyadic signature fourteen successive times. Perhaps this will be their last time to incarnate together, particularly now that we humans are collectively entering this present cycle of unity. Imagine the radiant joy as they release each other to eternity's pure graciousness.

This type of union produces a doubled energy spiral within the Dyadic signature by joining the final static expression of the signature with the beginning moment. Prior to this, the Dyadic signature was only aware of its final expression and the Universal Law of Attraction that was pushing it along to that completion, and little else. It was obsessed with its mission to form its place within the first vision. Because of this, it could never look back upon itself to know its origins. Through pure union with a Triad, the consciousness and energy of the Dyadic signature are now aware of their beginning moment as well as their eternal place within the vision of the First Moment. As to the benefit of such a union to Triads: until self-realized or illumined, Triads are constantly looking back to their origins without much consideration for the static nature of their First State uniqueness. By assisting Dyadic signatures through their final expression and lastly their ascension out of evolution, illumined Triads gain true knowing of their distinctive place within the vision of the First Moment.

~ The Ascension of Dyad and Triad ~

The pure unadulterated radiance of the ascending Dyadic signature imprints its double spiral signature upon the etheric body of the Triad, leaving the Triad with the ability to manifest any appropriate physical form within the genre of the imprint. This gives the Triad the ability to manifest a physical body without having to go through the natural birth and death cycle of the genre form it is manifesting. When it requires a physical presence on the planet, it uses the Dyadic imprint within its etheric body to manifest an age and gender appropriate form to complete its vision. The only limitation to the Triad is that it will only be able to manifest the genre forms of the ascension imprints it carries within the memory fields of its etheric body. If a Triad has only achieved illumination and assisted in Dyadic ascension in a singular dimensional realm, Earth for example, it will only be able to manifest bodies appropriate to that type of Dyadic signature, in this example, human bodies. Contrarily, the Dyad now exists as an Entity and is free to manifest any form it wishes from the entire range of genres expressing within the dimensional system through which it has evolved. It can do this by willfully impregnating a female from the other side of the veil, then living out the life cycle of that form, or by directly manifesting the physical form of its choosing. The Dyad, however, can only stay within the influence of the stellar presence through which it began its evolution. In other words, it is locked within the multi dimensional reality of its Grand Hostess. For the most part this is more than enough range of experience for most Dyadic signatures. To free themselves of this constraint, Dyadic Entities have been known to form unions with Triads as they transmigrate to other systems. Once there, the Dyad can observe that system from its etheric body or choose to devolve into matter. If there is a genre form from Earth's great catalog that is compatible with the new system, then the Dyadic signature is free to impregnate or manifest as it would here on Earth.

~ *The One as the One: Parthenogenesis* ~

When Triads assist in a Dyadic ascension, they are free to stay within that system, manifesting the physical forms they require, or are free to travel beyond the stellar influence through which the ascension took place. As the above-exampled Triad transmigrates to other star systems or other galaxies, becomes illumined within the circumstantial constraints of that system and assists in the ascension out of matter of a Dyadic signature evolving through that system, it receives the imprint upon its etheric form of that Dyadic signature at the time of the final radiance. Triads are free to manifest the forms within the species genre of that realm and they are free to manifest the genre gained from their experience on Earth. If they ever return to Earth, they are now able to manifest two different genre types, but only if both can live within the atmospheric circumstances on Earth. George Lucas' science fiction franchise, Star Wars, is a wonderful hint of this many-models-to-choose-from phenomenon.

Once a Dyadic line (genetic line) has produced an ascension event, the bloodline becomes singular, meaning, it is autopoietically determined through parthenogenesis, or reproducing itself at will or through agreement with an Entity (ascended Dyadic signature) or Triad wishing to experience asexual conception. This is only possible if the ascended Dyad gave birth to females, i.e., male ascensions[7] do not produce ascension bloodlines unless they father children who then reproduce. The ascension process is radiantly multi dimensional and moves forward along the genetic line for seven generations giving the females the ability to give birth through "immaculate conception." The priestly class of the Lemurians and Atlatians guarded these bloodlines to protect them from "corruption" in an attempt to produce several successive ascensions along a given bloodline. These "pure" bloodlines gave rise to many of the spiritual figures of history whom we think of as having a wide range of abilities, evenly tempered by great wisdom.

All mythology and spiritual history abounds with examples of those individuals born of "virgin" mothers who then go on to produce extraordinary shifts in the conscious perceptions of human kind. In the Akashic Records, Mary, the mother of Jesus, was immaculately conceived, as was Jesus, her "only"[8] so begotten son. This implies that a Triadic/Dyadic ascension had taken place somewhere along Mary's bloodline at least seven generations before her inception. According to the mystic theosophy of the Gnostics,[9] those humans born into an ascension bloodline were emanations of supreme beings up to seven subsequent generations from the first or last ascension, if there were multiple ascension points within one bloodline. In the Gnostic understanding, the Supreme (Creator God), as a male human, always manifests through a completely innocent female. The female establishes the vibration of purity and gives spontaneous birth to the male child, e.g., Mary and Jesus or Isis and Horus. In this sense, the female of an ascension line made it possible for a great male spiritual leader to emerge into the World. A little church history: when the Cesarean rule in Rome fell in CE 476, Catholic Christianity having become the state-established, ruling religion of the Roman empire in 387 AD, all written historical knowledge of Gnosticism, with its direct references to Dyadic (natural wisdom) and Triadic (a eon[10]) union, was destroyed. By the fifth century, all Gnostic gatherings were held in hiding. As a result, such mystical works as the Naghammadi Scrolls (buried in the desert around 325 AD) were lost until their discovery in 1945. These writings, as well as the Gnostic Gospels and Scriptures, were deleted from the original Bible during the reign of Emperor Constantine.[11] They have been labeled heretical by the Church ever since Christianity was made legal in 310-313 AD, as a result of co-emperors Constantine and Licinius' edict of Milan that, in essence, politically joined church and state. During this time Constantine was made the first official head of the Church as Pope Constantine I. In CE 323 he became sole Emperor of Rome and remained so until his death in CE 337 from a sudden illness which appeared as he prepared for battle. It seems Constantine and his queen, Theodora, wanted to march into the hereafter with diplomatic immunity intact. Shortly after CE 323, except for Mary's and Jesus' immaculate conceptions, no other references to virgin births were allowed. He also ordered any direct mention of reincarnation or the communing with Divine Spirits stricken from the sacred text that formed the early New Testament.

The Catholic Church teaches that Peter was the first Bishop (pope) of Rome, and that all other popes are Peter's successors. This, they believe, is supported by the verse in Matthew 16:18 attributed to Jesus, "And I say also unto thee, that thou art Peter, and upon this rock I will build my church; and the gates of hell shall not prevail against it." It states on page 254 in the Catechism of the Roman Catholic Church, "The Pope, Bishop of Rome and Peter's successor, 'is the perpetual and visible source and foundation of the unity both of the bishops and of the whole company of the faithful.' For the Roman Pontiff, by reason of his office as Vicar of Christ, and as pastor of the entire Church has full, supreme and universal power over the whole Church, a power which he can always exercise unhindered." Altering the text of the Bible to suit Emperor/Pope Constantine's wishes would have been easy, and, some might argue, a just reward for the single living individual who had stopped the public persecution of Christians by declaring Christianity a legal religion.

It was around CE 323 that the ascension bloodlines went into hiding to protect those who were giving spontaneous births, especially those descendant members in the bloodline of Ann of Sepphoris to Mary, to Chana and Ruth[12] through Jesus. It would have been difficult for the Church to establish Jesus' as the only virgin birth if, say, the sisters and brothers of Jesus, as well as his own children, including his son's daughter, were producing similar offspring. Out of great fear the matriarchs of the ascension bloodlines offered their female children to lives of celibacy and busied their males with jobs as far away from the scrutiny of the Church as possible. Many of the female saints were from such bloodlines, with St. Francis of Assisi the only male shown in the Akashic Records to have been from such ancestry and to have developed Christ awareness then publicly taught the teachings of his Nazarene ancestry. The Akashic records show that Saint Bernadette of Lourdes was the last female of such a bloodline originating with Jesus and Mary Magdalene. Both Saint Bernadette and Saint Francis were immaculately conceived.

This ascension phenomenon is extremely important to understand if we are to comprehend the true relationship of Triads to Dyads, First State to evolutionary matter. This is the mutual benefit of our union on Earth – Triads gain full awareness of their uniqueness within the creative template; Dyads gain a conscious bridge to their origin within the First Moment.

~ *Other Divine Births* ~

The story of Mary of Sepphoris and Jesus of Nazareth is a continuation of similar stories associated with ascension bloodlines that were "developed" in Atlatia and Lemuria thousands of years before the immaculate conception of Mary through Ann, then Jesus through Mary. The recounting of the births of Ishmael, Isaac, Samson and Samuel in the Old Testament was also the reporting of ascension bloodline births.

About two thousand years before Mary, Mut-em-ua, the virgin Queen of Egypt, gave birth to the Pharaoh Amenkept (Amenophis) III, who built the temple of Luxor, on the walls of which were represented the four conditions present with all such conceptions: <u>The annunciation</u> – The god Taht announcing to the virgin Queen that she is about to become a mother. <u>The immaculate conception</u> – The god Kneph (the Holy Spirit) mystically impregnating the virgin by holding a cross, the symbol of life, to her mouth. <u>The physical birth</u> of the grace-declared Man-god. <u>The adoration</u> – The newly born infant acknowledged by gods and men, including three kings or Persian Magi, who came offering him gifts, as in the case of Jesus. In this particular relief, the cross again appears as a symbol.

In an Egyptian temple, one dedicated to Hathor at Denderah, one of the chambers was called "The Hall of the Child in his Cradle"; in a painting which was once on the walls of that temple (now in Paris), we can see represented a Holy Virgin Mother with her Divine Child in her arms. The temple and the painting predate Christianity by hundreds of generations. As mentioned above, Horus was said to be the parthenogenetic child of Isis. In the catacombs of Rome, black statues of this Divine duo still survive from the early Christian worship of the Virgin and Child. When Christianity absorbed the pagan myths and rites, it also adopted surviving pagan statuary, renaming them as saints, or even as apostles. Statues of the goddess Isis with the child Horus in her arms were exported to other countries, where they are still to be found with new names attached to them. Those names are Christian in Europe, Buddhist in Turkestan and Taoist in China and Japan.

Divine mothers with their babe-gods are found among the oldest relics of Carthage, Cyprus, and Assyria. The followers of various sects knew such figures by a great variety of names: the mothers as Venus, Juno, Mother-Earth, Fortune, etc., and the children as Hercules, Dionysos, Love, Wealth, etc. In India similar figures commonly represent Devaki with the babe Krishna at her breast, while others represent various less well-known Indian divinities. Jason, who was slain by Zeus, was said to have been another son of the virgin Persephone and to have had no father, either human or Divine. Adonis, the Syrian god; Osiris, the first person of the principal Egyptian Trinity; and Mithra, the Persian god whom so many of the Roman soldiers worshipped – all had strange tales told about their births. Plato's mother, Perictione, was a virgin who conceived him immaculately by the god Apollo. Apollo himself revealed the circumstances of this conception to Ariston, the affianced husband of the virgin. The list continues with Horus, conceived by Isia through the "power" given to her by Thoth, the mind of the God of the universe; Nana, a virgin who gave birth to Attis; Hera who conceived and produced Typhon and Io, who was made pregnant by the Divine hand. Virgin births, or Divine births, were widely acknowledged from the time of later Atlatian culture until around 325 AD. Attis, Adonis, Dionysos, Osiris, and Mithra were the principal gods in their respective countries and those countries, together formed the greater part of the Eastern provinces of the Roman Empire and the culture of its chief rival, the Persian Empire. At the time when Christianity arose from cult status around CE 313, all of the above virgin-birthed gods were worshipped in various parts of the World. The official Church position on such births occurring prior to Mary's conception remains: they are an invention of the Devil, who, knowing the Christ would subsequently be born of a virgin, counterfeited the earlier birth miracles as a way of discrediting the birth through Mary of her only begotten Son of God, Jesus the Christ.

~ *Atlatian and Lemurian History* ~

The above examples of virgin births (parthenogenesis) take into account the twelve ascension bloodlines as they proceeded beyond the collapse of the Atlatian culture (24,000-11,000 BCE) some thirteen thousand years ago. The spiritual center of the global Atlatian society was based in what is now the Mediterranean basin with its primary temple complex located almost exactly between what are now the islands of Crete and Cyprus. The land bridge connecting Europe and the African subcontinent breached as seawaters rose some one hundred to two hundred meters due in part to the sinking of portions of the north African continent and in part to the global melting of ice plates from the last glacial maximum of eighteen to thirteen thousand years ago. The Mediterranean basin had remained a utopian paradise, much like the Garden of Eden depicted in the Book of Genesis, through most of the earth changes affecting that region until the deluge. Each ascension bloodline formed the spiritual core of the twelve families as they moved, three in each of the four directions, away from the valley that had been their home. Most of our collective memory of this period is held as mythological stories through the oral historical traditions that were necessary while humankind developed a written language to replace the telepathic communications prevalent during the Atlatian epoch.

Most Western stories of humankind's beginnings on Earth owe their origins to the survivors from Atlatia.

The Chinese culture is the remnant of the global Lemurian society (37,000-24,000 BCE) and is by far the oldest civilization on Earth with active historical references tracing back to the time of its global dominance. The Akashic Records show the Lemurians as highly advanced in every aspect of life as we know it today, with this one primary difference – Lemurians acknowledged individuals as part of an ever-progressing collective, thereby owing their existence to the continuation of the whole through a series of conscious incarnations. Children who could not demonstrate a knowing of their most previous incarnation were placed into slavery to those who could. They were looked upon as outsiders and were not educated or allowed to experience anything except the gross repetitious tasking of servitude. The Lemurian religion was referred to as The Way and focused on maintaining complete awareness of each incarnation as a way of better serving the collective. It was believed that this would ensure the proper harmonic balance central to their culture. Also, this promoted efficiency of purpose, in that, once one learned an ability in one lifetime he or she maintained that ability in subsequent incarnations. As a result, the Lemurians developed enormous medical, architectural and scientific capabilities. The downside was that fewer and fewer Souls, who could consciously recall their most previous incarnations, were reincarnating into the Lemurian culture. As a result, there were few who could actively administer the growing slave segment of the population. Souls were choosing to begin lifetimes in the Atlatian experience of Soul liberation through conscious unity as opposed to reincarnating into the genetically conflicted collective culture of the Lemurians. Those returning Souls who could remember naturally took their place as leaders. In an effort to keep their culture from being completely decimated, they used the enormous numbers of slaves to bury most of the culture's technological and architectural advancements, at least until such a time in their future when individuals would once again begin to consciously remember their Lemurian incarnations and bring back to the world a knowing way of life as was previously practiced.

In a very conscious response to the coming consciomorphic wave,[13] a group of individuals left China some 5,200 years ago[14] to break free of the choking intolerance of its "past-life" oriented culture. This migrating group was comprised of the finest farmers, builders, artisans, architects, doctors, and military strategists, as well as a large contingency of slaves. Their destination was the enchanted, seismologically volatile chain of islands off the coast of China, said to be home to the gods. The dominant belief at the time was that the islands were guarded by flesh-devouring dragons and if someone were lucky enough to avoid their detection, that individual would more than likely be destroyed by any one of the resident gods. It was the perfect hiding place for a group of conscious individuals wanting to establish a culture free of the persistently lingering Lemurian influences. This enthusiastic gathering of Souls founded the island nation of Japan. Instead of having to remember their most recent past lives as the prerequisite for cultural viability, individuals now gave honor to their most immediate ancestry by actively calling upon ancestral spirits to empower them in this life with the gifts the ancestors had acquired during their most recent incarnations. Their religion became known as "the Way of the Gods," to honor the many different gods thought to inhabit the land of their new home. This religion was cored with the ideals of gratitude for all blessings of nature, acknowledging all blessings of nature with sincerity and purity of consciousness through the performance of daily rituals designed to imbue body, mind and Spirit with ever-expanding states of awareness. This set into motion a constant awareness of the grand communion of Souls, both incarnate and disincarnate, who aid and guide all daily activity. In relationships, their religion encouraged being helpful to others, including all forms of life, through selfless deeds of service as a way of seeking the advancement of world consciousness through a life that mediates the active will of God. This binding of oneself with all others in harmonious union brought about a nation of individuals that flourished in peace and prosperity.

The Souls who formed this new cultural order did so with the highest ideals. As those originating Souls left Earth, their legacy slowly began to deteriorate into clans and tribes shuffling for power and dominance in an ever-increasingly unstable social order. In this state the natural use of chi[15] as a means of achieving effortless work goals was used as a weapon to inflict pain and suffering upon a perceived enemy. To ensure its continuation, the warrior class did away with all learned and overly able individuals, leaving the culture void of the richness of its founding members. Any individual with exceptional talents went into hiding in the priestly class, practicing his or her abilities within the safety of a growing network of shrines and temples. As a result, the religion maintained much of its original purity, but instead of recognizing the forces in nature as gods, over time the most powerful warriors, and eventually the emperor, were worshipped as gods. This need for fear-based power at the top of the social order ultimately led to the establishment of the Shinto religion as it is practiced today.

The ideas of modern science concerning our origins, cultural achievements and the global history of humanity are quaintly lacking in imagination and intuitive insight, primarily because in this current system any true advancement relies on the validation of past assumptions. Sadly, validation of past assumptions is the only crutch upon which we can lean as we begin to uncover more and more about who we are and why we are here on Earth. Unless we know who we are as Triads, and how it is we are derived in Creation, it is impossible to imagine, let alone accept for truth, the assertions of those who know of times past when humanity was at one of its many pinnacles. Only to again fall prey to the circumstances brought about by the continuous cycles of consciomorphic energy that overtake and reshape our awareness out here on the edge of Creation. If we are to hold onto our superstitions, not allowing a more expansive awareness of our birthright in Creation, then the concepts of ascension and parthenogenesis will remain lost. If Jesus remains the only Son of God and is relegated to Savior of the World through his blood sacrifice for humanity's sins, as taught by Christianity, then the ascension bloodlines will die out. This will leave us only with teachers who must shed conflicted genetic influences and gender and cultural loyalties, who through great personal effort, somehow unfold self-realization and enlightenment. Without a pure innocent teacher, such as Jesus of Mary, through whom the pure radiance of joy can pour out into the world, a fellow human whose very presence can effortlessly expand the boundaries of Dyadic awareness into Soul conscious, we humans will be at constant war within ourselves and at jihad with each other's wrongfully derived notions about who we are, how we were derived and our purpose in Creation.

Practice:

Actively call upon the Spirits of the Earth and Logos to work in unison with you as you awaken to knowing your relationship to this Realm. Just intending this is and stating it aloud is enough to set the unseen influences governing such declarations into motion as you move through your daily activities. Your physical body will respond to the added energy being pushed your way through this conscious command of such influences.

Genetics is 50% of the game of life. Five hundred years ago we only needed to sit and listen to the stories told by village elders to have an intimate knowing of our genetic origins. With the vast migrations of the last two hundred years, we have lost our family origins. Take the time to become aware of those individuals who make up your ancestry. Trace your family tree to where it began. Talk to the oldest members of your family to gain a more complete understanding of your family. Much of our ability to cope with life's stresses rests with our genetic make-up. Honor your mother and father, and their mothers and fathers. It would be very helpful if you could go back at least seven generations. Our bodies are our most intimate relationship. By knowing more about our origins, we know more about our physical, emotional and mental tendencies.

The following statement is helpful in realizing your connection to your body:

"I am ever more aware of the importance of listening to my body's continuing awareness. By listening to my body's accumulative awareness, I gain its wisdom through an intuitive bond that allows me to know the past, present and immediate future with clarity. In turn, I allow the continuing awareness of my body to view its origin through my First State significance."

Repeat this aloud as often as it seems to want to speak through you.

Thoughts:

In all ways, always be willing to understand.

Creation is constantly enfolding and unfolding itself through me as the accumulative awareness of matter evolving through space and time. Creation is constantly enfolding and unfolding itself through me as my awareness of timelessness and shapelessness.

My authentic response to life is evidence of my willingness to know beyond any boundary considerations.

Lifestyle Suggestions:

Meditation: It is impossible to meditate at progressively deeper levels if your body and mind are loaded with stress. Willfully directing life force energy, also named chi, ki, ka or prana, through your body is the most effective way to melt away years of accumulated stress and anxiety. Chi or prana is the fatigueless energy that permeates all matter, and in some beliefs, is the substance out of which everything is made. The ability to willfully direct this life-giving and life-renewing force is vital to Knowing.

In the previous Lifestyle Suggestion sections we began to focus on a complete yogic breath combined with the seven-one-seven-count breathing pattern. Refresher:

The yogic breath: allow each inhalation to pour into the body, filling up the lungs from the bottom up. Allow the lower abdomen to bulge outward as the breath begins. Lift the bulge upward, spreading apart your ribs, as the breath continues to fill your lungs. Expand your chest then slightly shrug your shoulders at the top of each inhalation. The exhalation should pour from your body beginning with the top of the lungs. Collapse your shrugged shoulders and chest expansion as you begin to exhale. Next, allow the mid-ribs to contract inward followed by the collapse of your lower abdominal bulge. Each breath should be slow and deliberately paced with a metronome – seven counts in, hold one count, seven counts out.

Before going on to the next phase of the breathing technique for eliminating stress and anxiety we need to first have a clear understanding of the anatomy we will be willfully affecting:

At the base of the brain and at the top of the spinal column sits the medulla oblongata. It is the lowest part of the brainstem and serves as the site of connection between the brain and the spinal cord. Located just above the foramen magnum in the skull and in front of the cerebellum, the medulla oblongata contains a number of nerve centers, which are responsible for controlling involuntary processes such as the heartbeat, breathing, and body temperature regulation. It is only about two and a half centimeters (an inch) wide and comprises less than 1% of the entire weight of the central nervous system. In spite of its small size, though, it is integral to the transmission of nerve impulses between the spinal cord and the higher brain. Many of the nerve fibers, which pass through the medulla oblongata, cross over, so that many impulses from the right side of the brain control functions on the left side of the body and vice-versa.

In metaphysical terms, the medulla oblongata, or, "Mouth of God," in ancient texts, serves as the opening in the body where life force energy (chi or prana) enters. The physical and etheric bodies are connected in twenty-one primary energy centers, seven within the physical structure and fourteen within the etheric structure. Each group of seven is lined up to form a vertical column, a pillar. The center column corresponds with the spinal column having the first energy center (chakra) at the base of the spine and the last at the crown of the head. The two columns of seven energy centers in the etheric body appear on either side of the physical body and behave in much the same manner as the chakras of the physical form.

We unconsciously affect this etheric opening at the base of our skulls during times of resistance by silently reaching a hand back to rub the top of our necks. The life force pouring through the center of our hands is enough to slightly encourage an increased flow, however, when we are overly uninterested in our immediate circumstances or emotionally tired, our physical and etheric bodies respond by expanding this opening through a yawn. Yawning increases the flow of prana or chi inward through the medulla oblongata and lungs.

Continuing with the technique:

As you breathe in (count of seven) through your nose lift your face upward while keeping the lower jaw stationary. This physical action will force open the metaphysical aspect of the Mouth of God. With your face still shining upward, as you pause for a count of one, with your imagination, your mind's eye, willfully force chi in through the etheric opening at the point where your head and neck join. Do this by imagining a stream of light moving through the back of the neck into the fifth chakra, then radiate it downward into the chest as you begin your count of seven on the exhale, allowing your face to return to the beginning position with your mouth closed.

Always breathe through your nose. Do this for at least fifteen minutes.

Diet: As always, eat less, and chew more. Make your food into a liquid before swallowing. This will eliminate the need for drinking during meals. Notice any cravings that become persistent. Make a note of any tastes, such as sweet, sour or metallic, that are present between meals. This could indicate certain medical conditions that should be attended to such as over toxicity of the muscle tissue, severe food allergies, etc. At night, while lying in bed, gently push your hands into the lower abdomen making a wide circular movement that includes the entire soft area your belly. Do this for about five minutes, increasing the pressure as you continue.

Exercise: Keep investigating those dynamic types of exercise that allow you to meditate while being active.

~ *Chapter IV Footnotes* ~

1 This primary conflict is metaphorically explained in Genesis as the moment when Adam and Eve, incarnating for the first time, felt naked and all at once overwhelmed in a sense-driven, instinctually motivated physical form. The consciousness of the physical body ruled over the knowing sovereignty of the Soul as a means of securing the race for future generations until such a time when the Soul would command the physical form from the experience gained through repetitive incarnations.

2 The Logos formed the energetic grid-like structure of the Akashic Records after its union with the Earth Spirit as a means for Triads to communicate an unbiased observation of the Earth realm. Because of this, little is known in the Akasha about the actual formation of planet Earth.

3 Amun-Re (Amun-Ra) was king of all the gods of Egypt. Helio-Gabalus was the term in ancient Greece.

4 Gaia is the goddess of the earth and mother of Cronus and the Titans in ancient Greek mythology.

5 Our understanding of Dyadic awareness has come a very long way since the Augustinian monk, Gregor Mendel, opened the way for the Human Genome Project to forever change humanity's view of itself. Most of this project's findings can be researched on the Internet at various sites.

6 Each genre's spiral signatures are identical until a mutation within a genre causes a new spiral signature and an evolutionary jump begins a new signature within the Records.

7 Most ascension happens only after several dedicated lifetimes that directly support the ascension process. With males, this usually means lives of celibacy.

8 The word "only" implies that Mary was the singular parent of Jesus.

9 Gnosticism is a pre-Christian philosophical and religious movement. Gnostics claimed to have secret knowledge about God, humanity and the rest of the universe of which the general population was unaware. It became one of the three main belief systems within first century Christianity, but did not flourish because it did not discriminate against other religions or women. Gnostics believed salvation is achieved through knowledge. This teaching was centered on I AM awareness and was forced into hiding from the fourth to fifteenth centuries by Christianity as it forced conversion on all other religions.

10 In Gnosticism – A Divine power or nature emanating from the Supreme Being which plays various roles in the operation of the universe.

11 Born to the Emperor Constantius Chlorus and Saint Helen in CE 278. He worshiped the Roman god Sol.

12 Mary Magdalene gave birth to three children, two daughters and a son, fathered by Jesus the Nazarene.

13 We collectively move beyond the midway point in the thousand-year-thick photon field/wave that begins the shift of human consciousness back to unity in 2011.

14 The leader of this group was a reincarnation of an illumined individual who had marched with Sananda some thirty-seven thousand years before. See Chapter Eleven.

15 Psychokinetically influenced life force energy driven by pure intention.

*"There are two ways
to live your life. One is as though
nothing is a miracle.
The other is
as though everything
is a miracle."*

—. *Albert Einstein*

Chapter V

~ Our Dimensional Communion ~

Thousands of years ago during the Atlatian period, a culture that predates the Fertile Crescent period,[1] mystics knew everything the biologists, geneticists, chemists, physicians, engineers, physicists and astrophysicists are "proving" today through scientific disciplines. This numinous knowing was the template used by mystics to bring thought into matter as a means of satisfying their purposeful needs and wants;[2] they did not, therefore, consume the matter of Earth. In short, Atlatian resources were mined from the etheric body of the planet instead of the physical matter body of Earth. The Atlatians used the knowing awareness of how creation was metaphysically and physically ordered, to live in complete harmony and balance with Earth's other systems of "life" and allowing that life to go virtually unspoiled. The Lemurians before them had consumed Earth's resources but in an extremely balanced manner, especially when compared with today's global use of natural resources. The greater knowing of the delicate nature of life influenced the Lemurians to keep their everyday living needs to a minimum. Like the Egyptians long after them, the Lemurians built their houses of perishable materials that would easily breakdown and return to the cycle of life such as mud and straw. Only buildings and below ground facilities dedicated to the greater knowing and used for the celebration of all life were made of more durable materials such as granite and metals.

Lemurian mystics, through reading the Akashic Records, knew the Logos had used an inconceivable amount of time to observe the extremely complex nature of evolving matter and its corresponding awareness, and that awareness' response to the constant cyclical waves of energy emanating from the center of Creation. Once the Logos were completely satisfied that the conditions on Earth were right for a Soul to enflesh, they integrated their observations within the Akashic Records of the planet as a future guide for incarnate Souls and opened the rays for incarnations to begin. This happened thousands of millenniums before the first Dyadic footsteps of a Triad appeared upon terra firma. This was not just a question of merely selecting which species would best serve the sensory observational needs of the Triads, it was also a question of how to assure Triadic release from this realm once the collective Souls had satisfied the assessment of Earth's three primary manifest realms; water, land

and air. The only effective way to accomplish this was to find a Dyadic relationship that would be as mutually desirous of expanding beyond its first vision evolutionary boundaries as Triads would be to migrate from this system to the next once they finished finding themselves through the different layers of matter. This mutually defining relationship, therefore, had to have within it a time boundary that would act as a prompt to both the Dyadic awareness and Triadic consciousness as to when it was time to allow the expansion to ascension and transmigration of Souls to begin. This system of observe, capture and release was the method used by Triads to explore other dimensional realities all across the Universe. The Akashic Records indicate this time barrier to be linked to the number of generations from the first Homo erectus mutation (Homo sapien) for Dyads and the grand cycles[3] of energy emanating from the center of creation for Triads.

~ *Our Earliest Forms* ~

As was stated, a vast amount of time[4] was spent observing the evolving forms, waiting for the exact conditions to spontaneously emerge within primates[5] for a perfect Triadic/Dyadic fit. Aside from the above-mentioned factor, primates were chosen because of the enormous potential held within their physical and mental makeup. There was another key – while all mammals experience emotions as part of an immediate response to their circumstances, it was the integrating of memories through emotional ties of one generation of apes to the next that was considered primary to the process of holding memories within the Dyadic/Triadic form. Balanced groupings of emotional memories are passed from generation to generation within primates as a means of preserving their evolving awareness. In other words, genetics ensures the evolution of the physical form; emotional memories ensure the evolution of awareness. This passing of emotionally induced memories went beyond instinctual behavior patterns, allowing several subsequent generations to use passed-on subconscious or pre-conscious memories as a means of securing a complete experience of Earth. These emotional memories became the intuitive messages that allowed a greater range of empathic communication through the sharing of urges or anthropocentric prompts.

The primate structures we Triads combine with today were sped along their early evolutionary track to create the exact simpatico needed to ensure the optimum conditions for longevity and the right ratios of conscious awareness to honor the linear time boundary set within the Dyadic/Triadic accord. This fast track process began some 250,000 years ago with the discovery, by the Logos, of a mutated primate form in the Homo erectus branch of early humans. The nervous and endocrine systems, along with the slightly larger brain of the mutation (called Homo sapiens), allowed the etheric body of the Dyadic forms to blend completely with the etheric body of the enjoined Triads, thus allowing a higher rate of chi exchange between the two forms. This increased chi, ki, ka, prana or life force energy, was used as manna for the inhabiting Soul and was also needed to repair the damage constantly created where the boundaries of the Soul intertwine with the boundaries of the physical form. This boundary damage is a result of the inconsistency of two divergent forms of Creation occupying the exact same space and time; this is the original conflict spoken of as the original sin. Before this, Triads could only briefly use Dyadic forms before the gaps and overlapping energies of their corresponding etheric bodies[6] caused emotional and mental traumas that ultimately resulted in physical harm to the Dyads, cutting life spans to approximately two decades. Once the new variety of human was discovered, Triads could spend increasingly longer periods fully integrated within the Dyadic form with only a minimal amount of harm because Souls fed off the increased gathering of chi shared through the endocrine/chakra system, instead of the subtle energies of the physical form. The Dyads gained from longer periods of combining through the increased exposure to memories held within the etheric body of the Triads; the Triads gained by way of the creation of more memory fields within their etheric bodies through the experiences afforded by the increasing longevity on Earth. Once the mutually beneficial relationship was fully established, ensuing generations of Dyadic/Triadic combining had even less resistance to each other, resulting in age spans of hundreds of years, as much as nine hundred during times of unity. The Souls associated with the planets of our solar system were the first to begin to explore dimensional reality on Earth, particularly those Souls who had already incarnated within the atmospheres of some of the satellite planets such as Maldec.[7] The first two Souls to incarnate in the new primate forms were Souls that had their origins on Earth, first as Dyadic structures, then as Entities and finally as Dyadic Souls.[8]

~ *The Science of Man* ~

Modern science has still not resolved the origin of Homo sapiens. Two extreme scenarios have been proposed. According to the first, the distribution of anatomical traits in modern human populations in different regions was inherited from local populations of Homo erectus and other intermediate forms. This multi-regional hypothesis states that all modern humans evolved in parallel from earlier populations in Africa, Europe and Asia, with some genetic intermixing among the populations of these regions. Support for this comes from the similarity of certain minor anatomical structures in modern human populations and preceding populations of Homo erectus in the same regions.

A different scientific model suggests that a small, relatively isolated population of early humans evolved into modern Homo sapiens, spreading across Africa, Europe, and Asia – displacing and eventually replacing all other early human populations. In this scenario, the variation among modern populations is a recent phenomenon. Part of the evidence to support this theory comes from molecular biology, especially studies of the diversity and mutation rate of nuclear DNA and mitochondrial DNA in living human cells. From these studies, an approximate time of divergence from the common ancestor of all modern human populations can be calculated to be at around 200,000 years ago. Molecular methods have also tended to point to an African origin for all modern humans, implying that the ancestral population of all living people migrated from Africa to other parts of the world – thus the name of this interpretation, the "Out of Africa Hypothesis."

The Akashic Records indicate that once the "new" form (Homo sapiens) emerged, was selected and proven over time as being able to withstand Triadic Soul influences, Souls began to migrate from several different star systems to begin their journey into the realms of matter here on Earth. As Souls began to arrive here from the Arcturus, Draco, Lyra, Orion, Pleiades and Sirius star systems, the Logos, along with the lead Soul groups from each system, shifted the basic genetic structure of the new primate to more mimic the Dyadic life forms used in those other systems. Each of the four genetic shifts, or alterations, created to refine the nervous systems of our ancestors to better accommodate the energy signatures of Souls transmigrating from other systems inadvertently formed new blood variations. These new variables gave us the blood types "A," "B" and "AB" from out of the base type "O," which was a natural result of the earlier spontaneous mutation process within the Homo erectus grouping. With the mutated "O" blood type of Homo sapien, more molecules of chi could piggyback on the red blood cells; the more chi, the more energetic and less reliant on physical sustenance the physical body became. However, the additional molecules attached to the red blood cells, as in the "A," "B" and "AB" types, gave less distribution of chi, causing the physical body to need faster burning foods and longer periods of rest. The added molecules of the newer, alien-derived blood types generated subtle inconsistencies of energy within the etheric body of the Dyadic form causing the original Dyadic to Triadic conflict to reappear but to a lesser degree than was present with Homo erectus.

Not all the subtle changes played as well here on Earth as they had in the other systems. Each new blood type[9] slightly altered the manner in which the body naturally distributes the chi to the organs and tissue it receives through minute openings between the Dyadic and Triadic etheric bodies. This chi distribution variation also altered how the combined Dyadic/Triadic awareness maintained the connection between the Soul and physical bodies, dropping life spans into the one or perhaps two hundred-year range. These newer bloodlines happened over a significant period of time, giving the Dyadic forms plenty of time to adjust before the collective of "arriving" Souls enfleshed. This adjustment period helped to lessen the Triad to Dyad conflict that was being regenerated by the genetic tweaking of Homo sapiens by the Logos.

~ *Adam and Eve* ~

The Dyadic Soul that incarnated as Mary of Sepphoris was the first fully conscious feminine incarnation into Homo sapiens form. She appears in Hebrew creation mythology as being Eve of the Garden of Eden (Eden is named Os Sira in the Akashic Records). Her entry as Eve into this dimension was made possible in part by the enjoined Soul balancing her feminine skew that had been the first Homo sapiens, called Adam in the Book of Genesis. Mary and Jesus as Adam and Eve had opened the doorway into this dimension as the first enjoined Souls[10] to incarnate as Homo sapiens. They then demonstrated the "way out" in their last incarnations through the ascension of their Dyadic forms. They had become Souls from out of matter, which then gained liberation from birth and death through the transmigration of their Dyadic consciousness/energy into the next more expanded dimensional reality adjacent to human awareness. Both of the Souls of Mary and Jesus were created here on Earth. Once created, they enjoined with each other to express the highest emanation possible on Earth – Christ Consciousness. Their enjoining allowed them to take human form through gestation within a womb without the need of egg fertilization. While Triads emanate Christ Consciousness when they enjoin in

preparation to incarnating, the emanation of energy from Dyadic Soul formations enjoining pulsates at a frequency identical to that of the Earth's matrix,
giving an enormous range to the aura field of energy surrounding such individuals. Enjoined Dyadic Souls are capable of moving mountains with a whisper because they have literally been the mountain and fully empathize with the
matter creating the mountain. The matter in turn is completely obligated to
reform itself to the will of a paring of enjoined Dyadic Souls. Jesus intimated
during his final Passover gathering, "When the Sparrow falls, I am there. I am
in the dawn and setting of the sun. Look under a rock and I am there. For as
you wrap your garment against the cold, you feel me, for I am the garment and
the cold alike. Eat of a loaf and I am there; sip from a dish of wine – I am there.
As I have passed throughout all of Earth's forms, the Father and I are one. We
are alpha and omega; one each as the other." (From the Akashic Records)

As previously stated, Triads are First State Beings that enjoin with each other
for the single purpose of incarnating into matter. Interestingly, the Akashic
Records do not refer to Triads as Souls unless they are enjoined. Because of
this it has been argued by some mystics that the phenomenon of Souls only
exists here on Earth. This is inaccurate to the greater knowing as Triads from
other systems are also referred to in the Akashic-type records of their worlds
as Souls without evidence that they are enjoined. It is also shown that in some
extraordinary cases, Souls can be created directly by Celestial and Solar deities. Such Souls are extremely rare, are imbued with the exact same qualities
of their creators, and, as all Souls, are eternal just as is with Triads of the First
Moment. While Dyadic Souls are comparatively numerous in our solar system, they are not indicated in the records of other worlds. As indicated in this
material, a Soul can be created when Dyadic awareness reaches and repeatedly incarnates as its final form, encounters and blends with Triadic awareness, then, through a series of incarnations with that Triad, ascends out of its
evolving state to become an Entity, and is no longer at the affect of the Universal Law of Attraction. When, as an Entity, Dyadic awareness is finished freely
and willfully, exploring the dimensional reality that gave rise to its existence,
it, without the influence of a Triad, ascends to its final incarnation to become
a Dyadic Soul. This type of Soul is not a First State Being in that it evolved;
yet, it is everything a First State being is, and more. It is Triadic, now being a
static state of Consciousness, Energy and Urge,[11] and this new Soul is also
fully conscious of its previous evolution through matter, such as with the case
of Jesus and Mary. These types of Souls are extremely rare in the overall population of Triadic Souls, owing their ultimate state to certain spontaneous con-

ditions that arise within the planetary systems through which they are evolving and the full empathic rapport with a Triad that allows them the knowledge of their origin from the First Moment. All Bodhisattvas are Dyadic Souls – born of this World, in this World and no longer of this World.

The Lemurian and Atlatian Souls who achieved this state were later inspired the images of and were revered as the goddesses and gods of early Greek and Roman mythology. As all the mythological stories report, these gods and goddesses were of superhuman ability. Such Souls could readily manipulate the matter of this world because they were the matter of this World. When need be, and usually in great times of human need, Dyadic Souls enter into and manipulate stone statuary or shape-shift to take the form of animals, or appear as one of the elements of fire, water, earth or water as a way of shifting the consciousness of a particular human consciousness.

Souls who are First State Triads in origin retain all their memories of combining with Dyadic forms, but do not have the firsthand experience of being an evolving form. They have the memories but do not link the memories together as wisdom. While Triadic Souls can easily manifest thought to matter, it is more difficult to freely and willfully alter existing forms such as is the case of Dyadic Souls freely shape-shifting themselves or other matter. Triadic Souls can achieve great feats through the boundless manifest power of their imagination, but seldom do they rise to the level of Bodhisattva or above. Dyadically originated Souls usually stay within the energetic confines of the planetary system of their origin and naturally have a complete knowing of all matter, awareness and consciousness within that system. They do commune with the Dyadic Souls from the other planets of this solar system as a way of allowing a greater knowing of all life within the energetic confines of the sun. Triadic Souls are not bound to a system through having evolved through its substance and corresponding myriad of multi dimensional awareness. Triadic Souls are little more than observers to the dynamic flow of consciousness and energy present within the realm they are observing and as such give added dimension to the Worlds they observe. They are completely free to incarnate and transmigrate individually or within a collective and are never bound by the natural laws that govern the system they are observing.

~ *The Soul's Entry into Form* ~

As has been stated, when Triadic Souls enjoin then enflesh, they produce a field of energy referred to as Christ emanation. This emanation is a gift of sorts having little to do with the actual workings of the human body. The phenomenon that allows Souls to enter a Dyadic form is the lowering of the harmonic pulse (rhythm or vibration) of a portion of this emanation into a cellular-like, pure-light energy mass that is equivalent to Earth's matter. This thickened ethrioplasmic[12] substance is produced and maintained as an imme- diate response to the incarnation intention of two enjoining Souls. Energy being just energy, the intention of the enjoined Souls gives the ethrioplasmic matter entering the body a magnetic field of sorts. This magnetic emanation attracts and repulses other forms of matter according to its polarization. To incarnate, each of the enjoined Souls gathers a portion of this pure cellular light in the form of a spiral matrix cord and extends this stringlet of jelly-like light particles into the thymus gland[13] of the physical body. The thymus gland lies in the upper part of the mediastinum behind the sternum and extends up- wards into the root of the neck. This silvery looking cord originates in the crown of the Christ body, and extends through the heart chakra of the Soul and Etheric bodies to the physical body, creating a thread-like attachment through all seven simultaneous forms – Physical, Etheric, Astral, Causal, Mental, Ce- lestial and Christ. As the cord touches the outer boundaries of the thymus, each enjoined Soul allows 144,000 of these individuated ethrioplasmic cells to descend into the physical body, with each cell taking up a specific residence within the energy grid that is the metaphysical expression of both nervous systems. These same cells ascend out of the physical body at the time of death taking with them a certain amount of physical weight,[14] between .75 and 1.75 ounces (21 and 50 grams). With children seven years of age, the weight loss at death is more, owing to the greater density of the ethrioplasmic field entering the body than would be present in an adult of seventy years of age. This im- plies that the number of cells remains at 144,000, but the congealed light matter's density lessens as the body ages. This density depletion is due to the conflict generated from the Triadic to Dyadic synthesis over time.

Each light cell, according to its unique harmonic resonance, aligns specifi- cally with one of the twenty-one chakras of the combined Triadic/Dyadic bod- ies. The wave properties of these cells allow them to gather and share the chi energy brought into the physical body on the breath and through the minute openings[15] between the etheric bodies of the Triad and Dyad as a response to the fluctuations in the ether tide.[16] This direct sharing of chi between these evenly spaced points generates a grid-like web in both the physical and etheric bodies that can be observed by mystics or other "sensitives" as non-electro-magnetic lay lines. Each of the light cells anchoring the grid is capable of working with any of the seven core chakras, as well as the fourteen secondary chakras[17] of the etheric bodies while maintaining a specific alignment with one primary chakra.

The primary physiological reaction to the passing of this ethrioplasmic sub-stance in and out through the thymus gland is the production of T-cells that allow the body to prevent and eliminate disease. Lymphocytes originate from stem cells (haemocytoblasts) in bone marrow. The ethrioplasmic molecules of the Christ emanation send out a "call" to the lymphocytes, which then begin their journey to the thymus. They then divide into two groups: those that enter the blood, some of which remain in circulation while some lodge in other lymphoid tissue, and those that remain in the thymus gland and are the source of future generations of T-lymphocytes. Those that enter the thymus mature and develop into the activated T-lymphocytes that respond to antigens en-countered elsewhere in the body. These thymic lymphocytes carry out three defensive functions. First, they stimulate the production and growth of anti-bodies by other lymphocytes. Second, they stimulate the growth and action of the phagocytes, which surround and engulf invading viruses and microbes. Finally, the thymus lymphocytes[18] recognize and destroy foreign and abnor-mal tissue. The physical body is incapable of functioning for very long if this vital aspect of the immune system is not activated at the time the Soul enters the physical form or is in disrepair due to the conflict-generated stresses of life.

As revealed earlier, a certain degree of conflict is present the moment a Soul enters a physical body. This natural conflict, with its resulting stresses, is the primary factor in disease and aging. Our physical bodies are meant to break-down over time – some two hundred and fifty to three hundred years. The added stresses of our lifestyles and our rush to maturity compound this core conflict, giving us rapidly aging organs and glands. The maturation of the thymus and other lymphoid tissue is stimulated by thymosin, a hormone se-creted by the epithelial cells that form the framework of the thymus gland. The onset of adolescence brings the involution of the thymus and with increasing age, the T-lymphocyte response to antigens declines, leaving the immune system less and less effective. To better illustrate the extent of this involution, the thymus weighs about 10 to 15 g. (about half an ounce) at birth with its maximum weight at around 30 – 40 g (around 1 to 1.5 ounces) just before puberty. By the age of forty, it has returned to its weight at birth, leaving our bodies to guard against the rapid process of aging with an immune system only capable of caring for an infant. This is why pathogenic viral diseases are particularly harmful to infants and the elderly – they cannot fight off a growing disease.

Metaphysically speaking, our physical bodies are impacted by much more than meets the senses or invades the body. We are vast beings with several surrounding dynamic layers of energy all working in unison to balance past, present and future influences. The most significant of these influences are the past-life memories held within the etheric field of our Souls that imprint general information onto the ethrioplasmic field of the physical body. These imprints include detailed information about previous health conditions and maladies. The physical body genetically carries forward bloodline predispositions that work in conjunction with our unconscious past-life health imprints, giving us a straight line of time from our birth to our death. To put the icing on the cake of our extenuating previous-lifetime health issues, future influences affect our overall harmonics in radiating waves of intuitive impressions regarding the immutable events established along the path of a given incarnation. These unchangeable events are placed within an incarnation by the Soul as a series of wakeup calls, so to speak, and are fully known to all humans at least ninety days prior to their unfolding.

Some general statements can be made concerning Triadic past-life memories, present-life genetic conditions and future intuitive insights generated by immutable events: If an individual incarnates quickly, say within a few years from a previous incarnation, the etheric memory imprints regarding the health of that lifetime will be very strong. These types of complaints often disappear after puberty and if they do persist, it is usually with a lesser degree of seriousness. Conversely, if robust health was experienced in the most recent past life, then that condition will prevail adding to the overall energy of the physical form.

If a present-life genetic predisposition is exaggerated by a past-life health memory, the result could be a rapid tendency toward that genetic condition. These types of cooperating influences often last the entire lifetime and can be as troublesome as they were in the previous lifetime. If the individual should come to know the past life as an influence to the genetic condition, the overall condition will lessen just through the realization of the source of the condition.

Should a Soul's body be prematurely killed, either through crime or in war, and the Soul reincarnates quickly into its next life, it will carry the wound(s) to the new body through some visible condition, such as a birthmark or in extreme cases a physical limitation. The effect will lessen as the Soul learns how to deal with the leftover resentments from the incident. Should the Soul incarnate with the perpetrator associated with that past life experience, the opportunity for recovery is greater through the sweeping tides of karma that will balance the inconsistent energy of the rift.

If a Soul leaves the body in an attempt to avoid the complexities of life, say through suicide, it will quickly incarnate to complete that cycle and will bear the "mark" of the previous self-inflicted exit: literally and figuratively. This type of influence is extremely hard to interrupt and can result in subsequent attempts to exit anguished circumstances through self-destruction. If a pattern of felo-de-se develops over several lifetimes, the Soul will be given opportunities to incarnate in other systems (planets within our solar system or other worlds within other star systems) as a means of breaking the cycle.

Present genetics can be altered and brought into balance when the inhabiting Soul accepts the intelligent awareness of the Dyad as being equally unique in Creation. This complete acknowledgment of one for the other is all that is required to completely shift the harmonics of the physical form. Once the body is brought into balance, all genetic information is recoded to the intentional cooperation of Soul and body.

Isolated fears and phobias can develop when the Soul has a contracted response to a future immutable event that could bring harm to the physical form. Once both Soul and body know of an immutable future event, the overall response can be expanded to include other outcome choices, which bring about different circumstances on the other side of the event.

The Dyadic awareness that survives death carries with it the general memory of the physical body it most recently helped to create. Because these types of memories are mostly instinctual and ability-oriented, they remain a small contributor to the general health conditions of the new body.

When in human form, we live according to the natural flow of chi energy and the harmonic resonance wafting from the enfleshed form as Soul combines with matter to bring about human consciousness. The amount of chi and the intrinsic nature of our harmonics are our localized Universal Law of Attraction – who we are, we draw to us. Influences and immutable events exist to reveal more of our presence within the Great Schematic; they do not exist to teach us about life on Earth. As Souls, we know beyond the events and circumstances of each successive life and have nothing to learn that would affect our Souls. Our Souls are complete in every moment.

By knowing our place within Creation – who we are, how we were derived and our purpose for being here – the effects of all external stresses are lessened to a very great degree, leaving us free to manifest our decided destiny. If we take care of our physical body in a conscious knowing manner, we will have the optimum amount of time allotted for this incarnation and we will attract to us all those things we purposefully want to complete in our revelation of this realm. Once we have this type of relationship with our physical forms, we can expand our conscious awareness into adjacent dimensions and begin the process of ascension. Knowing is the first step; manifesting is the second step and liberation is the third step toward ascension. The process of liberation for all Souls is the second birth, allowing the Soul to become twice born – first into the body and then encompassing the body.

~ The Collective Soul's Entry into Earth ~

As previously stated, with each individual human, a silver cord runs from the crown of the Christ body through the heart chakras of the other five bodies to connect in the physical body through the thymus gland. Apart from establishing the necessary energy grid for Souls to incarnate into matter, the Logos also serves as the silver corded connection between the seven levels of collective conscious awareness and the collective physical herd, and ensures that each age of humankind has 144,000 continuously active Dyadic Souls[19] on the planet to serve as guides. These Dyadic Souls serve as a representation from the collective of the exact number of ethrioplasmic cells descending into matter from an individual Soul into a physical form. Like their cellular counterparts, these 144,000 Souls take up ethereal residence on the planet (the body) to ensure that the balance and harmonic resonance of energy nurtures the body of humankind. This gathering of Dyadic Souls is our collective anchor here on Earth. The Earth Spirit works in complete unanimity with these Souls to bring about what is needed for our collective adventure, no matter what that need or outcome might be. The entry into the Earth of this collective silver cord happens at the exact point occupied by the pyramid complex of Giza, with the Sphinx being the energy vortex.

There are always exactly 144,000 Bodhisattva,[20] or Dyadically formed Souls on the planet at all times, just as there are always 144,000 cells from the Soul body manifest within the physical body. This collective outward expression of the Soul's connection to the physical body is necessary for our collective sojourn on Earth and our eventual ascension out of this World. Just as with the seven different bodies of each Soul's incarnation, the Bodhisattva express as seven corresponding levels of function to anchor the consciousness of the Solar Deity to the heart chakra of the Earth Spirit.

Practice:

Daily acknowledgment of a hierarchical structure that is actively ensuring your individual and our collective experience's needs through its representation of 144,000 Earth-born Souls is vital to expanding your/our level of conscious awareness. Each of us is guided and refreshed through our connection to one or more of these Avatar Souls. The good news, we do not have to be aware of their presence to enjoy the benefit of their manna,[21] we need only consciously acknowledge their gift to increase the flow.

Remember, it is important to honor your ancestry. The genetic lines concentrated in your body have brought you to this moment in time. In this regard, you are instructed to honor your mother, father, and theirs before them for a total of seven generations. As fully knowing beings, we are like children at play in a wonderful World of Souls who anticipate our needs and desires. Until we are sovereign, that is to say, until we take complete responsibility for each moment, we rely on these forces to govern our destinies. Taking sovereignty is our birthright and our eventual state of conscious awareness. We can hasten this through clearly stating:

"I am ever more aware of the vast presence of those Souls who join with me in my observation and ultimate self-revelation within this realm. I joyfully command to be awakened to the greater knowing of All That Is through my Divine Union with those who radiate pure joy from the seven levels of conscious awareness. I honor those who have come before and those who will proceed by commanding joy now as my complete experience in each and every moment."

Repeat this aloud during the day as often as it wants to speak through you.

Thoughts:

Joy is the radiance of knowing.

I am aware of myself through being observant of others. We are all mirrors to each other's journeys, reflecting the positive and negative aspects of our expectations and judgments in every exchange.

My nurturing comes from my willingness to command life from out of the ethers.

Lifestyle Suggestions:

Meditation: Being creative allows us the healing moments when we forget our concerns for life's many conundrums. Take a few moments during the day to be creative in whatever way is most convenient to your lifestyle. The greatest form of meditation is the simplest expression of activity. Watch how children play – they ooze complete confidence through their creative play. In their natural state, each movement is joined with emotionally driven thought to manifest the perfect meditation.

Buy a coloring book and crayons. Use your non-dominant hand to fill in the colors you feel are the best communicators of the feelings you experience when thinking of the object you are coloring. Avoid using colors that are automatically picked. Example: a child who has fallen from a tree might associate angry or hurt feelings with trees and therefore color a tree in an angry fashion with colors that depict his or her associated feelings. If allowed to express those feelings, the child will eventually replace those feelings with colors that are learned as being appropriate for the tree.

Diet: Continue with the practice of eating less and chewing more. All foods and liquids should be ingested in moderation. Eat raw foods or slightly cooked foods as often as possible. Eat foods that are natural, that is to say, foods lacking a list of ingredients or printed packaging. Some foods can harm the body's ability to defend itself against microbes. The following are just some examples of the foods that can dramatically lower immune system efficiency: distilled alcohol, tobacco, caffeine, nicotine patches, nerve stimulants, foods high in cholesterol, refined sugars, artificial sugar replacements, homogenized dairy products, food preservatives, food additives and most artificial vitamin supplements.

~ *Supporting the Thymus Gland* ~

A healthy thymus function is critical to a healthy immune system, which leads to better overall general health. As we age, the thymus gland naturally undergoes shrinkage; this shrinkage leads to reduced thymus function. Consuming diets rich in fruits and vegetables in addition to taking natural supplements such as vitamins A, C and E, selenium, zinc and thymus extract will support and improve thymus gland function. Herbal supplements can also improve the thymus function and assist the immune system. Each individual's dosage of the following herbs will be different: Echinacea, golden seal, peppermint, cardamom, cinnamon, cloves, spearmint, rose hips, oats, millet, carrot, bee pollen, wild cherry, slippery elm, chickweed, garlic, ginger, hibiscus, sage, orange peel, mullein, lemon peel, pleurisy root and feverfew.

The single most important activity to increase your immune system's efficiency is SLEEP. Get an average of between seven and nine hours. Better yet, sleep when you are tired. Some people can go for hours on twenty minutes' rest while others need a full night's sleep. Do not compare your needs with those of others. If you are in an intimate relationship, it is important to keep the same sleep hours. This can be difficult with differing work schedules. The term "sleeping together" is used to describe lovers. The physical body is the least real of all the bodies; intimacy happens at many different levels. Those who "sleep together" in addition to having sexual intercourse are achieving deep levels of intimacy within their preconscious awareness. Notice that there is a sense of emptiness if you have ever left the bed immediately after having had coitus. Conversely, there is a sense of completion when you fall asleep in each other's arms after having made love. Sleep and intimacy are extremely important to balanced health, more so than proper foods and general exercise.

Exercise: It is extremely important to begin forming a balanced approach to the body you are living within. Not all exercise programs achieve this balance. Being buff or pursuing a body-sculpting program might be attractive to those concerned with their physical appearance. It is important to listen to your body to get a better understanding of what forms and levels or exercise are needed by your body to maintain optimum health. This will take experimenting with many different forms and levels. Listening to your body is critical. If your body does not feel right or is outright complaining through chronic stiffness, pain or fatigue, then begin modifying your approach. If you have not been exercising, allow for a two-month period of recovery before deciding if stiffness or pain is chronic.

The one aspect of all exercise that is equally important to all humans is conscious breathing. Continue with the yogic breathing exercises from the previous chapter. Learning to breathe properly is vital to achieving an energetic balance within the body.

~ *Chapter V Footnotes* ~

1 The period designated by archeologists and anthropologists as the beginning of civilized humankind.

2 The Knowing practices of the early mystics (26,000-8,500 years ago) over time degenerated into the alchemy and magic associated with the Dark Ages (500-1000 AD). Even though these corrupted practices yielded very little, they did form the foundation of modern science.

3 Each cycle comes in thirteen thousand year intervals with the initiating wave itself being one thousand years in duration, giving a total of fourteen thousand years to each cycle.

4 The total amount of time, in Triadic terms, from the Logos joining to manifest a dimensional gateway into Earth's playground to the final ascension will be approximately 206,000,000 years. The first primate forms that allowed Triadic intrusion into matter emerged some ten million years ago. The final entry of collective immutable events into the Akashic Records is in the year 6,720 Gregorian.

5 Presently, there are twenty-eight animal kingdom phyla. Dyadic humans are classified animalia phylum chordata; subphyla vertebrata; class mammalia. We share this with lemurs, monkeys and apes. Several other mammalian forms could have been included in this phylum that became extinct between 35,000-15,000 years ago.

6 The etheric body of a Triad is static while the etheric body of a Dyad is evolving in response to the evolution of its awareness. The dominant static state of Triadic energy generates rifts within the evolving etheric energy of the Dyadic causing the nervous system to short circuit. In Homo sapiens, the physical nervous system, endocrine and corresponding chakras of the Triad perfectly align to form a blended field of life force energy that is both static and evolutionary.

7 This small Earth-like planet orbiting Jupiter was home to a vast civilization that destroyed itself through a true hydrogen detonation. The resulting shock wave blew away the delicate atmosphere of Mars rendering its surface useless for future habitation. At this time the sun was much hotter than it is today. Venus will be our next home.

8 Our solar system is the only known region where Dyadic Souls are generated.

9 In the early Twentieth century, an Austrian scientist named Karl Landsteiner classified blood according to two distinct chemical molecules present on the surface of the red blood cells. He labeled one molecule "A" and the other molecule "B." If the red blood cell had only "A" molecules on it, that blood was called type A. If the red blood cell had only "B" molecules on it, that blood was called type B. If the red blood cell had a mixture of both molecules, that blood was called type AB. If the red blood cell had neither molecule, that blood was called type O. He was awarded the Nobel Prize for this achievement. Each blood type also demonstrates certain behavioral tendencies and preferred abilities aligned to their alien origins. In modern times it was the Japanese Government that used these blood stereotypes characteristics to place typed individuals in certain jobs as they built their military capabilities prior to and then during World War II.

10 Dyadically generated Souls do not have to enjoin to take a human form. This was the very first and one of only a dozen or so recorded instances found in the Akashic Records where Dyadic Souls enjoined to enflesh.

11 The evolutionary Dyadic awareness of its final ascended form becomes its eternal Urge.

12 Ethrioplasmic matter is a gelatin-like elastic non-matter matter whose harmonic pulse is equivalent to the tonal frequency of Earth matter without becoming matter. If observed with the senses, it would appear to be a thick liquid jellyfish-like substance made of loosely congealed light particles.

13 The thymus gland has been called the Seat of the Soul, The Seal of the Soul, Soul Seat, etc. by mystics and spiritualists alike. Many healers use the Heart chakra as the beginning point for all healing.

14 Ethrioplasmic substance weighs an equivalent of 1-1/4 ounces or 35.5 grams per cubic foot. A cubic foot of normal pressure sea level air at 48 F weighs almost exactly 1-1/4 ounces.

15 The minute openings exist at each of the seven core chakras and serve as channels for the flow of chi into the body. In addition, there are two sets of three openings independent of this chakra network: 1) where the neck and head join as the primary chi point of the brain stem; 2) at the crown of the skull as the primary point of chi to the pituitary and pineal glands.

16 The gravitational and electromagnetic influences exerted upon the physical body's etheric form. The lowest point of this influence is around 3 AM in the morning.

17 The etheric bodies of the physical and Soul forms each have seven primary chakras that work in perfect balance and harmonic attunement with the seven core chakras of the physical form.

18 In the 1960's research showed that immature white blood cells would "incubate" for a period inside the thymus gland, and exit transformed into one of the specific types of T-lymphocytes, such as T4 helper cells or T8 suppresser or cytotoxic T cells.

19 These Earth born Souls naturally resonate with the Earth Spirit because they are of the exact same harmonic resonance. When manifesting thought to hand it is important to call upon these Souls.

20 Usually Bodhisattva are Dyadically derived Souls. In very rare cases, a Triad can become Bodhisattva. There are no current examples of this in the Akashic Records. The only cases every recorded date back to the very early beginnings of Triads on the planet when Dyadic Souls were not abundant.

21 From the Old Testament: the miraculous food that God gave the Israelites during the exodus from Egypt and during their forty years of wandering through the wilderness. Another definition is a sudden event that brings abundant good.

"It is this belief in a power larger
than myself and other than myself
which allows me to venture into
the unknown and even
the unknowable."

—. *Maya Angelou*

Chapter VI

~ *Body, Mind and Soul as One Harmonic Expression in Time/Space* ~

Each single Triad is an immense being. Yet, even with the twelve intelligent universes as its playground, on its own, it has finite levels of probability and possibility within its capacity to discover and observe. Alone, it is but one point of witness to Creation. When Triads enjoin with other Triads the probabilities and possibilities exponentially amplify as each manifold frame of reference shares the events unfolding from within the First Vision. When enjoined Triads bond with Dyadic substance, the union becomes multi dimensional multiplicity with very few limitations except for those imposed by a governing consciousness, such as the World consciousness,[1] which includes collective human consciousness. In the case of life on Earth, there are the collectively agreed-upon laws of physics, time/space boundaries and, with humanity, the law of willful potentiality (cause and effect). When fully knowing of their place within the First Vision, Triads are able to contravene all laws associated with the World and collective human consciousness through the purity of one harmonic expression as unified body, mind and Soul. This type of human presentation is the personification of the Divine Presence as is also witnessed with the Logos.

As enfleshed Souls sojourning on Earth in Dyadic forms, Triads are unique cells within the collective consciousness of humanity and, as such, together form the collective Soul of the human experience. This term is not meant to imply that enjoined Souls further enjoin with all other enfleshed Souls. This is meant as a description of humanity's collective efforts while enfleshed on the planet. Triads, in unison with the Logos and, at the invitation of the Earth Spirit, share all observational and exploratory experiences through the unbiased configuration of the Akasha (Akashic Records) at the sub and preconscious levels of knowing awareness. This is done to hasten their journey on Earth that they might then transmigrate to other ascertainable and observable systems.[2] Triads also freely share observations as a means of relieving the unresolved emotions, unfulfilled expectations and incomplete experiences of numerous individual and collective incarnations. It is through this unlimited sharing arrangement that each Triad is not obligated to experience every probable event, response and ensuing circumstance to have a complete knowing of sentient human life. As such, each enjoined Soul that has enfleshed in human form is aware of what it means to play out any given role within the framework of the human drama. In this sense, Triads only need one incarnation to achieve this knowing.

Just as each cell within a human body carries the schematic of sentient life, each human being is a complete expression of the whole of humanity, and as such, carries within its being all the knowing of the collective endeavor of humankind, from the first to the last incarnation. As for outwardly expressing this complete knowing, no one human is more capable than another, i.e., Serapis Bey, Kuthumi (Koot Humi), Quan yin, Babaji, Buddha, or Jesus is no more capable than any other human to express a fully knowing vision of the whole, this being more a question of willingness and openness than genetic wiring or esoteric initiation. The willingness to open to the core stream of consciousness formed when the six bodies of each Triad collectively join to compose the hexagonally tiered boundaries of the Akasha is simply a matter of choice. To be one in conscious union with the Earth Spirit and Logos through infinite knowing begins with a choice and fulfills itself through willingness. Willingness, followed by a deep abiding sense of gratitude, is the fundamental key to all higher knowing.

In certain New Thought circles, it is taught that each human has a lower and higher self. Through this New Age understanding, the higher self is deemed all knowing and therefore good or benevolent, while the lower self takes it on the chin for every selfishly motivated thought, word or deed of the personality/ego. This is an updated carry-over from the early Catholic ideas of heavenly inspired piety and chastity versus evilly stirred wickedness and carnal lust. While this concept of a lower and higher self is true to the condition of humanity, it is true only in this regard: the lower self is our physical Dyadic form, the higher self is our Triad or Soul; the lower self is not bad because of its urges to propagate, any more than the higher self good for its desire to purify and balance. These tendencies are natural functions of each aspect of the union, are without determinable value and therefore cannot be judged in any way.

It is shown in the Akashic Records that Dyadic awareness, the repeatedly incarnating energy of our human forms, craves being overloaded with primitive organic sensory experiences, this being its one true role in our Earthly sojourn as our observational platform. The full collective memories of each incarnation, from the very first moment of conception until the very last moment of release from the body, are kept within the energy framework of the Triad's (Soul's) etheric body, and collectively express as our personality/ego once the Soul is settled[3] in the Dyadic form. In the early years of a given incarnation (from conception to the onset of puberty), Dyadic awareness is dominant to the personality/ego as a means of establishing the incarnation through evolutionary survival behaviors. This is not to say that an individual is without personality and ego in the formative years. This notion of Dyadic dominance is meant to show that physical urgings dominate personality/ego until such a time as there is a conscious cooperation between the Soul and physical body. True human intelligence emerges as the more dominant guiding force when a conscious working relationship develops between Dyadic awareness and the Triad's personality/ego. When the linearly instinctual, sensory-prioritized Dyad remains dominant beyond pubescence, the personality/ego very quickly develops a need to be relieved from constant survival yearnings. Dyadic awareness, through the Triadic personality/ego, finds such relief through narcissistic and overly hedonistic behaviors. Interestingly, one of the highest forms of this type of "pleasure for pleasure's sake" involves placing the Dyad in life or death situations. This type of action defies the Dyad's instinct to survive, momentarily lifting the dominant Dyadic survival yearning, which in turn gives the Dyad a deep sense of renewed life as it is dangled on the edge of extinction. Conversely, our Souls express direct, clear, nonsensory-delineated knowledge void of any argumentative pretext as their one true role. Because they can recall every incarnation and know themselves to be constant eternal beings, Triads find relief from the incarnational union by bringing balance to body, mind and Spirit, experiencing the three as one harmonic expression.

Usually, Dyadic awareness develops a sense of itself as an ongoing entity (an awareness that survives death) only after incarnating into the same genetic pool over a period of several hundred lifetimes. However, because Dyadic awareness is based on repetitive tasking and has little direct memory of the emotional and mental details of those incarnations, it can only really sense its ongoing nature. This sense of self is not a true self-awareness until such a time as the Dyad attracts a Triad interested in repeatedly incarnating with it for at least seven successive incarnations. When these conditions are met, the Dyad's instinctual memory is expanded to first include segmented recollection presenting itself as increasingly occurring deja vu episodes, then full episodic sensory memory as flashbacks connected to future immutable events. This gradual awakening is necessary so as not to overwhelm and cause permanent damage to the sympathetic and parasympathetic nervous systems through the release of full streams of consciousness energy through the Dyad. At this time the Dyad experiences itself as equal to the personality/ego expressions of the Triad and begins consciously communicating directly with the Triad, bypassing the personality/ego, who, until then, acted as intermediary between the Dyadic and Triadic aspects of the union.

Unlike the evolving Dyad, our personality/ego is self-aware and knows of its ongoing existence through never having lost the conscious awareness of its place within the enjoined Soul's body. When the enjoined Soul is not incarnating, the personality/ego is actively at play within the dreamscapes of the Triad's etheric body, playing out "what-if" and "if-only" scenarios that relate to the immutable events of the most recent incarnations. The average time period for this completion of missed expectations is about four years in Earthly terms, with the between-lives period being an average of some thirty years. Some metaphysicians inaccurately view this between-life phase as Soul consciousness working within parallel probable realities. The personality/ego self is a direct byproduct of the countless incarnations of Triadic consciousness into surviving Dyadic awareness and is often associated with the lower self because it only appears to be actively present when a Soul is enfleshed.

It is through this continuously conscious awareness of the personality/ego that we Triads do not have to start from square one with each new incarnation, but can consciously bring forward and incorporate selected memories and abilities as current life needs arise. We can also unconsciously bring forward behaviors or learned abilities when externally influenced by events or circumstances. The dimensionally fluid mechanism of personality/ego allows the Soul to effortlessly organize the enquiry of a given incarnation through the senses of the Dyad. As a result, the personality/ego is more closely associated with the lower survival harmonics of Dyadic energy, while imagination and intuitiveness are connected with higher harmonics of Triadic energy or Soul consciousness. In this regard, the lower self develops a need to be right as a strategy for survival; the higher self seeks to be precognitive as a means of helping the lower self maintain its purpose. The higher and lower selves together constitute the overall intelligence of a given incarnation. The notion that one aspect of the whole is better than the other, or somehow more important to the greater knowing is fruitless. In unison, without the insanity of guilt or shame, the pair is capable of feats only limited to the agreed commandments of World consciousness and collective human consciousness.

~ *Metaphysical Time/Space* ~

It is impossible to offer a clear understanding of the greater knowing of time[4] as a thought responsive-medium; individuals must experience that level of knowing for themselves as they become more and more enlightened to the truth of creation. In this offering, we will confine the discussion of time to the necessary components needed to produce a pathway to a greater knowing as it relates to the blending of body, mind and Spirit. Space as a medium of manifestation is clearly discernable to a human with sensory perception, and the true nature of space is more expansive than the senses report. In short, time and space behavior for us according to our beliefs and our beliefs determine the range of our ability to perceive time and space. If we expand our knowing regarding the medium of creation, its boundaries will widen beyond our sensory perception.

The nature of time being more a ball of yarn than a string of yarn, Soul gatherings join across interlocking, moment-specific junctures within a set of given dimensional probabilities – Earth being only one of seven "real" worlds. Our shared consensual observation of Earth is a collective effort with each individual human obligatorily following the rules of the whole until such a time as the individual awakens to his or her knowing place in creation. Once awakened to knowing, the individual becomes unified body, mind and Soul as one harmonic expression in manifest form and has his or her existence outside all the governing principles of collective humanity, including the boundary of time. When the time barrier is broken, the illumined being is free to move conscious awareness along all intersecting planes expressing as moment-specific junctures of time/space as it gathers the information needed to fulfill its purposeful needs. These intersecting planes form the time/space realities for separate incarnations and associated parallel probable incarnations. An awakened Triad's physical body is only just barely confined to a specific consensual time plane, meaning the physical body itself cannot freely move between past and future incarnational time planes; it can, however, move freely within the physical space of its present consensual time plane, free of sequential time as a constraint. Without consensual linear time holding the Dyadic form to a past or present state, it becomes pliable and free to shape to any desired conditions suggested by the Triad. This liberation of body, mind and Spirit from separately functioning forms into one harmonic expression takes on a new dimension, as the physical body's velocity becomes the speed of thought. Distance, as in moving from one place to another, is no longer based on linear time, giving the knowing human form the ability to move non-sequentially within its given time plane. In this sense, a knowing individual can visit past and future moments within the current incarnation, not only in mind but in body as well.

The only public demonstrations of this occur infrequently with the magi and Sadhus of the Hindu culture of India, the monks and priests of Tibetan traditions in China, the magicians of the Shinto priesthood in Japan and with some spiritually awakened indigenous peoples in Africa, Australia, South America and North America. The seeming reason for this lack of non-sequentially presenting Dyadic forms and thought velocity awareness in the Christian, Judaic and Islamic cultures is found in the need of individuals to please the collective cultural mind as a way of promoting linear self-assurance. Remember, personality/ego is Dyadically associated in time/space with the senses used first to satisfy core beliefs and then consensual time/space boundaries. If strong, narrow-minded, societal or cultural beliefs reinforce the similarly contracted core beliefs of an individual, that individual's senses will only be used to validate those beliefs, thus giving a fanatically biased view of past, present and future moments. In this state, the multi dimensional qualities of this world flatten into one-dimensional findings that are used to further narrow the cultural/individual core beliefs, thereby stopping the individual from any authentic observation of creation. The individual relinquishes his or her true uniqueness to a pattern of thought behaviors that retentively reinforce themselves. This is demonstrated perfectly in religiously empowered cults such as those organizations that use covertly exclusive indoctrination techniques to control their members. It is important to know that what an individual believes is true is dominant over the greater knowing of creation. This is possible because the Soul is created in the image of the First Moment (Creator God) and therefore dominant in this Dyadic dimension. Until such time as a human is cosmically illumined, the Soul works through the personality/ego. Because Soul's consciousness is outside the duality of right or wrong, it empowers beliefs and visions without prejudice, thus empowering the personality/ego as the director of those beliefs and visions.

Once a Dyad and Triad are working in complete unison, they can begin to influence all matter within a given time plane. (The subject of transmutation and morphification will be covered in detail in future chapters.) The New Testament records several excellent examples of this with the miracles attributed to Jesus the Nazarene, such as transmutation of illness and decay into health and vitality, the reanimation of Dyadic matter through raising of the dead, the reversal of gravity by walking on water, molecular morphification by turning well water into wine, etc. Other cultures have stories of masters who have demonstrated the ability to willfully command time and space to the extent of appearing in different shapes and being in several places at the same time. To give an example of this, a story has been told and retold about a crew of interested filmmakers from Los Angeles that was documenting the daily life of the avatar Babaji back in the late 1950s. Their time with this Bodhisattva extended beyond the usable film they had brought with them, prompting them to sadly announce their need to return home without some of the more interesting healing rituals being caught on film. Babaji, upon hearing of their purposeful need, quietly asked them the name of the store where they had purchased their film. The next morning they awoke to find the needed film along with a receipt from the Ventura Boulevard film shop they had described to Babaji. When the film crew returned they immediately visited the shop where they showed a picture of the avatar to the sales clerk whose named appeared on the receipt. Babaji was identified as the strange little man who insisted on a certain type of film but only in waterproof containers. The clerk went on to state that this old man was wearing western clothes and not the robes as shown in the picture. He also told how the old man had quietly disappeared when the clerk went to the store's back room for the proper change of a hundred dollar bill.

~ *Shifting Time/Space Velocity* ~

Three primary shifts occur within an individual's consciousness as he or she gently steps beyond the last barrier of social, cultural and human collective consciousness into enlightenment and liberation. First, and most startling, the individual realizes that he or she is uniquely here in the present moment guilt-free of any wrongdoing and, through the release of conflict, is balanced within body, mind and Spirit. Now all cells within his or her physical body responds directly to each thought seeking to bring that specific thought form into physical dimensional form through the power of joy within the Divine Urge. Next, the psyche becomes absolutely still, single-mindedly focused, intuitively alive in precognition and willfully content. Finally, the Triadic energy of the Soul moves through the cells of the Dyadic body, refreshing every molecule, bringing the vitality of the First Moment into every thought, utterance and deed, cleansing the etheric bodies of the Triad and Dyad and harmonically attuning the newly illumined being to the All within the One. From the purity-driven force of joyous unity, each thought, through the command of voice, now manifests to its completed form. The latent energy pooled at the base of the spine is released upward through all of the energy centers and finally outward through the crown chakra where it joins with the vital ethrioplasmic fluids of the other six Triadic bodies. In this state, the shifted Soul is twice born: once in flesh through the womb and once in Divine essence through the liberated body.

For Triadic Souls to be linearly aware as a singular expression of human consciousness, moving Dyadically in time equal to space and space equal to time, the influencing precepts at play between the conscious and subconscious minds manifest in concentric waves of alternating expansion and contraction. In all humans, the momentary exchange that happens between the conscious (Triadic) and subconscious (Dyadic) minds takes a thousandth of a microsecond. To give an example of one sensory moment:

- As awareness (conscious or unconscious) contracts around sensory derived information, the subconscious mind expands into associative current life past, present or future memories[5] while Soul consciousness simultaneously integrates all connected past, current or future life's past, present and future memories as they relate to that particular sensory experience.
- The conscious mind then contracts the sensory feed into the core belief template used by the personality/ego to organize the present incarnational inquiry.
- The subconscious mind's associative memories create sequential time and space-adherent delineations of discernment around the data in the preconscious mind's memory fields. This is done by the personality/ego to organize the data into streams of conscious awareness that can be readily shared with others through common observation points within a given frame of reference.
- The subconscious mind responds to the contracting organization by expanding into more associated memories as a means of having enough information to make the most creative choice within the stream of awareness.
- The conscious mind then contracts to sequence present time/space correlations in context of the sensory information being examined.
- The subconscious mind then contracts disassociate memory streams

in deference to the appropriate space/time adherents allowing the conscious mind to expand into now and the future outcome-derived projections being skewed by the personality/ego.

- The unconscious, multi directional acts of sequencing discernments are the foundation of the intellect or conscious mind and are therefore time derived; while associative memories are non-sequentially stored in the electromagnetic mass of physical etheric body and randomly accessed as subconsciously held space associations. Human consciousness first uses the senses to validate individual core beliefs concerning dimensional reality and then to corroborate collective consensual reality ideations.

This is important: the subconscious mind controls space, i.e., matter energy; the conscious mind controls time, i.e., sequencing of associative responses and behavioral strategies. Linear time exists solely as a function of response to stimuli. What you know in your subconscious mind is experienced as your overall relationship to matter, what you know in your conscious mind you experience as consensually delineated time. The two combined give full time/space awareness to consciousness.

To shift consensual time/space you must be willing to live the rest of your existence outside consensual reality, beyond the ideas of gender, family, community and culture. The first step to achieving this is the understanding that you as a Triadic Being are without boundaries of any nature and that you have grace-inspired dominion over all Dyadic substance. Living your life from this knowing requires great care, in that, rushing toward this knowing may cause a rift in conscious consensual awareness that would lead to irreparable dimensional delusion. You must be willing to allow this expansive realization of dimensional creation to progressively infiltrate the substance of your Dyadic form. As you consider the boundlessness of your true nature, you will begin to glimpse this possibility of pliable matter and thought velocity as a more natural state of existence. Once you open yourself to this knowing, somewhere in a moment, the culmination of this continuing movement toward enlightenment and illumination takes hold of your conscious awareness through Divine epiphany and instantaneously transmutes your Dyadic substance.

For the illumined and actively enlightened human being, life is a series of manifest realities with associated probabilities radiating in both directions along a given time plane. Time is no longer a boundary to conscious awareness as it applies to past, present and future in that the being has the ability to join all consensual, interlocking, moment-specific junctures as a time/space singularity or constant now. Unconscious time is no longer experienced as the illumined being moves freely without conflict. Lifetimes seem more like days with birth being the morning and death being the night, and the in-between a dream of parallel prospects. The being willingly experiences the total sum of all events and responses from each incarnation of every combined Soul-to-Dyad encounter. With this ability, even historically accurate "facts" are known to only be consensual probabilities, each with their own parallel potentialities. The Dyadic aspect of the illumined human being is quickly and completely aware of itself as an eternal force taking renewed forms as a means of evolving to pure energy, free of conflict and finally expressing as a completed aspect of the first vision. Now the Dyad acts as a resonator for each new Triadic thought, amplifying its harmonic vibration through the ethrioplasmic substance of the firmament. Each movement of the Dyad becomes a sacred geometric radiance that influences all matter and substances to form to the purposeful needs of its liberation; each utterance is a command to completion. The Dyadic form now serves as a gathering point of attraction for the manifestation of thought into form. In this state, the Dyad is fully precognitive and fearless regarding the circumstances surrounding life and responds without hesitation to the calling commands of the Triad.

~ *Two Primary Time/Space Core Beliefs Influencing Knowing* ~

Most of the information stored within the etheric bodies of the Triadic and Dyadic forms concerning our relationship to space and time is placed there through our direct witness of dimensional reality. The remaining percent, and perhaps the most influencing, comes to us subconsciously through our inclusion within the collective human mind. This is further reinforced through the core beliefs of our specific cultural subset where we get collective time/space attitudes unconsciously as visual and auditory cues from family and community through cyclical patterns of behavior. If we are to ever expand our consciousness beyond the limitations of societal and cultural cycles, we must first know the somniferous-like suggestions that collective concepts of time have on our psyche.

In our wrist-watched modern global community, time regulates every aspect of our societal and cultural lives. With the advent of computerized mechanization and miniaturization, time has become a tradable commodity in that it is the primary valuation of performance used by all competing cultures. After all, time is money; money is potential power. In past cultures such as the Venusian-inspired Mayan civilization of Central America, time was worshiped as a Deity whose existence was the very foundation of that culture's ideas of creation. Using the orbit of Venus around the sun, they calculated the exact point in the future when time itself would no longer be a boundary for human consciousness – the winter solstice of 2012.[6] Calculations of modern physicists, such as Albert Einstein, indicate that time theoretically gives way to space as velocities approach the speed of light. Mystics know that the distortions of time by space directly indicate that, without time, space would become fluid and foldable, rendering the distance between two separate points insignificant when thinking in terms of light or thought velocities.

As we all know, cultural ideas of time were derived primarily from terrestrial, lunar and solar cycles and were used for the reckoning of events over extended periods. The Gregorian calendar formulated by Pope Gregory today serves as an international standard for the emerging global market place. After the previous shift marking the end of the Atlatian epoch, calendars were used primarily as calculations for spiritual or religious celebrations. Taking into account the numerous specialty calendars restricted to particular religious or cultural celebrations, and all the major local cultural variations of the three primary calendar systems of solar, lunar and lunisolar, there are presently about thirty-five different calendars used in the world today. In the case of the lunisolar Chinese calendar, years are counted in cycles, with no particular cycle specified as the first cycle. Some cultures eschew year counts altogether and name each year or period of years after an event or leader that characterizes the year or period of years.

The interpersonal system we use to celebrate the passing of the year is actually established through the bloodline biorhythms of family, then extended into community and finally culture. All culturally imposed calendars do little more than give a common reference point for the communication of ideas as they relate to past and future collective events. Bloodline rhythms are established when a Dyadic group maintains a specific geographical location over several hundred generations. It is logical to assume that seasonal changes in climate establish the bulk of the community and cultural cycles through collective survival activities. However, it is the daily rituals of life, such as those idiosyncratic actions associated with a family's habits, when they awaken, bathe, eat meals and retire, that are primary to time valuations. Biorhythmic blood-line patterns directly tied to regional seasonal cycles deeply imprint within our psyche as the fundamental observational dynamic of our personality/ego aware-ness. This is the first core belief used to organize our observation.

No matter where we travel after leaving our families, we retain that initial idea of time as the first core belief that organizes our individual inquiry. Example: If an individual spends the first third of life in his or her place of birth then leaves the family, community and culture to move to another society for an extended period, for example, ten years, the individual will retain the original time dynamic. Each time the individual revisits the original culture during that ten-year period it will seem as though he or she had never left. Personal body timing and language syntax will quickly and effortlessly fall back into rhythm. This is also true for an individual who moves within the same culture and for various reasons has trained himself or herself to repress stereotypical regional timing peculiarities. Once home, the individual immediately exhibits the original timing tendencies in physical and verbal language. It is safe to say then that time stereotypes can be applied to differing cultures. Example: The majority of individuals born in the United States of America operate on a want-it-now basis, whereas someone from an island culture close to the equator will readily accept tomorrow as a relevant time frame for having a desire met. Individuals from less developed cultures will expect longer times to achieve similar ac-tivities than their more technologically driven counterparts in first world na-tions, no matter their socio-economic circumstances. The saying goes, "Ameri-cans believe two hundred years is a long time. Europeans believe two hundred miles is a long distance."

Then there is the issue of gender balance and time/space. The second core belief affecting an individual's observational experience of sequential time/space is gender identification. Depending upon the gender base of the culture, that is, whether a culture's gender dominance is matriarchal or patriarchal, time will be somewhat different for males and females, even when they share identical bloodline biorhythms. It can be observed that males, even in a matri-archal culture, tend to naturally exhibit an intrinsic knowledge of time as a commodity and will trade that currency between other males, but not with the females of their culture. Time only becomes a currency to the female gender when competing with males for the same goods and services or securities. In observing predisposed gender tendencies it can be generally stated that:

- Dyadic females are "being" oriented and experience time/space within an emotional context. This "being" within time allows more of the mysterious nature of time to reveal itself as a pliable dimension – past or future can present itself in any given moment through precognitive shifts in awareness. With the feminine, time is a ball of yarn with a generally inconsequential beginning and ending, where beginnings and endings join through overlapping circumstantial threads. To the feminine, time itself has value only as it relates to family, village and overall community within issues of security.
- Dyadic males are "doing" oriented and intellectualize time by assigning it a comparative power value. Examples: racing against time, besting a previous personal performance, producing more output in less time, etc. In "doing" time, males can fully examine the power contained within the limitations of space as it correlates to an established beginning and ending or primary coefficient. This allows time to gain importance as a commodity.

It can be metaphysically argued that we are equally male and female, in that, Dyadic matter is charged with a feminine skew and non-matter matter (Triad) is skewed to the masculine. Taking this metaphysical slant a bit further, it must be established that a single Triad is genderless. However, the Akashic Records indicate that as two Triads enjoin they unintentionally generate a matrix of energy that appears to have a specific polarized charge. The ethrioplasmic substance produced as their Souls combine either releases a masculine positively-charged essence or a feminine negatively-charged essence. This gender skew of a Soul has nothing to do with determining the gender the physical body as it develops in the womb, and it can determine sexual orientation and gender preference from very early on in the incarnation. In general, a positive charge produces expansiveness, or an outward flow of observable experiences, while a negative charge produces a contractive or an inwardly flowing observable experience. That being established, when a masculine Soul incarnates into a feminine Dyad it has a greater range of possible time/space observations, the same being true for the feminine Soul incarnating into a masculine Dyad. Contrary to popular belief Souls do not pick the gender of the body they will inhabit. Because the Soul is dominant over the Dyad, its gender essence or emanation will always override the gender of the body when it comes to observing dimensional creation.

This does not mean that natural Dyadic gender traits will be compromised if an opposing Soul is in an opposing body. Examples: Marilyn Monroe's Soul orientation was masculine, she was considered by many to be the personification of feminine wiles; Mother Theresa's was masculine, yet she nurtured. Golda Maier's was feminine, and she assumed a very masculine role as protector of a nation. Outwardly feminine Elizabeth I of England and Catherine the Great of Russia, both had Souls with masculine skews. Pope John Paul II's Soul orientation is feminine as were Gandhi's and Winston Churchill's. There is no real worth in assigning gender valuations when observing a Soul's lifetime contributions. If anything, gender roles slow the progress of a society by limiting balanced contributions and by dictating a range of interests. After all, where would humanity be without Rosalind Elsie Franklin as a scientist or Mikhail Baryshnikov as a performer? When humanity as a collective is finally at peace with societal gender assignments, it will begin to incorporate a more expansive view of creation through knowing the inherent forces available to a mixed Triadic/Dyadic skew. Same-skew Triadic/Dyadic unions, masculine-to-masculine or feminine-to-feminine, produce equally powerful human expressions with gender tendencies amplified along stereotypical gender characteristics. Examples of such individuals would be: John F. Kennedy, Lady Diana, Madame Curie, William the Conqueror, Cleopatra and Mao Tse-tung. A knowing human utilizes the power generated by opposing or similar skews to bring into manifestation his or her purposeful needs and the needs of others.

A Soul's skew affects the manner in which it relates to the information being collected by the Dyad's senses. For example: In a raw uncivilized culture, if the Soul's skew is masculine, the information will be heard in terms of protector or hunter irrespective of the physical gender. The skew has no other real significance on a given incarnation's gender except to unintentionally gender-spin the sensory data being witnessed and observed. Gender balance is lost when a Soul repeatedly incarnates several times in one Dyadic gender or the other. When a Soul shifts genders after a long series of same-gender incarnations, the imposition of cultural gender bias will skew the personality/ego to the point that it is overly agitated with the biological and societal tendencies of the new gender, even if the new physical gender is the same as the Soul's gender skew. In this case, time and space delineations will seem somewhat delusional and out of context, leaving the new human with the feeling of sensory betrayal. Example: A Soul with a feminine skew incarnates five times into male-gendered physical bodies, then in the next incarnation it takes a female-gendered form. The masculine time and space tendencies brought in from the past five lives will color the present female perceptions making it

difficult for the female to trust her time and space impulses, especially culturally mentored instincts. In this case, when the female hears a sound or detects
a smell it will seem unnatural and out of context to the moment because she
will want to prioritize that data as a hunter/protector, not as a gatherer/nurturer.
This effect will lessen over time, allowing for a full gender experience, but
usually only toward the end of that particular lifetime.

Continuing along the same train of thought as exampled above: if a surviving
Dyadic awareness has helped to form five male physical forms, then helps to
form a female physical body occupied by a Soul who has been successively
male, the out of place/time feelings will be overwhelming. In this case, the
human might become antisocial or even develop unexplainable psychotic tendencies. Very little real therapeutic help can be given to an individual through
psychiatric means, unless the attending physician takes into account the considerations mentioned above when diagnosing and treating an individual for
such misalignments. The example given is the extreme and rarely happens.

If a Triad which has incarnated several lifetimes within one culture then abruptly
incarnates on the other side of the globe into a society it has never previously
encountered but keeps the same gender, it will feel out of contextual time.
Even though he or she might be born into a family gathering with Souls it has
known in several past incarnations, he or she will still feel out of place, even
within that family unit because his or her basic idea of time would be signifi-
cantly different. The only conditions that would make this cultural shift more
difficult to integrate would be if the migrating Triad exampled above had only
male incarnations in the previous culture and chose a female form as its first
incarnation into the new culture, or conversely with female to male. Reversing
genders after a prolonged series of incarnations as one gender or the other is
very difficult in that, the general tendencies of the previous gender carried in
the surviving personality/ego will tend to override the gender tendencies of
the present incarnation. In this case, the personality/ego's lack of identification with the present gender will be exaggerated by the time disassociation,
causing both influences to last the duration of that lifetime.

In the reverse gender example above, we have a Triad's personality/ego carry-
ing forward a dominant male gender identification into the new culture because of a long series of incarnations as male. If the Soul's gender skew and
the surviving Dyadic awareness that formed the new body are inclined toward
the feminine, the male-oriented personality/ego will struggle against the body

for dominance, creating unpredictable psychological issues. The emotional and mental conflicts of this individual will be greatly enhanced if the family, community or culture is intolerant of the unexplainable condition. If the personality/ego and Soul's skew are identical, the new, opposing, Dyadic gender will be experienced as a mistake with little or no Dyadic gender identification, resulting in an asexual or, in extreme cases, a trans-gender orientation. Each of these exampled situations is extremely difficult to experience and requires great care and knowing to facilitate the balancing of body, mind and Spirit. It must be noted that once balance is brought to the individual, he or she has the choice to demonstrate either set of gender tendencies.

A side note: With the vast number of Souls seeking to incarnate onto Earth at this time, the number of such incidences is out of proportion to the total. Fortunately, our modern world has developed certain abilities to deal with most of the issues exampled above. Unfortunately, the most popular solution is the use of mood altering pharmacological remedies over wisdom-driven compassion.

In a knowing individual, an opposing Triadic/Dyadic gender skew is used to give both an emotional and intellectual awareness of time/space, while a similar Triad/Dyad gender skew is used to enhance the focus of either the emotional or intellectual component. For the knowing individual, collective consensual notions of time and space need not be validated through beliefs but instead are experienced as developing agreements. As has been stated, we are here to joyfully observe Creation in all its many forms and to exercise profound clarity in our grace-inspired dominance of this realm. Because we are dominant to all Dyadic forms, animate or inanimate, and because time/space adherences only exists to satisfy our collective need to sequentially observe this reality, we can individually and/or collectively agree for all life on Earth to shift the boundaries of observable time/space. As awakened Souls, our sovereignty, in combination with the Earth Spirit and Logos, allows us to reform energy (matter) to suit our needs and wishes. The manipulation of matter, the intentional alteration of its presentation to the senses, is achieved when we understand that time is directed through the conscious mind, and matter is directed through the subconscious. We can then begin to alter the two greatest influences we experience – Time/Space. We, in unison with the Dyad, are the observer/witness; through us, the observed knows itself to be existent. We are Souls, embraced by flesh, imbued with the Divine Spark, and as emissaries of the First Moment, are incapable of making a mistake. We are sovereign to the degree that we allow it for ourselves. Most of our experience when in human bodies is done automatically. We need do very little to have an incredible experience on Earth.

~ *Dyad/Triad Observer/Witness Space/Time* ~

The term observer operates through the Dyad and applies primarily to the senses, whereas, the term witness is multi dimensional and defines the essence of Triad consciousness. The senses are driven by both the conscious and sub-conscious minds. This is fully demonstrated during hypnagogic induction when a patient has lost the use of a given sense, such as hysterical blindness, and it is restored to full function through posthypnotic suggestion. The sense connection to the subconscious mind is primal and acts on the brain stem (instinct) whenever we find ourselves in a situation that has no corresponding memory held within our etheric body. Here we respond to life from what has been loosely termed, the belly brain or lower three chakras – base chakra or procreation; spleen chakra or external power over others and the solar plexus chakra or internal personal power.

Another aspect of observing is the act of being fully vested in a given sequence of events or stream of consciousness. The most effective way to do this is to completely forget who we are as human beings and throw ourselves into the heart of the melee. This is a very personal form of observing, that, more often than not, becomes the death of us, quite literally. Why do this then? Forgetting who we are allows the senses to operate at full capacity. When we think of ourselves as only human in a world filled with peril, unsure of where we are on the food chain, we become extremely good observers or die trying. Enacting high-risk resolutions when faced with a personal dilemma allows for a greater sense of knowing as it momentarily sets aside the rehearsal tendency within our personality/ego.

It has been experienced that the more knowing we become, the less sensual we are. This seems to be true but is hardly a rule. As we begin to awaken from the hypnosis of Dyadic awareness, the general tendency is to become isolated in the immense comfort of Triadic consciousness for a period of time. We are less distracted by sense-oriented yearnings as we shift from the dominance of contracted Dyadic awareness to the expansiveness of Triadic consciousness. Knowing allows us to experience ourselves beyond the value of an exclusively sense-driven existence. Once we are fully in command of our sense-driven observations, we then incorporate sensual pleasures as a catalyst for igniting Cosmic Awareness or Nirvana.

Practice:

Reduce the number of clocks in your home to one and notice how many times a day you check to assign the right time to a given moment. Be aware of how you calculate distance in relationship to time. Observe your personal relationship thoughts as they relate to time.

As a journaling practice, research as much as you can about the rituals and gender dominance within your family during your first few years. Notice if the gender dominance is different from your culture's gender bias. Be observant of your gender biases and how those beliefs alter your perceptions of time/space. The more you uncover, the more you will expand into knowing.

Everyday for two weeks, make a notation each time you encounter a personal preference that is centered on belief-oriented expectations. Check your thoughts and associative feelings as you delve into each expectation. Remember, until you are awakened, your sensory existence is a series of preference-driven expectations and little else. To expand beyond this dynamic you must be willing to investigate the subtle aspects of your personality/ego.

During this exercise it is helpful to release preferences by just being aware of them as they surface and by repeating an affirmation such as,

"This preference for _____ satisfies my expectations of _____. This is no longer a part of my observation and witness of Creation. I release the habitual belief in this preference, setting it free that it will evolve to a more expanded level of completion."

Examples:

"This preference for soothing music satisfies my expectations of peace and joy. This is no longer a part of my observation and witness of Creation. I release the habitual belief in this preference, setting it free that it will evolve to a more expanded level of completion."

"This preference for organized surroundings satisfies my expectations of being in control. This is no longer a part of my observation and witness of Creation. I release the habitual belief in this preference, setting it free that it will evolve to a more expanded level of completion."

Thoughts:

Time is an agreed-upon reality with no real boundaries.
Space is openly subjective and relies solely on the fulfillment of sensory expectations to be real.

Gender is without definition or singular contribution, being instead a biological condition or attribution of deliberation. To assign gender attributes to another human is to deny their uniqueness as a sovereign being.

Lifestyle Suggestions:

Meditation: Anything and everything becomes a meditation when you lose yourself in the rhythm of what you are doing. This can be exaggerated when you chant or move in a consistently deliberate pattern. Not long ago migrant farm workers toiling in a field could be heard singing as they repetitively moved through their work. At the end of the day, they were less tired and more focused than those who were supervising their work.

Find a CD of music that speaks to your physical body – you know, gets your toes tapping. Create a consistent, deliberate, repetitive action that fits the rhythm of the music and practice it for the duration of the song. If the music has a vocal track, then sing along. Gospel music is an extremely good choice for this exercise. Make certain that the motions of your body and the sounds of your voice are complementary. Singing in a loud high voice while moving your body slowly will bring an imbalance to this exercise. The louder the voice the more erratic the movements should become.

Quickly relax in a very still position as soon as the music stops. Notice any bodily sensations as you calmly relax. Be aware of any places in your body that are contracting or twitching. Be aware of your emotions as you relax at deeper and deeper levels.

Diet: Approach the meal table with gratitude. Be wholly aware of your emotional and mental states as you eat. If you have not already done so, then begin the process of food combining. A convenient chart is located at the back of the book on page 276. Eat fruits and sweets separately and at least a half an hour away from all other foods. Avoid combining starches and meats. Eat proteins with other proteins; no liquids with meals unless it is a single four-ounce serving of red wine. Notice any cravings as you alter food combinations.

Fasting: Serious students of all spiritual disciplines eventually use some form of fasting as a technique for cleansing consciousness and awareness. Fasting, when used to bring the body, mind and awareness into alignment, is the most effective way to gain a deeper understanding of the relationship of food to our bodies – physically and emotionally. Make certain to always approach fasting with a playful yet serious intent toward renewal. Your beginning attitude will set the tone for the fasting period. If you dread the fasting process, your fast will be loaded with dreadful moments. It is extremely important to consult a medical professional to determine if you are inclined to low blood sugar or hypertension. Do not fast unless you are healthy. Read up on fasting techniques and follow the rules of the road when coming off a fast. Do not fast to lose weight. If you do this, you will gain the weight back – and usually more – as you come off the fast. Juice fasting is one form that everyone can experience with little or no adverse effects.

Be smart about this very important tool. Learn as much about fasting as is comfortable before you begin to explore the emotional and physical realities of why you eat.

Exercise: Walk. Walk silently with a friend, Dyad or Soul. If you are aware of your guides and spiritual mentors, ask them along. While in their environment, invite any unseen elementals or devas to join your tour. Soften your vision by not focusing on the details of your pathway. This will allow them to show themselves.

Be aware of how your body moves as you walk. Relax your hips and use the inside of your feet first. Walk over varied surfaces to open all the nerve channels in the feet and to allow the major muscle groups to work in unison. Again, watch your breathing and consciously bring chi or prana in on every breath.

Imagine the life force suspended in the atmosphere directly in front of you. Envision it as small energetic points of light. Draw that light into your lungs then push it down through your body, allowing it to gather in the base chakra as a ball of energy. Imagine the energy glowing a bright red hue then extend it further downward into your legs to the soles of your feet. With each step, imagine yourself leaving a red glowing footprint of energy.

~ *Chapter VI Footnotes* ~

1 The sum total of all the consciousness and awareness of all life on Earth, whether animate of inanimate.

2 These en masse transmigrations of Souls from one system to the next usually correspond with the immense waves of energy that foretell the shifting of thirteen thousand year cycles.

3 A Triad is attracted to a specific Dyad through the release of a certain harmonic energy as the male's sperm breaks through the outer layer of the female's ovum. The Triad actually enters the physical body in the last trimester of gestation or can enter the body as late as seventy-two hours after the birth. The Triad gains a complete memory of the embryo's gestation experience once fully established in the Dyad.

4 Steven Hawkins' study of time and time dimensions is an excellent starting place for expanding views on time as an intellectual construct.

5 Memories are held within the etherioplasmic substance of the Soul and physical etheric bodies. Memories regionalize within the etheric bodies according to completeness. These memories are accessed through the associative stimulus in the brain by way of the hippocampus.

6 The Akashic Records indicate that consciousness will "see" beyond time just before entering the leading edge of the next cycle of unity that began to overtake humanity some five hundred years ago.

THE *KNOWING*

*"As we express our
gratitude, we must never
forget that the highest appreciation
is not to utter words, but to
live by them."*

—. John Fitzgerald Kennedy

THE *KNOWING*

Chapter VII

~ The Divine Plan for Earth as Each Soul's Expression ~

The human will is the most powerful of all the Soul's natural resources. Nourishment, water, sleep and breathable gases support the evolving Dyadic awareness, however, it is sheer human will, derived solely from the Divine Urge to be, that continues human life on Earth. With other life forms, those lacking self-awareness, life continues as a response to instinctual survival patterns locked within the genetic code of their bodies. Some biologists and behavioralists argue that instinctual survival behaviors are, in fact, the will of an organism to continue. However, the type of will expressed in the human experience is substantially different from the instinctual forces that drive evolving matter to completion. Soul consciousness blends with Dyadic forms as a means of using the observing mechanisms of those forms to completely witness evolving matter. The style of observation, or the Soul's expression, depends on the unique unalterable characteristics of the Soul in the moment of its Creation, the positive or negative skew of the Soul as that propensity applies to Earth's dimensions and the retained incarnational memories that establish the boundaries of an incarnating Soul's personality/ego.

As a Soul awakens to itself, that is to say, becomes illumined or spiritually liberated while enfleshed in human form, the Soul's expression becomes a dynamic creative force that radiates into the world as unlimited will, influencing all evolving Dyadic[1] matter in much the same manner as the First Moment/First Vision influence that began our Universe. In this state, a Soul is experienced on Earth as a direct expression of that very First Moment or in terms of this work, Creator God, the two being one in the same. The Divine plan for each Soul's expression in this dimension is to radiate the unlimited brilliance of that First Moment – Creator God – as its gift to evolving matter. Through this demonstration, Dyadic matter then knows its originating moment and is able to connect its beginning with its completion.

During cycles of unity, such as during the Atlatian epoch, all incarnate Souls are in perfect communion with the knowing that they are direct expressions of that First Moment (Creator God). They also understand that each and every consideration (thought), word (command) and deed (action) move waves of energy out through the layers of thought[2] that surround the Earth, altering these primal and life-essential bands of thought energy, thereby altering Earth's systems of manifestation. These essential, steadily vibrating bands of harmonically resonant thought energy are held into place through the Universal Law of Attraction and are used by the Earth Spirit to manifest Its micro and macro-ecosystems. In terms of energy, thought waves exist as a narrow and very limited spectrum of harmonically resonating oscillations whose existence is experienced simultaneously as both stimulus and response. Thought energy, like light energy, exists both as particles and waves, therefore, every band of thought energy is a wave, while each singular individualized thought form is a holographic-like projection from that wave. By way of example, an animal form (let us use the example of a cat)[3] is a specific thought projection (particle) within a set range of thought harmonics (wave) we refer to in this example as a species of animals. All cats, big or small, wild or domestic, spotted or striped, single or multi colored convey the details peculiar to collective range (wave) of Dyadic energy manifesting as the cat family. Moreover, this wave to particle dynamic applies to every animate or inanimate form manifest on Earth. As Dyadic energy manifests, it takes on a life of its own, so to speak, in that it behaves in a manner peculiar to the harmonics of the thought wave and also behaves in a manner that responds to the most recent past incarnational (particle) memories held within its etheric body. Its behaviors are also constantly adapting to changing environmental circumstances, which in turn influence the harmonics of the wave originating its form.

Each separate wave of thought energy held within the Earth's matrix makes up a greater harmonic resonance that denotes a life signature for the planet. Just as is the case on the millions of planets that support life in the Milky Way Galaxy, the Earth's life signature is unique and attracts a certain type of Soul to observe its many manifest forms through enfleshing within its evolving structures. These "certain" Souls seek to incarnate here out of empathy for the life signature of Earth and as such can be said to be of a particular harmonic resonance, one attuned to the thought waves generating the overall energy field surrounding Earth.

As has been stated in this work, evolving Dyadic awareness survives the death of its previous form and seeks to establish a new form, usually within the same species and most preferably, within the exact genetic line it last experienced. In some scientific circles, the forward dynamic of evolution, at the very least, constitutes a species' motivated will to exist. Because most animate Earth manifestations lack self-awareness, they also lack self-motivation and are instead ushered forward by the whole life signature of the planet with each one making up the details of the manifest forms that constitute the Earth's total ecosystems. If left alone, this progressively morphing interdependence, through each symbiotic or food chain relationship, gives balanced evolutionary signals to each of the essential bands of thought surrounding and permeating Earth. In response, the harmonics within the band alter as a means of manifesting the variations needed within its manifest life forms to sustain the species and its place within the ecosystem. If a given band of thought energy lacks the proper conditions to manifest forms, it will begin to blend with adjacent wave harmonics, and its life forms will begin to present similarities peculiar to those adjacent waves or become altogether extinct. If a global natural disaster takes place, such as the extinction level event (ELE) that happened at the end of the Cretaceous Period sixty-five million years ago, the energy field surrounding the Earth will undergo rapid shifts in harmonics. In the case of the Cretaceous Period ELE, the thought waves producing the reptilian forms began to morph with adjacent waves presenting quick and severe mutations within the manifest forms (particles) of adjacent waves. Fossils showing large lizards with feathered torsos and wings, sudden reptilian-type mutations in early mammals, or amphibious reptiles taking on mammalian characteristics are examples of such crossover harmonics. In such extreme cases, each manifesting thought wave would undergo rapid harmonic shifts to accommodate the void created by the natural disaster or ELE.

This is a little different with Triads enfleshed within Dyadic structures. Souls are from their first moment self-aware; Dyads, in their highest expression, evolve to self-awareness. As First State, completely self-aware beings, we are custodians to all life on Earth. In this sense, our host forms are not subject to the automatic mutation or morphification that takes place when an adjacent species within the same thought wave becomes extinct, such as the other great apes[4] or other fellow primates. Our Triadic influence, or human will, keeps the Homo sapiens form we inhabit as it is. We do however mutate at the behavioral and emotional level with each and every mammalian extinction, especially those we cause[5] through our misunderstanding of life and the order of creation here on Earth. Interestingly, our will to remain outside the influence of adjacent morphing wave-harmonics isolates us within the mammalian thought wave. The more we isolate, the less empathy we have for other forms of life. In this sense, our will to remain the same, as life around us changes, is the cause of even greater and more severe changes within the thought waves surrounding Earth.

~ *Pure Unadulterated Will* ~

Pure will, knowing will, fluid will, as it relates to nonconflicted human expression, is the vital stream, the force of the Soul's creative expression and is felt through all human endeavors as the choice of willingness. Human life, in all its duality, is strictly a matter of willingness. Abilities can carry over from lifetime to lifetime either through memories stored within the Soul's etheric body or the surviving Dyadic awareness forming the new human body, or both. Should a Soul inhabit a Dyadic form that carries identical abilities from its most recent past incarnation as those abilities or even ability memories of that Soul's past incarnations, those abilities will be enhanced beyond measure. To illustrate the impact of such Triadic/Dyadic circumstances we could use the examples of Michelangelo, Saint Germane, Amadeus Mozart and Leonardo de Vinci to name just a few illustrious lives. Side note: Human history is littered with other such male and female incarnations whose names would lack historical significance due to the absorption of their cultures by conquering groups. In Egypt, it was a common practice for each successive group of pharaohs and priests to place their names upon the accomplishments of the previous scientists, engineers, and artisans and destroy any evidence of the former contributions. The Akashic Records indicate that almost all of the truly great lifetimes, those lives dedicating to joyful selfless service, were not recorded for posterity but instead were jealously disregarded or claimed by successive rulers or conquering hordes.

It is our will that allows us to be imprisoned by the framework of the collective mind's observational boundaries, just as it is our will that liberates us from collective limitation and finally individual bondage. Our will keeps us physically alive and keeps us locked into place within the mental and emotional boundaries of the human experience. Our willingness to incrementally progress through time/space as a means of sharing our observations with others is our communion with All That Is in this realm. As we awaken to our place within the communion of All That Is, we evolve a previous sense of obligation to the mutually agreed-upon laws governing the collective human endeavor into a knowing willingness. The force of the Soul's creative expression is then conveyed in waves of gratitude and sincere joy at the mystery of being human and at the actively contradicting complexity and simplicity of life itself.

For Triadic consciousness, life itself springs from the force of willingness or the Divine Urge. When human will is pure through illumination or self-realization, that is, unimpeded by conflict, it can literally move mountains. If an individual knows how creation is ordered, knows his or her place within the Grand Scheme, is without conflict within the vision of possibilities for life and is open to being in complete partnership with the Divine agencies that work on his or her behalf, that person then commands all he or she observes. Should that person also be about the business of helping others find a greater sense of themselves, then anything, ANYTHING, is achievable in relationship to that purposeful need and Divine desire.

~ *Creation Perception* ~

As has been stated, humanity tends only to perceive creation through its senses, which are used by the intellect to validate through met expectations, individual and collective beliefs or assumptions. If we would allow ourselves to exist as a stream of consciousness, that is to say, without the hindrance of expectations, with a wide-open, amorphous, intellectual boundary beyond the concerns of validation, we could also experience color as electromagnetic frequencies instead of just reflected rays of light energy. Shapes would also include the less solid boundaries of ethrioplasmic substance, giving us a full view of all multi dimensional creation. We would also become aware of sound as billowing waves of pulsing air pressure that turn every molecule into harmonic chimes mixing and blending in three hundred and sixty degrees of frequency awareness. As observing platforms of streaming consciousness, fragrances would also present themselves to us as varied molecular shapes easily differentiated in the nose and on the tongue from all other gaseous and liquid matter. Five very distinct tastes would be experienced with each mouthful of sustenance, giving us a full empathic connection to nourishment. The cellular structures of our skin would experience the elasticity of matter, as fingertip touch would give way to yielding waves of intelligent energy awareness emanating from all substance allowing us to feel matter before we touch matter. Outside the boundaries of our intellect-driven observations we would travel at the velocity of thought, leaving time as a linear static as opposed to a homogenous blur of condensed energy. Beyond our sensory-dependent intellect, all consciousness and energy would reveal itself as existing in an eternal now, relative within the confines of an elastic continuum of interdependent wave-like energy structures. Within these wave-like oscillations exist the stringlets of matter/non-matter energy that make up all that is discernable within the void.

Once we realize how matter is defined through our acquaintance with the First Moment, we can know how it is commanded into existence as the ultimate means of creative self-expression.

Through science, we have come to know that all basic exchanges in nature arise out of fields of interacting particles and that all particles are concocted from stringlets of pre-matter. The Akashic Records corroborate these findings and show that dimensional reality is composed of both non-matter matter (dark matter or virtual matter) and various material structures comprised of electrons, positrons, neutrons and protons. Both forms of matter exist simultaneously in a supple medium of unlimitedness or continuum as potentiality. All the various structures of atomic matter have a negative over-charge;[6] specifically, our physical body (matter) has a negative charge. All non-matter matter has a positive over-charge; specifically our Soul (non-matter matter) has a positive charge. All matter is feminine and all non-matter matter is masculine. In the First Moment (vision – inertia – positive) was the First Sound (vibration – motion – negative) released into the void. Much like the ethrioplasmic emanation of two adjoining Souls, the interaction between matter (motion – negative) and non-matter matter (inertia – positive) gives off an energy radiance that defines the Universal Law of Attraction, which sets into motion/inertia all that exists within the elasticity of the continuum. A side note: There are points within the continuum where the interaction between matter and non-matter is inert with the potentiality of such an interaction being reserved; there are also points of super-interaction through which the exchanged potentiality is expressed in measurable outputs, such as black holes or stars. Scientists believe the continuum to be mostly filled with non-matter matter or dark matter (80%), while the Akashic Records show the two primary First Moment components to be wholly balanced, each having the same quotient.

Throughout the continuum, there is a balance. As a potentiality moves from inertia into motion, matter comes into existence; as matter becomes inert, it converts to potentiality. Everything moves through the cycles of potentiality and manifestation back through potentiality into manifestation…ad infinitum. This is the elasticity of the continuum. Each thought is a positively charged form of non-matter matter and is therefore inert potentiality. When a thought is spoken through a First State Being, a Soul, it is placed into motion through the intentional utterance (word) associated with that thought form. Because the uttered thought is spoken into the creative medium, in this case, the etheric fields surrounding Earth, that exact thought is no longer an inert potentiality but has become a dynamic projection of non-matter matter into matter by way of a whole vision on the agency of the intention and utterance. The energy released through the projection of positive into negative reforms the less dominant, in this case the negative etheric energy field, into an image of itself. The whole vision, that is to say, a vision without conflict, contained within the singular thought is the image of the manifest form's first moment. If the energy release is conscious, purely intentional and without conflict, the thought (positive) will instantly form matter (negative) to the intention (complete vision) held within the thought. The intention acts as a template to manifest or reform existing matter and to complete the transaction of vision to form, of positive to negative. The only conditions required to manifest thought into form outside the confines of time are to know that we are First State Beings and as such have no need to learn, but only have to command manifest reality to our purposeful needs.

~ *Macro to Micro* ~

The Soul of Earth is a First State Composite Being enfleshed within the circumstantial limitations of the evolving Dyadic matter that gathered through the Universal Law of Attraction to form the terrestrial body of planet Earth. Each enjoined Soul's manifest presence in dimensional reality is an exact microcosmic mirror of Earth's own macro-multi dimensionality – First State static presence infused within evolving substance. In the case of Earth, we have its three dominant bodies of life as water, land and air. Our physical bodies are made up of same essential ingredients of Earth's three dominant bodies of life' with most of our bodies being made up of water, then gases, with non-fluid matter making up the least mass.

Yet, it is the force of macro/micro-duality that gives rise to the subtle awareness needed to sequentially suppress conscious awareness into the creative forces of Earth's Spirit, in complete unison with the emanation of the Logos, allowing singularly enjoined and composite Souls to play within the vigorous confines of Its duality, time and space. Once we know our place within the duality of dimensional reality, we can begin to command all aspects through the known powers contained within the limitations of duality. Science has been very successful at unraveling the limitations of our material world for some time now. Before we know how Consciousness, Energy and collective Urge align, we appear to be at the mercy of certain minor forces, such as the

Laws of Karma put into place by the Earth Spirit/Logos as an aid to our ultimate awakening. Once we know, once we have resolved our conflict with who we are in creation, we have stepped outside the limitations imposed by the forces of physics and all other collectively agreed-to limitations, and we then begin our command of this dimension as sovereign beings. As sovereign beings, we are complete and whole in each moment, free to manifest or transform existing structures to our purposeful needs.

The study of metaphysics as it applies to space and time allows us to observe Creation outside the boundaries of traditional physics, because in metaphysics we are not attempting to replicate yesterday's discoveries or beliefs through reproducing standardized validations. Instead, we are allowing creation to show itself as itself, as opposed to what we have decided it must forever be. And, it will be through the astounding advancements of science, through physics, that humanity will see itself as Souls enfleshed within evolving matter. The deeper we look into space, the more we will know about our origins. The new mystics, those that know who they are within creation, will be physicists. They will have given up the need to be right and will have become righted. Knowing is beyond the need to be right about what is, or is not. Remember, the Earth Spirit, the Logos and their enjoined emanation, the Holy Spirit, are very obliging in manifesting whatever we want to observe. You decide, they oblige. If you decide there are subatomic particles at the base of all life, they will show you subatomic particles. If you believe in gravity, they will show you gravity. In the book, *The Holographic Universe*, Michael Talbot investigates the phenomenon of cosmically fulfilled expectation. His basic position is that we suggest and the universe complies. Mr. Talbot's investigation touches on the constructs of non-matter matter and speculates that science will eventually confront other types of energy in the same manner as Dyadic substance. Unless humanity collectively embraces the notion of surviving Dyadic awareness as the driving mechanism of our inquiry here on Earth, or the reincarnation of the Soul into flesh, little progress will be made in this direction. The lack of knowing how to observe creation will continue the deep inner conflict propagated by science and religion.

The first sentence of this chapter is of enormous importance to the work presented in subsequent chapters. Conflict of any nature keeps a Soul from fully utilizing the human will. There is a natural conflict generated when a Soul enters a human form, this is the original conflict spoken of in the Old Testament of the Holy Bible as "original sin." Organized religion keeps us locked into the original conflict by asking us to believe that we are morally reprehensible because of its existence. In this regard, each human is doomed before conception. In many Christian rituals, the congregation is asked to verbally affirm their unworthiness before God Almighty either through reciting a verse or through singing the words of religious songs. Referring to oneself as a sinner and therefore not worthy of God Almighty's love intensifies that original conflict. Surprisingly, thinking of oneself as just a Soul without a knowing regard for the body, or as just a physical body without a Soul, neutralizes the original conflict. In other words, if we believe our "true home" to be in heaven at the feet of God Almighty, or, believe agnostically that whoever we are and whatever we know completely stops at the exact moment of death, the original conflict is counterbalanced. This has been the purpose of religion and science. The only way a Triad/Dyad can be <u>fully released</u> from this original conflict is to know that their relationship to one another - Soul to physical body, physical body to Soul – is Divinely ordered through the Holiest of Unions. Each human being is a Divine expression of the First Moment – Creator God. Living life in each new moment with this knowing understanding lessens the intensity of the natural conflict, thereby reducing its disruptive influence on body, mind and Spirit. Once we begin to acknowledge our existence as Divine beings, equally Souls, equally Dyadic Awareness, we fully regain our human will through the agency of the Holy Spirit and we become the Son/Daughter of Man/Woman. In this state, we are commanding our life experience. In Matthew 16:26-28, Jesus the Nazarene speaks of this the Son of Man,[7] *"For what is a man profited, if he shall gain the whole world, and lose his own Soul? Or what shall a man give in exchange for his Soul? For the Son of Man shall come in the glory of his Father with his angels; and then He shall reward every man according to his works. Verily I say unto you, there are some standing here, which shall not taste of death, till they see the Son of Man coming in His kingdom."*

To give further meaning to the verse: *"For the Son of Man shall come in the glory of his Father with his angels."* Once we know the greater truth, have released conflict and are working in unison with the Elemental, Devic and Angelic Beings, we truly reflect the First Moment – Creator God – into this realm through our understanding of the hierarchical structure of creation. Jesus and other mystics often use the Father, as in this verse, as being analogous to the First Moment. The Father rewarding *every man according to his works* simply means that when we know the truth and command life accordingly, we are rewarded with unity of body, mind and Spirit and live effortlessly through our emanation of the First Moment into this realm through us, as us. The phrase: *shall not taste of death*, is shown in the Akashic Records to mean: end most or final incarnation. *"Verily I say unto you, there are some standing here, which shall not taste of death, till they see the Son of Man coming in His kingdom,"* is interpreted to mean that there were those present with Jesus the Nazarene who would not have their last incarnation until the coming unity.

Once we are illumined as unified Soul consciousness/Dyadic awareness, we become the emissaries of the First Moment, the Sons/Daughters of the First Moment – Creator God. The phrase, Son of God, is recognition of this demonstration. The life expression of Jesus the Nazarene was to reflect into this realm the gracious magnitude of the First Moment – Creator God and nothing else. Jesus was just that, a Divine emissary of that First Moment above all other things. Free of conflict as Divinely willful humans, we are liberated to express the true nature of our Souls by commanding thought to matter to our purposeful needs. It is the simple knowing of how Creation is ordered, and where we fit into that order, that makes the effortless manifestation our Divine contribution. As Sons or Daughters of Creator God we are in the world and not of the world.

Practice:

Evoke the presence of the Earth Spirit to open your senses to the unlimited boundaries of space. Evoke the presence of the Celestial Spirits within our solar system to open your personality/ego's intellectual orientation to linear time.

During your day, take several moments to quietly focus on your breath, allowing each breath to be fully felt in your body as in a complete yogic breath: begin the breath by inhaling deeply into your belly, extending the lower abdomen downward and outward. Expand the lower ribs outward as you steadily fill your lungs. Your chest should expand more to the sides than with an upward lift as the air continues to fill your lungs. At the top of your inhalation, shrug your shoulders slightly to extend the inspiration to the extreme top of your lungs. Once you have done this for a few minutes, begin to focus your attention exclusively on the moment when each phase of the breath becomes the other: the moment when the inhalation becomes the exhalation and the exhalation becomes the inhalation. On at least three exhalations express in a very monotone voice:

"I evoke the presence of the Earth Spirit and command that my senses be allowed to behold creation as it is. I release the ego and behaviors of the physical body that have kept me from knowing creation. I am in conscious partnership with the Earth Spirit and the Holy Spirit representing the Logos in all my thoughts, words and deeds."

As Triadic/Dyadic union, we are events within the confines of time and space. When we fully know who we are and why we are here, we begin our true purpose: to joyfully liberate all imprisoned intelligence, animate or inanimate. In this, we give all who experience us a greater sense of their own journey toward completion. Experiencing deliberate thoughts about our place within the confines of dimensional reality helps to move us toward completion and illumination. Silently repeat the following affirmation:

"Consensual space and time allow me to interact with other Souls as I form and then share my inquiry of this realm. This is the only need for consensual time and space. My knowing of creation exists within and beyond the continuously reinvented constructs of consensual reality. I am now prioritizing my abilities to experience this realm with clarity and ease. I rely on knowing first, intuiting second and rely on sensory input third."

This declaration will begin to rearrange and reorder how you observe your immediate environment, how you relate to family and friends and how you respond to circumstantial influences that seem beyond your control.

Invocation:

Each thought we have is formed of loosely tied-together stringlets of ethrioplasmic or non-matter subatomic substance. These infinitesimally miniscule particles are the base of all manifest forms. It is important to know that every word you state into the ethers influences these stringlets of particles releasing, small portions of their pure energy into the etheric substance of Earth. An illumined Soul knows the value of each word and always seeks to speak directly and clearly without hesitation. There is a patter (cadence) and overall manner in which an individual may speak into the ethers which heightens the energy release effect of those stringlets. We then bid that released energy to gather in whatever manner we so commanded through the intention of calling a desired thought to form.

As a preparation, several times each day for the next week look at life around you and quietly but clearly whisper:

"The pureness of my being is illumed in every detail of life. The substance of the World reflects a pure image of my being back to me. All this I AM, and more."

Commanding thought to form is very important if you are to know yourself as a sovereign being.

Before the practice of calling thought energy into, it is important to build a pure field of energy through which to command vision into matter. The grand invocation written below, when spoken in a deliberate monotone voice in the key of "C", will prepare the waves of thought permeating the space around the caller by setting the conflict free intention of Soul consciousness toward the manifestation of purposeful need. Read this invocation several times before you say it aloud. It has been carefully updated from the original form to better reflect our modern understanding of Creation. The patter should be in a tempo akin to reciting a short poem or childhood limerick. Look at the words and be sincere when reciting:

"Through the Holy Spirit indwelling on Earth,

Upon the call of the Twelve Logos:

I AM enjoined and manifest.

Hallowed be the name, I AM.

I AM sovereignty come,

I AM grace expressed will be done.

I AM on Earth, even as

I AM in all kingdoms.

I AM this day giving life to all Creation, even as

I AM all Creation giving life to me.

I AM this day releasing all conflict, even as

I AM all conflict releasing me.

I AM the judgeless witness to each unfolding moment.

I AM compassioned power, and

I AM glory graced, from

Everlasting unto everlasting. All this

I AM."

Thoughts:

All around me Creation is unfolding itself to my Knowing. In return, I allow Knowing to guide my intuitionally driven physical senses to perceive everything that is vital to my attainment of self-realization and illumination.

My authentic response to life is evidence of my direct experience of Spirit Earth and the Twelve Logos. Our exact correspondence reveals life, as life itself.

Lifestyle Suggestions:

Meditation: If you do not already have one, it will be important to purchase a pitch pipe. Very few people have the ability to hit a musical note on command. A pitch pipe will ensure the quality of your tones.

Each of the seven core chakras (energy centers) resounds with tone and color. It is easy to use your voice to activate the energy centers with the intention of bringing balance to your body, mind and Spirit.

Sit with your spine lifted by mentally putting a slight space between each vertebra. Take a moment to focus on your breath, watching the point between breaths. Begin this chant in a slow rhythm. The pace might want to change on its own after a few minutes. Let it.

The first sound, "LAH," is whispered in the key of "C" and is spoken with full attention on the base chakra at the base of your spine. Feel it as heat at the base of the spine; see it as a deep red hue spreading around your hips. As it moves upward let it become a reddish orange.

The second sound, "BAH," is normally voiced in the key of "D" with your attention moving upward into the spleen center just below and slightly left of your navel. Feel it as warmth and see it as a bright orange disk of light that extends from the top of your pubis to your middle waist.

The third sound, "RAH," is growled in a low-pitched key of "E" emanating from the solar plexus. Say this sound from deep inside your body. See it as a bright yellow ball of light centered on your body and feel it as the radiant warmth of the sun on a bright cool winter's day.

The heart chakra is a happy sound of "YAM," (Yah-Aum) and spoken joyfully in the key of "F." Command this sound in a sincerely happy and firm tone. Imagine it as a deep green field of waving grass and feel it as a nuzzling sensation that chases away feelings of isolation and abandonment.

In the key of "G" shout "HAH" as the life force moves through your heart up into your throat. Imagine waves of light blue energy swooshing over your body in a fresh wave of mint energy.

In the key of "A" sigh the sound of discovery, "AHHA," as the energy continues upward toward your crown chakra and comes to rest in the third eye. It is midnight blue and feels indifferent to all sensations.

Alternating the keys of high "D" and "B" make the announcement, "AUM." Feel your whole body vibrate with a mighty (Au-Um) as a brilliant purple light surrounds your head. The feeling is complete contentment and the liberation of concern.

Repeat this for twenty minutes. The intention of this exercise is to immediately balance your energy centers, mind and Spirit.

Diet: Eat less, chew more. Continue to eat in gratitude and joy. Infuse everything you touch with gratitude and joy as you prepare your meals. Drink water with the sure understanding that this fluid is life. Without the gift of water, you would quickly be miserable. Some need as much as three liters a day. Think thoughts of enlightened people, such as your teachers or any avatars, such as Serapis Bay, Kuthumi, Moses, Buddha, Jesus or Mother Theresa while you cook or clean. Whispering their names draws their energy close to us. They, through their individual demonstrations of life, are blessings to us as we go about our effortlessness.

Fasting: Continue investigating the different forms of fasting. It is important to know when and how to use fasting as a tool. Check out all the book titles you can on the subject and be sure to seek advice before you expand your fasting experiences. Juice fasting, that is, slowly chewing a fresh vegetable juice concoction for meals for fourteen days allows the body to detoxify at a very fast rate. Fasting for up to twenty-one days on water and vitamins can be very eye opening.

Exercise: Be as active as is possible for your circumstances. Push yourself to new limits and accomplishments. Keep investigating those dynamic types of exercise that allow you to meditate while being active such as the Six Tibetan Rites illustrated at the back of this book. Stretch and use your body's weight to actively build endurance.

During your day, take a moment to focus on your breath, allowing each breath to be fully felt in your body as in a complete yogic breath.

~ *Chapter VII Footnotes* ~

1 Static Dyadic matter, as in a Dyadically formed Soul, is not affected by illumined Soul consciousness.

2 Thought energy exists as the graduated radiance emanation of enjoined Souls. The bands of thought energy surrounding Earth are the sum totaled graduated radiance emanation of the enjoined Earth Spirit/Logos in union with the Dyadic substance of Earth.

3 The biological designation for the cat family is - Kingdom: Animalia - Phylum: Chordata - Subphylum: Vertebrata - Class: Mammalia - Order: Carnivora - Family: Felidae

4 The term "ape" refers to a small number of large tailless primates found primarily in Africa and Asia. These are Gibbons, Orangutans, Gorillas, Chimpanzees, Bonobos, and Humans.

5 Sea mammals are included in this.

6 Non-matter matter and atomic matter structures give off an energy essence or overall harmonic signature that is observable as a consistent emanation condition.

7 The reference to Son of Man occurs in 196 times in 192 verses in the Old and New Testaments.

*"Religion is an illusion,
and it derives its strength from its
readiness to fit in with our
instinctual wishful
impulses."*

—. Sigmund Freud

Chapter VIII

~ *Thought Manifestation as Creative Self-Expression* ~

Being is the activity of Soul consciousness just as doing is the action of Dyadic awareness. Being is skewed to a feminine polarity and doing is polarized as the masculine expression of human awareness. Being is associated with the upper three chakras: the throat, the brow and the crown, while doing is tied to the three lower chakras: the base, the spleen and the solar plexus. Doing implies that there is something undone that requires your efforts to be done. Being on the other hand is expressing the fullness of what you know. Doing attempts to bring completion to circumstances and conditions; being is the personification of balance. Unconscious, repetitive doing in the absence of being is an unaware herding gesture. Consciously being to escape from doing creates the emptiness of isolation. Buddha's Eightfold Plan was offered as an antidote to the unbalanced human experience when doing and being are forced into polarized expressions. When and individual is balanced he or she emits an energy from the heart chakra that is a perfect blend of the vertical Earth energies rising upward as the kundalini[1] through the chakras (physical endocrine system) and the horizontal celestial energies moving downward through the silver cord that connects all seven bodies. When these forces are equally flowing through the heart chakra, the individual commands and influences all life with every word uttered and every action made. This is Quan Yin or Mer Ma,[2] Moses or the Buddha, the Christ or Maitreya fully expressing – Being/Doing – as emissaries of the First Moment. It is said of individuals who achieve this state of knowing that they are Divinely inspired and tirelessly available to all who seek them out. Their influence is at all times unmistakably authentic and always neutral, lacking any manipulation of body, mind or Spirit or outward intrusion. The knowing individual will empower others to their own conclusions and resolutions through being a source for them to draw upon when they have purposeful need. The unknowing individual, when just awakening from the sleep of conflict and the need to be right, begins to naturally draw energy into the etheric and physical bodies and depending upon the polarity skew of the Soul, will draw energy first from below or then above in unequal portions. If the Soul's orientation is feminine he or she will draw more of the vertical Earth energies, conversely, if the Soul's orientation is masculine he or she will draw more of the horizontal Cosmic energies. It is observed of these

individuals that, while still in the unbalanced state, they are either predomi-
nantly seductive (feminine skew) or charismatic (masculine skew). Because
most individuals are too afraid to go against the dictates of the collective mind
(family, community or culture), the opinion of others keeps them from acting
overly one way or the other. So, as they age, they become eccentric as they act
out repressed authenticity. Because the two primary energies are not balanced,
their influence will be inconsistent and will be experienced as positive then
negative influence, or negative then positive, and passive then aggressive. In
this sense, their efforts will be more of doing than being nature, as is most
certainly experienced with an unbalanced individual.

As an awakening individual begins to manifest to his or her purposeful needs,
the manifestations will have a polarity that reflects the Soul's orientation. Again,
the use of the terms positive and negative does not imply good or bad. In
essence, a negatively skewed Soul, while not completely balanced, will manifest forms that give off a feminine essence while a positively skewed Soul will
manifest forms that give off a masculine charge. The quality and duration of
an individual's manifestation is completely dependent upon his or her true
intention and completeness of vision respectively. Quality and intention are
one and the same, just as duration and vision are equal. If the intention is to
empower all who would enjoy the manifestation, then the quality of a manifest
form will be of the highest order, giving off a more balanced polarized energy.
If an individual intends and calls into form a manifestation used to manipulate
or directly influence others to his or her will, the quality will be lacking and
unless there is a strong vision holding the manifestation in time/space, the
manifest form will diminish rapidly into formless ethrioplasmic energy.

When a fully knowing individual manifests thought to form, the manifestation
lacks nothing and is experienced by all as a pure, Divinely inspired form that
enthuses and empowers everyone at his or her individual level of knowing, all
Souls being equally unequal. The inspiration offered through such manifestations opens unknowing Souls to the possibilities of liberation from the mundane, inspiration being one of the Soul's gateways to joy. We need only look
to the early Sumerian and Minoan, Greek and Roman or Chinese and Japanese antiquities to know the effect on our Souls of the Muse-stirred[3] inspiration still permeating the art and architecture of those cultures. When viewed
with an open heart these works can expand our consciousness even to this day.
Imagine the depth of inspiration and joy when an unknowing individual experiences a called form, a form that has been manifest from thought to hand: the

effect can be wonderfully joyous and instantly catastrophic. When tourists visit the city of Florence, Italy, they are warned of the depression that might overtake them after a day of visiting the numerous museums dedicated to the art and architecture of the Italian Renaissance. The tourists who suffer the most from this malady are aspiring or would-be artists. To an unproven artist there is awe and inspiration, immediately followed by self-doubt and comparisons as to their capabilities in light of the works of art they are viewing. If an individual experiences the profound beauty of a called form, for example, the chalice of Jesus the Nazarene referred to as the Holy Grail, that individual will instantly be elevated to the highest level of knowing his or her Soul is capable of achieving. This sudden shift in knowing could be devastating to the personality and ego aspects of the Soul, leaving the individual vulnerable to all manner of influence including profound self-doubt. All inner conflicts would rush into view, begging to be resolved or released. It is because of this that the manifest artifacts and many of the surviving personal belongings of saints are usually kept from common view. By way of example, the remaining artifacts from King Solomon's temple, or the Ark of the Covenant, or artifacts of the crucifixion of Jesus the Nazarene and Buddha's begging bowl and prayer beads were all called into form from out of the ethers to the purposeful needs of each avatar's grace. To touch or be in the immediate presence of such works is to be in the presence of the one who called the form from out of the ethers.

To better illustrate this phenomenon, consider that the Nazis invested millions of dollars sending teams of pilferers to confiscate church and temple belongings in all occupied lands as a means of reinforcing the metaphysical powers of the Third Reich's leaders. It is believed that Hitler had personal possession of the Spear of Destiny, also known as the Spear of Longinus and the Holy Lance, which is one of the most important Christian relics relating to the final moments of Jesus. It is first described in John 19:31-37 as the instrument used by a Roman soldier to ensure that his prisoner was dead before he took him down from the crucifixion stake. The Jews did not want to have his body hanging on the stake during Passover. This artifact was valued above the crown of thorns or burial shroud of Jesus because it had been directly covered with his bodily fluids.

The first miracle attributed to the spear was the healing of the eyesight of Gaius Cassius, a centurion who was an early Christian convert. It is reported that the spearhead passed into several of Europe's prominent political and military leaders, including the Visigoth king Alaric, Emperor Charlemagne,

Constantine I, Frederick of Barbarossa (Holy Roman Emperor Frederick I), Frederick II, and the Frankish general Charles Martel. All of these individuals believed in the legend that pronounced the possessor of the spearhead to hold the destiny of the world in his hands for good or evil. They believed beyond doubt that any leader who held the spear would be invincible; Charlemagne and Frederick of Barbarossa were both undefeated in battle until they let the artifact fall from their possession.

Adolph Hitler first saw the Spear of Destiny as it was displayed in the Hofsburg museum in Vienna, Austria in 1909. As a young man he had been fascinated with the legends of courageous German knights questing after the Holy Grail. Richard Wagner's opera, Parsifal, was Hitler's favorite story of ninth-century knights and their quest for the Spear of Destiny. Through a series of twisted circumstances, Hitler became fixated on the occult, particularly the imagined mystical origins of the Germanic race from Atlantis, or Thule as it was so called by Adam Rudolf Glauber, who later took the name, Baron von Sebottendorf). The inhabitants of Atlantis (Thule) were thought to have extreme magical powers. Hitler convinced himself that he was a direct descendant of Thule and knew possessing the Spear of Destiny would enhance his imagined magical bloodline powers. The very first act of Hitler's S. S., as Germany annexed Austria on October 12, 1938, was to seize the spearhead and other spiritual artifacts from the museum in Vienna. He saw this act as confirmation his long held belief in himself as the German Messiah and eventual world conqueror. The artifacts were taken to Nuremberg, where they were placed in perpetual care at Saint Katherine's Church. Hitler was in constant, sometimes daily, contact with the guards who protected the Fürher's most treasured artifact.

The artifacts, in particular, the Spear, stayed on the main altar in Saint Katherine's until 1944 when they were moved to a secret chamber beneath the church to protect them from Allied bombs. On April 30, 1945, two hours before Hitler's alleged suicide, the vault was discovered by American troops and the spearhead removed.

~ *Manifesting from Gender* ~

At the present time, in the current thirteen thousand year cycle of conscious duality, the gender of the human body is only significant for reproduction and has little to do with an individual's femininity or masculinity and therefore nothing to do with the quality or duration of his or her manifestations. Men cannot manifest more proficiently than women and vice versa. When a human is balanced in body, mind and Spirit, that is, when the individual has released all conflict and given up the need to be right, he or she is observed as behaviorally non-gendered or even perhaps asexual. This does not mean that the individual is or should be sexually inactive. It simply means that he or she no longer needs to be right and therefore becomes right in all ways, not needing to prove anything or conquer anyone. Human sexuality is often used to prove or conquer. This non-feminine/masculine presence is due in large part to the unfettered harmonics, the unlimited consideration of life, or Divine emanation felt at the absence of conflict and the nonattendance of intolerance and judgment. These individuals are often asked to be spiritual leaders, those who actively represent a version of a cultural ideal of purity as it relates to Creator God. This is so because their life demonstration appears godly, Divine in nature, or inspired by forces unfamiliar to the average individual. Often, this role is heaped with lifestyle expectations as to how that individual must present himself or herself to the world in exchange for elevation to such an important role. Over time, the weight of such expectations can become a burden, so much so, that the individual, wishing to be liberated, will begin to disrupt his or her role as Divine emissary by acting contrarily to collective expectations. Through the sabotage, the formerly balanced individual then finds himself or herself in the midst of deep personal crises of inner conflict that shift the harmonics and corrupt the energy emanating from the heart chakra. Usually this distortion of heart chakra energy is expressed through extreme passive/aggressive behaviors such as those witnessed in the Christian religion when gospellers slip from the pedestal they were placed upon by followers who wish to assign the responsibility of their spiritual experience to another. This type of heart chakra distortion most often results in suppressed yearnings for externalized inclusion and validation that is expressed in overly exaggerated feminine or masculine traits of seductive or charismatic willfulness. Societal expectations for spiritual leaders run contrary to the nature of Soul enfleshment, pure joy of Life. Sexual expression is the driving dynamic of all feminine/masculine relationships, even when that force is dormant due to a balanced body, mind and Spirit, or is inactive in that place between incarnations where the enjoining Soul has generated a polarity.

While enfleshing on Earth, our Souls are skewed in orientation to masculine or feminine; the more at peace with ourselves we become, the more we harmonize the doing with being, the analytical with the creative, the external and internal, the conscious and subconscious minds and the masculine and feminine polarities. It is extremely difficult to be unbalanced during a cycle of unity, such as the next cycle beginning in 2011, but it is possible. The skew of a Soul can be exaggerated at any time if that is the desire of the Soul. In other words, even when completely balanced, neither this nor that, we can knowingly put a skewed spin on a manifestation to achieve a certain effect. The reasons for this would be tied to the intention of the illumined Soul and would be of little real value to anyone else unless they knowingly joined with the intention. The inspiration felt from the skewed form would stimulate the same skew within each person experiencing the manifest structure. The completely balanced priests of the Atlatian period demonstrated this intentional skewing in an attempt to prepare individuals for the coming period of separation as they entered the thousand-year-thick transition wave that preceded the present cycle of duality. This skewing was needed because the individuals in Atlatia were completely unaware of polarized energy. The priests were preparing those who would survive the intensity of the transition wave for what was to befall them in the age of duality. Most of the Souls of the Atlatian epoch, as human incarnations, had never experienced a polarized physical form. Just as we are now beginning to feel the lighthearted liberation of the coming unity, five hundred years into the transition the Atlatians began to fully experience masculine and feminine polarity and were at once struck by the pressure it created within their etheric bodies. The slowness at which thought was manifesting, combined with the sudden comparative listlessness of their Triadic to Dyadic relationships was overwhelmingly preoccupying. They were being forcibly evicted from the paradise of unity into the captivating narcissism of duality. For the first time in their long existence, they felt the actual weight of their physical bodies and the sluggishness at which they moved under the influence of duality. They suddenly had to exert effort to get from one place to the next. The lightness of joy and unlimited love that flows through a balanced manifest body overrides the laws of physics making life effortless and grace filled. The approaching age of duality even demanded that the Atlatians communicate with their physical bodies as opposed to exchanging information at a nonphysical, nonverbal level. They needed language and symbols to move thoughts into realized form.

~ *Manifesting From Unlimited Love* ~

When a human is no longer caught in the cycle of pleasing or manipulating others, they exude the purest of all human energy – Unlimited Love – Divine Love. To the uninitiated, unconditional love seems to be the highest form of human expression. We are taught that unconditional love extends to all life without exclusion. In reality, unconditional love is a sacrificial love in that it asks us to love through conditions that might otherwise have us withholding our love. The manner in which humans express "unconditional love" is to allow feelings of love in spite of conditions. This is not unlimited love but is more a continuation of a victim mentality, in that unconditional love dictates that one individual love another in spite of conditions that would otherwise interfere with his or her own joy and peace. This sacrifice is akin to the idea that it is more important to give than receive, which perpetuates the unbalanced condition present in most relationships. It is impossible to give unless we have received, just as it is impossible to love without conditions when we are unknowing. Unconditional love has its limits because it is based on conditions. Once we know the unlimitedness of love as our common day-to-day expression, then our consciousness has its reality beyond all conditions. Unlimited love is the normal interaction of Souls and is the single factor that equally allows all humans balance and grace. The energy that moves out from us when we are balanced and existing within a complete vision of possibility, while expressing our authenticity in the moment, is the purest form of human energy. In the mystical knowing this purest energy is unlimited, without boundary or definition of any condition. Those who believe unconditional love is the highest form of human expression are living a misunderstanding. Remember, we are representative of the First Moment: we are created in the image of that First Moment – unlimited in any way. Therefore, what a person believes is true here on Earth, supersedes what is true even to the point that we can impose that belief on all Dyadic substance. If our beliefs align with the greater knowing, then we have life effortlessly and abundantly; if our beliefs do not align, we become distracted by the contradictions, and the ensuing conflict manifests within our body, mind and Spirit.

Joy, then love, is the purpose of each and every Soul, whether enjoined and enfleshed in a dimensional realm or not. Thought manifestation is the highest form of creative self-expression for Souls while they exist in human form; joy is the highest form of creative self-expression while a Soul is outside the confines of dimensional reality. You need only look deeply into the eyes of an infant to experience the unlimited joy of its Soul. Souls achieve the state of manifest creativity while human by first giving up the need to be right. Giving up the need to be right alone ushers into our hearts (heart chakra) the vertical and horizontal energies needed to become sovereign beings and thus the diviners of our own manifest destiny through joy and love. In this state, we are true lovers of the vision of possibilities within the First Moment because we become a demonstration in every moment of each day of the First Moment. Human love is what is felt in our personalities and egos when our heart chakras open through the blindness of invulnerability. Unlike Divine Love, human love is vulnerably circumstantial, and it is the closest most humans ever get to knowing Divine Love and liberation. Divine Love is invulnerable because unlimited love exists beyond any conditions or limitations. If you have to remember to love a person in spite of circumstances or conditions, then you do not love; you are simply practicing a high form of tolerance. Tolerance is a wonderful condition that is very much needed in the world of today, to say the least. Just like unconditional love, tolerance is the act of getting along in spite of differences. Jesus the Nazarene did not teach unconditional love, he taught unlimited love through his instruction to, "Love each other as I have loved you" – without reservation, with active enthusiasm. Exclusion is foundational to both tolerance and intolerance and is at the root of all religious disparity. For the mystic, it is hard to imagine a god, let alone the supposed One and Only God or the One and Only Son of God Almighty, that would be jealous, revengeful, displeased or angry. The mystic's version of love is unlimited and all-encompassing no matter the circumstances or conditions, no matter what is transpiring. The master teacher, Jesus the Nazarene, demonstrated this openly when he said of those men who were nailing him to the cross, "Forgive them for they know not what they do."

Tolerance, like courage, has very little to do with knowing who you are and why you are here, or your true purpose on Earth. It does not take courage to live a balanced life: it takes commitment to a vision of what is possible for your Soul while it is clothed in human form. Courage is very limited in quality and duration: courage is situational and conditional. Commitment is unlimited and without boundaries. If you are committed to a knowing vision, then all will fall into place. If you have to muster up the courage each and every day to face the purpose you have chosen as a life mission, then you will be old and tired by the journey's end. If you live a commitment that is based on knowing who you are and why you are here, then you will be blessed and grace filled until your departure into those between-life realms adjacent to our Earth's dimensions.

True creative self-expression is the ability to manifest from unlimited joy and love, without hesitation, those forms needed to bring balance to your vision of possibilities for this life experience. Most individuals connect a purpose with an occupation or avocation. The purpose of being here on Earth has little to do with any act of doing. True purpose is without definition, just as joy and love are without limitation. Doing is the detail of how we survive from day to day while being is the vision of life everlasting in each new moment. Doing by itself is of little true importance, in that mastering an ability is not required to become enlightened or illumined. No one need do anything to become all-knowing – it is every Soul's birthright within the First Moment of their creation. Souls do not evolve to knowing, they are born as knowing beings. On Earth, being, in and of itself, has little meaning without the dynamics of doing. To come to fullness and Divine ripeness, the threads of being are woven into a tapestry of doing. In this state, no matter what activity you undertake, no matter what career path you choose, no matter your talents or the degree of your proficiencies, you are on purpose through the joy of life.

If an individual experiences a lack of purpose, it is usually fueled by a lack of vision. Those who lack vision have to muster up courage to get through the circumstances of their lives, usually to reach an illusory future moment built only on past patterns of success and failure. Vision is a continuous process of becoming that is based upon a knowing of the possibility of life in all its circumstantial form as it directly relates to an individual or group. Life is truly simple and trouble free when you know who you are and why you exist, and little is possible except to continue the drudgery of existence lifetime after lifetime if you do not know who you are and why you exist.

This is taken from the Atlatian Codes: *The natural order of* knowing *Triads enfleshed* in this realm *of forms is to call into existence through the Earth Spirit, Logos* and their intermediary, *the Holy Spirit, that which is needed in each moment* to ensure *revelation and liberation to all who partake of such* adventure.

It has been stated that knowing (gnosis) does not make you immune to all the influences of this world. Complete immunity happens when we are in the World and not of the World. By this, it is meant that we no longer gain sustenance from this dimension, but exist here in physical form without taking nourishment, with the exception of ingesting water. It is also true that ignorance of how the system works is no defense for inadvertently bringing harm to oneself and others. When you know how the system of manifest thought works, you will only use it in extraordinary measures; the ability to manifest thought into immediate manifestation will not become an amusing form of entertainment for family and friends. Those who know, use their acquired abilities very wisely, exercise great care, and use clear caution in calling matter into existence or reforming Dyadic structures from inanimate to animate matter.

~ Knowing Those Who Set The Table Before You ~

By now you have begun to know yourself as much more than previously imagined. You are Soul consciousness uniquely formed and unalterable from your First Moment, undeniably conscious of the eternal reality from which you were formed. At the same time, you are evolving Dyadic energy or human awareness constantly seeking the perfect expression of your final place within the Great Schematic that was the first vision of Creator God. As such, you exhibit multi dimensionality and uniform feminine and masculine polarity when enjoined with another Soul for the intention of enfleshing into form. Once enfleshed, your one true purpose is to fully enjoy all of life without reservation or hesitation, without guilt or shame of any type, giving in exchange the unlimited flow of energy from that First Moment. Analogy – Life is like a five-star restaurant. Your role is to be served as you so command. You are shown your place in the establishment by the maitre d'hotel. A waiter both informs you of all the choices available on the menu and acts as your intermediary to the chef and chef's assistants, who organize and arrange your selections according to your tastes. There might be a wine steward to offer other selections or to enhance your previous choices. Your presence at the table is your only role. It is up to you to make clear and direct selections.

You are a guest in this realm of forms, but because you are a First State Being, you have command over everything in this realm, save for the Earth Spirit and Logos. This ability to command is not an entitlement; this is a birthright: the difference between a usurper of the crown and one born to rule. The agencies that work with you to bring thought into appropriate form will know the difference between a demand and a command, force and power. When Jesus the Nazarene called his friend, Lazarus, who was dead for four days, from the tomb, he did it by commanding the agencies capable of such feats. He was properly aligned with those dynamic forces that would respond to his command. He did so without hesitation, with the full and unadulterated knowing that he and his Creator God were one and the same, the First Moment enfleshed. Had the Nazarene demanded it to be done of his own will, without the grace-inspired etheric forces gathered about him to do his bidding, he would not have been able to make it instantaneous. It would have taken longer and the aftereffect would have been questionable. The quality and duration of a calling of thought to form and the actuality of its manifestation are dependent upon intention and vision. The time is dependent upon the forces at play to bring the calling into form. If Jesus had intended to take control of the Jews as their king, he would have performed the miracles ascribed to him on his own without the help of the agencies at his disposal. He then could have rightfully said, "Follow me and no one else. For it is I and I alone who do these wondrous miracles." Jesus always publicly acknowledged the forces gathering about him as he performed miracles by stating, "It is not I but the Father within me who does these things."

Back to our restaurant analogy: You have obviously chosen the particular restaurant[4] to satisfy a hunger or taste sensation. Because of this you pay very close attention to what is offered and how it will be served, especially if this is the first or one of a few times you have dined at this restaurant. This careful attention will bring you a knowing choice. Clarity of choice is therefore your assurance of having what you command. There are beings who escort you to your place within the restaurant, other beings who see to your basic needs and still more beings, in this analogy, in the kitchen, out of sight, who work to bring your choices into the expected form. You do not need to know the names of these beings or anything about them to have the utmost experience while dining. You do, however, need to acknowledge their presence, quietly listen to their tutelage, courteously accept their attention to your details and graciously thank them for their awareness of your needs. It is your place within this analogy to be the most gracious diner possible within the range of the unique properties of your Soul. Your sheer gratitude is payment in full for the experience. These helpers need nothing of our world to soothe them.

~ *Past Gods and Present Guides* ~

The restaurant analogy above illustrates the dynamics through which thought manifests into form. Without the helpers at our restaurant we would have to initially come to the restaurant days ahead of time and write in our reservation. Upon arriving on the day and time, we would welcome ourselves, open the door, check our name off the ledger and grab menus at the maitre de station, then seat ourselves. We would then begin the process of educating ourselves as to all possible combinations of selections available by perusing the restaurant stores for ingredients. We would then fill our water glasses, reseat ourselves, take our cocktail order, go to the bar fix our before dinner drinks, then reseat ourselves. Next, we would take our hors d'oeuvre order to the kitchen, prepare the order and reseat ourselves. Next, it would be time to decide on an entrée, select a wine for our entrée, go to the wine seller, retrieve the wine and reseat ourselves. Whereupon we would then select a salad, prepare the salad, reseat ourselves, order our entrée, and go back to the kitchen to prepare the meal. Once finished we would reseat ourselves. Midpoint in the meal we would refresh our water and wine, we would check with ourselves to make certain everything was to our liking and begin to ponder dessert. Shortly after that, we would leave our meal to prepare our dessert selection, and, once finished, return to the table to serve our next course. Just before beginning our dessert we would decide on an after-dinner drink of coffee, leave the table to prepare the coffee and then reseat ourselves. We would then check again to make certain that all had met our expectations and get up to prepare the bill, at which time we would present ourselves with the statement of damages to our pocketbook, collect our money and return to the cash register with payment. We would then present the change and thank ourselves very much for choosing this establishment. We would bus our table to prepare the tabletop for the next guest and retreat to the kitchen to wash the dishes. Once the dishes were washed, dried and put away, we would leave the building for home.

If this were a true representation of life, few would ever return. There are those among you who not only do this for yourselves, but also do this for family members day in and day out. Thanks! We have helpers who watch over us (even those of us who are performing double and triple duty), working diligently with our with every thought and word. Some of these helpers have existed before human beings. These are all the Elementals and Devic Beings that play within the dimensional boundaries around time and space. Some of the watcher/helpers are Dyadic Souls of various abilities, while some are here as a result of our command for them to exist. Through the millenniums since the end of the Atlatian epoch, humans have called into service all manner of Beings and Entities that do not incarnate but exist solely to serve humanity. In our analogy of the restaurant, these Beings are wait-service professionals and chefs who busy themselves with manifesting our purposeful needs. In true human fashion, we have elevated some of these called Entities and Beings to the positions of gods and goddesses to guard over and protect us from all manor of real and imagined calamities.

This is important: after thousands of years of worship, the gods we had invented long ago to oversee the unexplainable details of our lives and make safe our passage through time in space literally took on lives of their own. We called them into partnership to aid us in our journeys, elevated them to more knowing positions than we, worshiped them by sacrificing to them as devoted servants, then abandoned them in favor of a single off-world god who resides in heaven or in hell or some other perpetual mystification. These Entities and Elementals evolved from the Dyadic matter of Earth and aid us in our manifestation through their intimate knowing of this World. Now that we are once again able to comprehend the greater knowing of creation, it will be to our advantage to have these Beings in a knowing partnership. If we think them to be myths or fairytales, it will be at our own undoing. It is reckless to assume that any of the lesser gods[5] would immediately have our greatest interest at heart. After all, we created them and then abandoned them as we grew in working knowledge of this realm and the universe around us. As our ability to explain the natural forces at work around us grew in efficiency, we, some more reluctantly than others, tossed aside those who had taken us through the midst and mists of our early journeys in this cycle of duality. We outgrew our god and goddess-creations by choosing rational thought over emotional response, by separating thought and feeling. We separated thought from feeling and, in doing so, created greed to fill the void. Instead of incorporating these unwavering spiritual colleagues into our new understandings, we decide to keep up with the Joneses. They still exist and will welcome anyone who has eyes to see and ears to hear.

During the period when humanity was creating gods, we created gods to govern everything under the sun, moon and stars. We had goddesses of planting and harvesting, gods of weather and petulance; we had deities to govern and care after every detail of life. We even pitted these called gods against each other creating jealous gods, especially our gods of war who are very seductive and then very destructive. Currently we think of them as wild imaginings, impossibilities in light of scientific revelation, and superstitious inventions of a time when the average individual knew very little truth of life. Now that we are again coming into a unity cycle, when once again our knowing will be fully realized, they will be known to us as our manifestations. As such, they are duty bound to our commands, just as the staff in the restaurant analogy. Knowing that they will respond if called upon is extremely important. Ignorance of this is no excuse for the harm that may be caused over an idle beseeching. As you begin to release all conflict and balance your vital forces, these lesser gods will quickly respond to each command, especially if that command is to manifest to a Soul's purposeful needs. Make it a point to become familiar with the historical gods pertinent to your region of the world. Go back to times before the current dominant populous. Even though men do battle and cultural boundaries change, the gods of the vanquished are still in force. All native peoples of all continents called upon disincarnate Dyadic or Triadic Souls of ancestors, Saints and Sadhus, Angelic Beings, other Dyads or Elemental Entities such as Gnomes, Sprites, Fairies, Brownies and Elves. By knowing your place as a Triadic Soul in Dyadic awareness you can employ these forces to actively work with you to manifest thought to form.

In most of the World's religions, there are deities and avatars whose names are used in the pleading prayers of the faithful. A knowing individual may use the presence of such great beings to aid in manifesting to any need, purposeful or otherwise. Be mindful of the saints and gods of your religion. They will aid; and be well advised to put off the aid from forces unknown to you while calling into form your heart's desire. As well as the many different gods, there are any number of disincarnate beings, Triad and Dyad alike, who would love nothing more than to join in your joy with promises of rapid manifestation in exchange for sovereignty over you. Do not enter into such arrangements. You are in command through gracious compassion and enduring joy. Ask the intentions of any force that might want to join in your manifest joy. Patience, especially in the beginning, is an essential ingredient to successfully manifesting thought into form. After your first full manifestation experience, the temptation to rush into joining forces to ensure a called form's immediacy will be a distant memory. Jesus the Nazarene was tempted by all manner of devils during periods of prayer and fasting with offers of everything from the simplest immediate comforts to global rule, and consistently replied with, "Get thee behind me, Satan." Satan, in this case was the designation of a lesser god, a god of manipulation. Interestingly, Jesus kept his purposeful needs directed to others and not to himself. The Akashic Records indicate that this was his way to put aside the unbelievable forces gathering about him that were knowingly being called into form by the Zealots to overthrow Roman rule and restore sovereignty to Israel. Once John the Baptist acknowledged Jesus as the messiah, the Zealots had a point of focus around which to manifest. The ethers around Jesus and his disciples were crowded with beings waiting for an opening through which to attack. They found such an opening in Judas Iscariot. Had Jesus once manifested for his own direct needs, even a simple piece of bread, he would have been consumed by those forces and Christians would more than likely be called Mithraists[6] because the gentle teachings of Jesus the Nazarene would be little more than a historical footnote.

All this sounds very dramatic and smacks somewhat of dark, underground, Stephen King-like images. It is important for you to know that through our misconceptions and ignorance we have called into form many different deities whose existence continues the confusion and conflict we have regarding creation. All the gods of ancient cultures still have form and force. These creations are not just mythical images. There were also more practical forms called into existence to aid us in our daily concerns. Example: In the United Kingdom: Wales, Ireland, Scotland, and parts of Normandy and Brittany, one can still witness the fierce doppelganger forms called into existence by the Druid priests to guard their grove temples in the highlands and valleys. These forms presently guard designated parameters around forests to keep out wayward intruders and will continue to guard them until they are called out of existence by those who called them into form, or by modern mystics who know the Old Religion that created them.

~ *Calling Thought Into Form* ~

It is impossible to manifest thought to hand without the appropriate posturing of body, mind and Spirit. Gratitude is that correct posturing and is the first essential ingredient of all willful direct manifestation. It is important your gratitude be given first to the Earth Spirit and Logos as opposed to a lesser Deity that might aid you in the actual manifestation of the form. It is important that gratitude is likewise directed to all who help in your undertaking, be they in physical bodies or etheric forms. Your intentions will be known to them and will carry your gratitude in their direction. Singling out the Earth Spirit and Logos is good manners and a matter of protocol in the process of manifesting form. In the early days of this epoch, priests would offer sacrifices to the greater forces. This act was never necessary and was wholly repugnant to those forces. In those cultures and times this was the highest form of gratitude or tribute that could be paid – giving to those forces helping to form life before taking any bounty for self, family members and community.

In all manifestations of thought to hand, this one point is the single most essential ingredient: you must be willing to live out your existence as your manifestations. This ensures your continued joy and sovereignty over what you call into being. As a caution, it is important to know that you cannot abandon a manifest form just as you would never abandon a child. You can transmute a called form, especially a form that has a very specific task, such as one you have called into existence as an aid in a distance healing. Once the healing is complete the form is either recalled to another task or reintegrated within your greater being. This was the case when Jesus the Nazarene did his healings. In John 4:46-54 we read, *"Jesus came again into Cana of Galilee, where he made the water wine and there was a certain nobleman, whose son was sick at Capernaum. When the nobleman heard that Jesus was traveling from Judea into Galilee, he went to him, and pleaded with him that he would come to Capernaum to heal his son: for he was at the point of death. Then said Jesus, "Except ye see signs and wonders, ye will not believe." The nobleman replied, "Sir, come or my child will certainly die." Jesus said, "Go back home; your son lives." The man believed what Jesus had spoken to him, and without hesitation went his way. As he was returning home, his servants met him, and told him, "Your son lives." He asked them the exact hour when the boy began to mend. They replied, "Yesterday at the seventh hour the fever left him." So the father knew that it was at the same hour when Jesus said, "Your son lives": and himself believed, and his whole house. This is again the second miracle that Jesus did, when he was traveling out of Judea into Galilee.*

The examples of Jesus' healings as reported in the New Testament, Dead Sea and Naghammadi Scrolls are well documented and widely accepted not only by religious authority but also by scientists. You can enjoin called forms to a higher purpose, meaning that two or more different forms called into existence at different times can be enjoined if the new form equally benefits the previous form. If the intentions of both forms are identical, it would not matter if the quality of both forms was not the same. A lesser form can be integrated within the intentions of a greater form at the willful command of either originating Triad. This is so even if different Triads called the forms. Triads have complete sovereignty over all forms called into purpose by uninitiated individuals who are familiar with the teachings of the Way of Truth and Light and have inadvertently called a form into existence to do a bidding.

In the beginning, it will seem as though there is a lot of work to learning the art of effortlessness. The basic rule is clarity over intention. Intention will not change and it can gather intensity, whereas clarity is whole and complete before the calling. It is extremely important to know what you want and to be without hesitation of any kind once the calling is begun. Therefore, it is important to set everything into motion is a prescribed manner. This formula was first put into motion by a small grouping of Souls who had lived in the unity cycle of Atlatia, and remained awake during the transition to separation some thirteen thousand years ago, for use during this epoch when they would have to survive in life. The most commonly used procedure of the Atlatians for commanding thought into form is taken from the Atlatian codes and Akashic Records as follows:

- Remember who you are and why you are on Earth – *you are a direct expression of the First Moment and eternal Joy is your radiant purpose. You, as a First State Being, are without equal in this world of forms.* There is nothing to fear, for as enfleshed Souls you are incapable of harm or mistake. All is as it should be.
- *Gather about you all those who will aid you in your day's endeavors. Do this before you arise from your bed.* Calling upon the Earth Spirit and Logos to clear your near and far vision will ensure the correctness of your spiritual companions. *Know that Divine Will attracts to your clear intentions only the finest of all guides and angelic entities.*
- Balance is important to manifesting neutral forms. *Release all conflict or judgment and embrace the eternal now as your rightful place within creation. Everything, all that has brought you to this moment of knowing, is as it should be or it would be otherwise. Live as though you are in The Moment – the First Moment – Creator God.*
- Be well aware of your true intentions for the calling of matter from out of the ethers. *Intention, as a primary force, drives the process to completion by setting the harmonics of your calling. All adjacent harmonics will inadvertently empower your command through the Universal Law of Attraction.*
- Visualize the completed manifestation without being paralyzed by the details. Do this by *becoming completely involved with your manifestation through your senses – See it, feel it, taste it, hear it and smell it. Letting your senses fill in the details* will allow you to be as clear as possible as to how the called form will appear in matter.
- Every word uttered is a sacred vow. Every sound, syllable and word.

With the power of your voice, *call to those outside powers* – Avatars, Angels, Beings, Elementals or Entities; *surround yourself with those agencies that will help you complete the details of the vision through their intimate knowing of Dyadic energy.* If their names are known to you, then speak them aloud as you call them to you. *Know that they stand ready to take your calling as their own undertaking.*

- Gathering the vertical Earth energy and horizontal etheric energy of the six other bodies in the heart chakra[7] is vital in manifesting thought into matter. *Focus your thoughts and emotions on the intention and vision of your manifestation as you gather these two vital energies at the heart center.*

- *Speak aloud in a clear unhesitant voice that which you care to manifest. Feel the unlimited energy of the First Moment as it surges through you into the now.* Release the calling through the gratitude gathered in your heart.

- Empower those agencies that do your bidding (your guides and all angelics) to bring the form of your manifestation into specific time and space. *Do this by simply knowing that your calling is being handed to you as the completion of Divine Grace in the moment it is called. This is the fullness of the giving and receiving nature of duality.*

- *Only command this manifestation once.* (Often, you will instantly and momentarily forget what was just commanded to take form. This is natural as you release the energy of the calling.)

- At the end of each day, *gather about you all those unseen entities and forces who prepared the way for your Divinely inspired call to manifest to purposeful need. Do this as you fall into slumber.*

When calling thought to form, it is important to distinguish the difference between a demand and the act of commanding. The definition of command in this particular case is to grasp the subtle relationships within all presenting circumstances and to effectively demonstrate your authority as an enjoined Triadic being who has grace-inspired dominion over evolving forms through the power of selfless gratitude. This naturally happens as you know your place in Creation. A demand is more akin to a claim that something is yours without the demonstration of ownership. Demands are filled with life force-draining details and stipulations that require constant supervision. On the other hand, commanding a manifest form, a situation or given set of circumstances, is to allow the details to present themselves within the context of naturally appearing conditions. A demanding person will need to control each aspect of his or her desire; whereas a commanding presence will bring order out of chaos with little or no effort. This is often the difference between being a leader of people (commanding power) and the general of an army (demanding through force).

Calling thought to form is the act of giving. As we give without expectation, in grace-inspired gratitude, we expand our ability to express our Soul's nature by calling into form those things of the Spirit realm and those things of this World. This is the moment when positive and negative, Spirit and form, enjoin as one expression – so above as below.

Practice:

Each time you use the phrase "I am," you set into motion the mechanism of manifestation. "I am hungry," sets into motion those streams of consciousness that bring you nourishment. "I am happy," sets into motion those streams of consciousness that ensure you connect with Joy. "I Am That I Am," is the spontaneous statement made at the moment of illumination and is the most powerful statement a Soul can make while in human form. Each and every word that follows the "I am" declaration will be lived out.

Interestingly, "I am not feeling well," sets into motion those streams that bring you health. The reason for this is that the subconscious mind, the part of your conscious awareness that aligns the creative forces within you, is incapable of acknowledging disclaimers such as "not." In this case, the subconscious mind would hear, "I am (blank) feeling well," and would set into motion those agencies needed to bring balance to your physical body. If regularly repeated over a short period, you would begin to feel well. As you have guessed, this unintentionally sets up conflict, in that, your intention is to acknowledge not feeling physically well and yet your words betray or run contrary to that intention, so you are left with the opposite of your calling. If you regularly repeated this over a long period, say a few years, the inner conflict generated between your intended statement of not feeling well and its immediate effect of getting better would eventually generate disease and you would become a self-fulfilled prophecy of illness. This type of confusion of "intention to outcome" is prominent in our world culture and is the basis for most of our non-core conflicts.

Think of how many times each day you use disclaimers: I do not (don't), I will not (won't), I cannot (can't). How many times have you heard someone say, "I won't ever do that again," only to watch the person proceed to do the very same thing. The agencies, your guides and spiritual aids, which help you with every aspect of your life, hear your command as, "I (blank) ever do that again." The word "ever" means: still, yet, constantly, continually, always and forever. Until we know the relationship between the disconnect aspects of language to the intended outcome, we repeatedly confuse our experience in life through verbally misstating intentions. Again, "I do not..." is the declaration that you will not act toward a certain result. The creative agencies acknowledge the disclaimer as a void and work to bring about the subject of the calling or statement. Your words state one direction and the outcome is the polar expression. With this you will be conflicted and the process will be befuddled. "I will not (I will it not)..." is a declaration of your desire to keep something from manifesting. This is also a form of a curse. "I will it so (So mote it be)..." is a direct manifestation command. "I cannot..." is a judgment of inability: you have failed to develop that ability and therefore are unable to act to conclusion.

For a week just observe your use of words. Do this without changing any words or combinations. Just observe. Becoming aware of how each word is used to bring about purposeful needs is essential to actively manifesting thought to hand. After your week of observing, watch each word that comes from your mouth, especially those words that will add conflict to your creative process. Only use phrases that command power through clarity and joy. Keep a journal of how your circumstances change. Make sure that you choose your words carefully when making personal statements that begin with, "I am."

Invocation:

From the last chapter: Each thought we have is formed of loosely tied-together stringlets of ethrioplasmic or subatomic substance. These infinitesimally miniscule particles are the base of all manifest forms. It is important to know that every word you state into the ethers influences these stringlets of particles, releasing small portions of their pure energy into the substance of Earth. These stringlets are like joined stem cells; they are the foundation of all form. An illumined Soul knows the value of each word and always seeks to speak directly and clearly without hesitation. There is a patter (cadence) and overall manner in which an individual may speak into the ethers to heighten the energy release of those stringlets and then command that released energy to gather in whatever manner is so needed through the intention of the one calling a desired thought to form.

Once you have begun to balance your etheric and physical bodies through conscious and dynamic meditation, you will want to begin building a vision that you can command with complete confidence. It is not important to consciously know all the details of the vision, for somewhere in your consciousness, tucked away for just this moment, are all the details you have gathered from all your lifetimes that are akin to your vision. You do not have to be aware of their existence for them to be real; you need only know they exist. Let us use wealth by way of example: in several past lifetimes you might have been wealthy or been from a family who was wealthy. The details of those lives are tucked away and will fill in the details of your "wealth" vision without your having to call them forward out of time. In other lifetimes, you might have been poor. How you felt about wealthy people will also help to form the details of your vision. If in those less fortunate lives you robbed from the rich, you will need to forgive any injustice you felt in those lives, whether the injustice was real or only used to justify your actions.

Several times each day look at life around you and quietly but clearly whisper:

"The pureness of my being is illumed in every detail of life. In my balanced state, the substance of the World reflects a pure image of my Soul to me. In my balanced state, I reflect unlimited Joy and Love as my gift to all the details of life. All this I AM, and more."

The invocation written below, when spoken in a deliberate monotonic voice in the key of "A," will open the three subtle energy channels at the crown of the head as a preparation for Soul consciousness to permeate the three upper chakras. Repeat the invocation once for each of the three upper chakras. As in all invocations, even the ones you will eventually write for yourselves, it is important to read this invocation several times before you say it aloud. As before, the patter should be in a rhythm akin to reciting a childhood limerick or riddle. Look at the words and be sincere when reciting:

"I am open and willing to allow my Soul consciousness to express in me, through me, as me. I am open and willing to allow my Soul consciousness to express in me, through me, as me. I am open and willing to allow my Soul consciousness to express in me, through me, as me."

Thoughts:

The Divine is all there is. Nothing is out of alignment to the purpose of the Divine.

My authentic response to life is evidence of my direct experience of the agencies that bring about those things I command.

Lifestyle Suggestions:

Meditation: Repeating the meditation technique from the previous chapter and adding a new element. Again, if you do not already have one, it will be important to purchase a pitch pipe. A pitch pipe will ensure the quality of your tones.

Each of the seven core chakras (energy centers) resounds with tone and color. It is easy to use your voice to activate the energy centers with the intention of bringing balance to your body, mind and Spirit.

Sit with your spine lifted by mentally putting a slight space between each vertebra. Take a moment to focus on your breath, watching the point between breaths. Begin this chant in a slow rhythm. The pace might want to change on its own after a few minutes. Let it.

The first sound, "LAH," is whispered in the key of "C" and is spoken with full attention on the base chakra. Then take a moment to intend to clearly hear your next words and say in the same tone and cadence, "I am sexually power-ful." Then repeat that statement with even more fervor, "I Am Sexually Pow-erful." Then repeat it a third time, "I AM SEXUALLY POWERFUL. I AM JOYFUL WITH MY SEXUALITY." Feel your words as heat at the base of the spine. See your words as a deep red energy spreading around your hips. As the energy of your words moves upward, let the energy become a reddish orange.

The second sound, "BAH," is normally voiced in the key of "D" with your attention moving upward into the spleen center just below and slightly left of your navel. Then take a moment to intend to clearly hear your next words and

---

say in the same tone and cadence, "Others know me as a sexually powerfully being." Then repeat that statement with even more fervor, "Others Know Me As A Sexually Powerful Being." Then repeat it a third time, "OTHERS KNOW ME AS A SEXUALLY POWERFUL BEING. I HONOR THEIR SEXUAL POWER." Feel your words as warm energy and see your words as bright orange energy radiating out from the top of your pubis to your middle waist. (Note: Be aware of any sexually forceful feelings like the desire to overpower others sexually. Ask to be shown the origins of those feelings.)

The third sound, "RAH," is growled in a low-pitched key of "E" emanating from the solar plexus. Say this sound from deep inside your body. Then take a moment to intend to clearly hear your next words and say in the same tone and cadence, "I am physically powerful." Then repeat that statement with even more fervor, "I Am Physically Powerful." Then repeat it a third time, "I AM PHYSICALLY POWERFUL. I ACKNOWLEDGE THE PHYSICAL POWER OF OTHERS." See your words as a bright yellow ball of light centered on your body at your solar plexus and feel the energy as the radiant warmth of the sun on a bright, cool winter's day spreading out from you in all directions.

The heart chakra is a happy sound of "YAM," (Yah-Aum) and spoken joyfully in the key of "F." Command this sound in a sincerely happy and firm tone. Then take a moment to intend to clearly hear your next words and say in the same tone and cadence, "I am joyfully nurturing." Then repeat that statement with even more fervor, "I Am Joyfully Nurturing." Then repeat it a third time, "I AM JOYFULLY NURTURING. I AM EMPOWERED AS I IN TURN RECEIVE NURTURING." Imagine your joy as a deep green field of waving grass and feel it as a nuzzling sensation that chases away feelings of isolation and abandonment.

In the key of "G" shout "HAH" as the Life Force moves through your heart up into your throat. Then take a moment to intend to clearly hear your next words and say in the same tone and cadence, "I am joyfully commanding." Then repeat that statement with even more fervor, "I Am Joyfully Commanding." Then repeat it a third time, "I AM JOYFULLY COMMANDING. I COMMAND ALL I PURPOSEFULLY NEED." Imagine waves of light blue energy calling every word you utter into form.

In the key of "A" sigh the sound of discovery, "AHHA," as the energy continues upward toward your crown chakra and comes to rest in the third eye. Then take a moment to intend to clearly hear your next words and say in the same tone and cadence, "I am knowing." Then repeat that statement with even more fervor, "I Am Knowing." Then repeat it a third time, "I KNOW BEYOND REASONING. I AM A KNOWING BEING." The energy is midnight blue and feels indifferent to all sensations and senses.

Alternating the keys of high "D" and "B" make the announcement, "AUM." Feel your whole body vibrate with a mighty (Au-Um) as a brilliant purple light surrounds your head. Then take a moment to intend to clearly hear your next words and say in the same tone and cadence, "The First Moment and I are One Knowing." Then repeat that statement with even more fervor, "The First Moment And I Are One Knowing." Then repeat it a third time, "THE FIRST MOMENT AND I ARE ONE KNOWING." The knowing feeling permeating your body and radiating outward into the world is complete contentment and the liberation of concern. Repeat this for twenty minutes. The intention of this exercise is to immediately balance your energy centers, mind and Spirit.

Diet: Practice what you have come to enjoy.

Fasting: Take one day off each week to fast for others. (This means no food just water. If you orally take daily medication, it would be wise to have a glass of milk to buffer your stomach.) Be specific in your fast. Fasting for another's joy or health is very powerful. Fasting for world peace is a bit grandiose and is open to a very broad interpretation. After all, being forced to live in another's idea of heaven would be hell. Be very conscious that you are not attempting to change anyone or any group. This is more for the process of elevating conscious awareness so that illumination can work its magic, whichever direction it wants.

Exercise: As always, be as active as is possible for your present circumstances, knowing that as you increase your endurance, you will increase your activity. Keep a written record of your accomplishments and push yourself to new limits. Again, keep investigating dynamic types of exercise that allow you to meditate while being active, such as the Six Tibetan Rites illustrated at the back of this book. Stretching, stretching and more stretching will add good years to your life.

Several times during your day, take a moment to focus on your breath, allowing each breath to be fully felt in your body as in a complete yogic breath.

~ *Chapter VIII Footnotes* ~

1 Ethrioplasmic substance that moves upward along the spinal column from the base chakra to the crown chakra. This vertical energy stimulates the chakras giving vitality to the body, mind and Spirit.

2 Phonetic spelling. A female individual who lived in the Sumerian city of Ur, today Tall al-Muqayyar (or Mughair), about two hundred miles (three hundred km) southeast of Baghdad. She was completely illumined.

3 The forces of creative imagining attributed to the nine daughters of Zeus and Mnemosyne.

4 This would be analogous to choosing a time period to incarnate – time being both a string and a ball.

5 Any deified non-incarnating Being, Entity or Elemental who is given influence over human beings.

6 Adherent of Mithraism.

7 See the standing breathing technique illustrated at the back of the book. This breathing exercise is extremely effective in building the energy streams at the heart chakra.

THE *KNOWING*

*"I would rather
have a mind
opened by wonder
than one
closed
by belief."*

—. *Gerry Spence*

Chapter IX

~ Thought Manifestation as a Collective Force ~

The constant self-abuse of inner conflict creates an underlying sense of worthlessness and unworthiness that, left undiscovered, is held within the Soul's etheric body for seven generations, seven incarnations. At the time of each death, there is an immediate release from the compounding conflict associated with that life, and the controlling behaviors of self-centeredness and self-aggrandizement are greatly diminished. Yet, the greater dynamic of the personality's and ego's baggaged conflict remains quiescently intact during the between-life period. In this sense, we carry within our Soul's etheric body a continually building notion that we are somehow less than the completeness of our Souls. The personality/ego frames this as imperfection of body, mind and Spirit. This inner conflict has us searching all of creation for the place where we are meaningfully right or correct. Within the influences of a cycle of duality, such as is during this current epoch, we collectively create the forces of good and evil, and then take sides, based upon a given lifetime's cultural values, as to which is right in the eyes of our current culture's created gods. Being on a determined "right side" only reinforces the seven lifetimes of conflicted energy dragging behind us and does nothing to alleviate conflicted inner feelings. Being right then becomes our Divine obsession, to the extent that we create intricately woven ideas and notions of who we are in creation and our purpose in the world. In this, we endlessly labor and labor and labor until death steals life away, leaving those who survive us to once again ponder the true meaning of life at their loss of our company. No matter the culture, no matter the geological location, this is the human predicament as it has come to be known. Many of us would rather be right than joyfully authentic.

Our inner conflict, that place that is driven by the uncertainty of who and why we are, generates our individual and collective need to be right or correct. Over many lifetimes we come to equate being right with being loveable. This, combined with our core belief that we are imperfect, gives humanity a collectively developed need to be right about how wrong we are. Religion does help release the pressure of our inner conflict by giving us a place to be loved no matter how worthless we deem ourselves to be. Religion is always just a Band-Aid to deeper wounds: a place to encounter a force greater than ourselves that is capable of looking beyond our flaws and inconsistencies, but a place that also works in such mysterious ways as to allow suffering and strife. Jesus the Nazarene would heal others by bringing balance and unity to an individual's body, mind and Spirit, then instruct the person to, "Go and sin no more." This prescription for correcting the conflict that was surfacing as a physical illness was also the cure for the release from the generations of conflict generating the imbalance within the ego and personality: "Go and sin no more," a short statement, so simply spoken and so increasingly difficult to achieve as we approach the inevitable shift back into unity beginning in 2011.

We all have the original sin as the conflict generated when a Soul enters a physical form. This type of conflict (sin) is a causation of dissimilar combining forces, physical matter (atomic substance) and non-matter matter (etherioplasmic substance) within the exact same time/space, as opposed to a willfully driven intention of thought energy or intentional behavior that is the source of the ego and personality's conflict. In one sense, we are always going to experience a degree of conflict as original sin while in a physical form. Some mystics believe this causation conflict is the source of humanity's suffering, as in the dynamics of karma, while others see the original conflict of Soul enfleshment as the dynamic that moves humanity forward through life. Whatever the belief, humanity is compelled toward conflict; the degree of conflict beyond the original sin is completely a matter of choice by individuals and collectives. To feel safe, our Dyadic awareness seeks to build a new body within the same bloodline as the previous incarnation it had helped to form. It knows the genetically imposed behavior range and physical limitations, so it feels less vulnerable and less conflicted within those implied boundaries. Our Soul is unconcerned with how each physical form deals with the compounding conflict held within its etheric form. If it were concerned, it would also seek out the same bloodline as a way of predicting the next body's reaction to its collections of opposing energies. The Soul experiences itself as complete, and therefore is unaware of any real or imagined conflict. Interestingly, our ego/personality chooses to replicate behaviors and actions from the conflicted sets of past incarnations as a means of relieving feelings of conflict, even if those behaviors were only peculiar to the previous Dyadic awareness. Once we are aware that we choose conflict as a means of feeling more familiar with life, we can then begin to choose the level of conflict we allow into the present life from past lives. In deciding, we also can release conflict as we bring it forward into the moment. Gratitude for the discovery of conflict is the key to releasing conflict.

Allowing the knowing that we are at once and forever complete from our beginning moment, that we are unparalleled in our uniqueness and forever held within the grace of the First Moment as unalterable to penetrate our ego and personality begins to free us of our need to be right. Needing to be right is the projection of our inner conflict onto the world through our ego and personality. We are now and have always been "right" as First State Beings. Learning the incarnational boundaries within a given dimensional system is wholly different from attempting to become Spiritual Beings. We are first and forever Spiritual Beings. While enfleshed, we still need the discernment we have gathered through all our incarnations to guide us through the subtleties of life, just as we need the wisdom of our Dyadic forms to instinctively maneuver us through the survival of each day. It could be said that discernment is foundational to our existence. Giving up the need to be right allows us to shed the lifetimes of conflict that we keep alive by choosing to forget who we are and why we are here. It is not important to identify each and every conflict held within your Soul's etheric body. It would take several lifetimes of continuous, uninterrupted conscious ego/personality to unravel the intricately woven spider's web of self-deceit manufactured by layers of competing conflicts. Or you can consciously give up the need to be right and allow joy to fill in the voids created by the released conflict.

The details of a conflict become unimportant in light of the release of the conflict, just as the details of manifesting thought to a given form are unimportant in relationship to the release of the command to form. However, knowing the core nature, not the details, of a conflict begins to shift the dynamic of that energy, just as knowing the complete intention of a manifestation to a specific purposeful need gathers the energy of the final form as its matrix. Consciously knowing that the core conflict for humanity is the need to feel loved, expressing as the need to be right, is the simple alchemy of the shift from proving to knowing. The alchemical effect upon the collective ego and personality will be immediate, and this shift, of course, is not always a pretty sight. Notice how humanity is acting out as we approach the new age of unity beginning with the year 2011: personal conflicts moving out through family and extended family relationships, individuals in conflict with their communities, territorial disputes between cultures and ideological wars between religions.

In the next several years, it will become extremely important for the human ego and personality to allow Soul consciousness to equally guide the actions of humanity. In its natural state, the physical body only seeks survival and then comfort. In our modern world of leisure, Dyadic awareness gets an unprecedented opportunity to explore the hidden recesses of the individual and collective psyche. In cycles of unity, nothing is hidden from our knowing and the ego/personality is used to develop abilities as opposed to defending beliefs. In separation cycles, almost everything is hidden from conscious view through the veil of anticipation and expectation fulfillment and external validation. In this state, abilities are developed to ensure inclusion and success.

~ *Being Fully Present in the Moment* ~

The inherent nature of physical body awareness is to progress toward a perfected state. Souls are in completed form and as such are the reflection of the First Moment, or Creator God. The fact that we Souls, when expressing collectively as humans, labor so industriously to assist matter into perfection by affording it a glimpse of that First Moment is wholly an act of unlimited love. We Souls love Earth and all of its many systems of life, even earlier when we still had a more active part within the food chain. History is filled with stories of how humans, from all cultures and lifestyles, have gone out of their way, even to the point of giving up their own lives, to save an animal that was in harm's way. Simply, we Souls adore Earth and Earth adores us.

Each manifest energy formation on Earth, animate or inanimate, began its existence from within the primary[1] bands of thought energy permeating the non-matter matter of the Earth's etheric body. These early bands of thought are the true celestial soup from which life, as evolving physical awareness, sprang. Without these primary thought forms harmonically reverberating within the etheric body of Earth, the microbial life forms brought to this world through countless comet impacts would have remained a slushy primordial muck that lacked the imagination to morph. Over the course of evolution, animated life began to add its distinctive thought energy to the primary bands of thought. This additional sharable energy gave imagination its origins. When we awaken to our true nature, we will once again fully project the completeness of the First Moment – *the moment* so often spoken of in ancient texts. While living from, or as it is currently stated, *living in the moment*, each of our generated thoughts begins to build layers of ethrioplasmic substance that form the foundation of our entire perception-based dimensional experience. Jesus the Nazarene stated, *"By way of the great comforter, and through the Father, I go to prepare a place for all who will to follow the way of truth and light. This place I so prepare is for the twice-born who so will as to forsake the way of the flesh,*[2] *thereafter enter the eternal realm of Souls. This is the gathering of the faithful of the way of truth and light, lest no one enter this manifest place except through my preparation of the way as the Son through whom acts the Father as Holy Spirit.*" (as interpreted from the Akashic Records on the teachings of the Nazarene Master)

As we live in *the moment* (live from the knowing of the First Moment) – the eternal now – every thought manifests as an immediate projection of the command of the First Moment. The term, the moment, refers directly to the First Moment – Creator God. For an individual to be *in the moment* means, he or she is one with Creator God – the First Moment. In this manner of existing, all the circumstances of every moment are complete in the moment they are formed. Manifest thought is outside the immediate influence of similarly expressing evolutionary matter – Dyadic forms – because called matter is the condensation of non-matter matter into matter-like energy matrixes. As such, its origins are off-world – not of this world. As Souls we are commanded to be in the world, not of the world. If we consume the world's resources as our sustenance, we are generating additional conflict. Of course, we need drink and nourishment from the Earth until such time as we are illumined and fully liberated.

This is important: Creator God would not hesitate to live out Its eternal existence as one of Its Creations. To manifest thought to hand, just as Creator God, you would be unhesitatingly willing to live out your eternal existence as any of your creations.

If left to our natural inclinations when in a physical realm, we Souls would want to replicate our completed state and bring thought to form in one single expression. Instead we labor under the idea that we have to do something to have our needs met. Until a Soul is completely balanced, illumined, it is obliged and otherwise shrewd to follow the dictates of the collective mind by taking care of its needs in the best way possible and to the highest degree of spiritual ability possible. Once liberated, the Soul is then free of the constraints of the collective and can begin to manifest in its own image, just as Creator God manifested us in Its Image. A Soul is prudent to release the shackles of the collective mind very cautiously lest it errs on the side of haste. Jesus the Nazarene's demonstration of the miracles of life was a very limited presentation of how we, as both the sons and daughters of man (Dyadic awareness) and the sons and daughters of Creator God (Soul consciousness), are to live daily life. Without exception, every Soul is capable of knowing why it exists and how it was derived; every Soul is capable of illumination.

~ *Divine Posturing* ~

So often, we are given explicit instruction on the Creative Schematic only to misunderstand the more subtle levels of the teaching. It is not our fault but more a product of our conditioning that has us looking only for those things that openly support our prejudices. Such is the case in the following statement concerning group manifestation in which Jesus the Nazarene gives an unambiguous teaching concerning our relationship to manifestation: *"In truth I say to you, whatsoever you shall bind on earth shall be bound in heaven: and whatsoever you shall liberate on earth shall be liberated in heaven. Again, I say to you, if two of you shall agree on earth as touching any thing that they shall ask, it shall be done for them of my Father, which is in heaven. For where two or three are gathered together in my name, there am I in the midst of them."* (Matthew 18: 18-20)

Whatever we manifest on Earth, we take from existing forms: in this case, thought forms held in the memory fields of our individual and collective etheric bodies. Jesus is stating openly that whatever we "bind," or unite, in form cannot exist on Earth as Dyadic matter without having a directly corresponding form in Heaven as primary non-matter matter. Notice in this passage from the New Testament that the word heaven is not given any formal regard. In those days, the more common use of the word "heaven" literally meant "sky," or the unseen forces that create the wind, or metaphorically, the unknowable forms that shape nature and influence all life as in the will of Heaven. In Medieval times alchemists referred to this as the ethers or unknown malleable agencies. The term "bind" is extremely important to the mystical study of manifest thought and means to amalgamate, to fuse both the forces of consciousness (vision) and energy (command) that are needed to bring compliant form from the heavens (ethers). Jesus states that whatever we let loose on Earth, we also liberate in heaven, implying little difference between the real workings of those two dimensions. As the maxim states: as above, so below. *"Whatsoever ye shall loose on Earth shall be loosed in Heaven,"* means to completely liberate from all obligation that which is united in form through your command to be. When you call a form into matter from out of non-matter matter, it is liberated and moves forward in time from that first moment, free of any mandatory connection to you, and you remain sovereign to its existence. The only power that can release a command to take immediate manifest form is pure gratitude.

In this teaching the Nazarene goes on to affirm: *"Again, I say to you, that if two of you shall agree on earth as touching anything that they shall ask, it shall be done for them of my Father, which is in heaven."* This is extremely important when working with groups: you all must agree on the final form to the degree that each separate vision of the completed form would be as one. In this sense, you are within the realms of vision and intention "touching" the form. This form of touching is experienced as a shiver by most or a quickening of the flesh, as it is often described in older texts. Asking is the proper posture for the language of Jesus' time. Commanding is more from the knowing state of consciousness and applies to any initiate of the mystical path. This is important: The "Father" Jesus refers to is not Creator God, but rather the combined presence of the Logos and Earth Spirit existing in the form of a complete, unified knowing that permeates all consciousness and energy, all thought and matter here on Earth, Biblically referred to as the Holy Spirit or Great Comforter. On a separate occasion Jesus also stated, *"I and my Father are one."* In this pronouncement, he openly made known his integration of the Earth Spirit and Logos emanating through him as an aspect of himself. He became the personification of the Holy Spirit. Because of this, he was also able to state, *"For where two or three are gathered together in my name, there am I in the midst of them."* The Soul of Jesus was born through Dyadic matter. He is able to state, *"...there am I in the midst of them,"* without hesitation. In very rare cases when a Triad integrates body, mind and Spirit, then integrates Earth Spirit and Logos, It becomes as the wind, in that, just as the wind shifts a field of grass, It is a part of the unseen forces that shift and shape the collective mind of humanity. If you individually call the name of such a Being, It responds without hesitation and with full attention to work with you in Divine partnership. If you collectively (two or more) call on such a Being, It empowers your intention and manifestation beyond an ability to fully comprehend, with each member of the collective receiving the direct benefit of this added dynamic.

Previously it was mentioned that some of our earlier gods were called into existence as a means of helping humanity with all the different aspects of daily life. It does not matter if you call upon a conjured being, an elemental being or a cosmic being to empower your intention, collapse the time boundaries around your command and give space to the ensuing manifestation. If we "make up" a being[3] and then collectively empower that being through devotion, it becomes a part of our collective memory, and as such, it takes on a life of its own. If this Being is called into form by a group of humans, it has multiple attributes that were assigned to it upon its inception. Those attributes, through the group collective memory, will come into play to empower the intention of the manifest helper. This is important: You are custodial to all called forms and if you manifest as a group, you are equally responsible for the actions of your collective creation. Remember, you are only responsible for someone else's "sins" if you willfully cooperate in their commission of the "sin." A "sin" is any act that feels unnatural or goes directly against your core values and knowing and is committed anyway. Keeping the company of like-minded persons is very important to your recovery from conflict. Meanwhile, getting back to the lesser gods, it is important to know the assigned attributes of each of the lesser gods that you might use in commanding your thoughts into form. If you do not know their attributes, do not use their names in your invocation, calling or command of thought energy to form. These beings are very real and very powerful.

To give a better idea of what is meant by very real and powerful, most of the images and ideas of Jesus the Nazarene (4 BCE – CE 29) that come down to us through time are without full basis in truth and as such are false witness to Jesus as a teacher and Master Avatar. This is the same for Moshéh or Moses (13th century BCE), prophet of God JEHOVAH, for whom there is no real historical basis, but without whose presence there is no Hebrew religion or law. Except for Theravada Buddhism in Sri Lanka, the teachings of Siddhartha Buddha (566 BCE), princely prophet of god MAITREYA,[4] have been reordered into thousands of sects worldwide. As for the followers of Mohammed (CE 570) the sources of Mohammed's biography are too numerous to be wholly trusted, with the work itself crowded with fictitious details, legends, and stories. Like all spiritual leaders, none of his biographies were compiled during his lifetime, the earliest written one hundred fifty years after his death. The Koran is perhaps the only reliable source for the most important events in his career as self-proclaimed prophet of God ALLAH.

In this regard, over time and devotion, Hebrews, Buddhists, Christians and Muslims have created their spiritual Hosts to fit their need for someone who would never let them down in a world filled with deceit and betrayal. Moreover, all who join the thousands of millions devoted to their individual god creations take on the conflict associated with the continual updating of each religion's masters. It is the distortion of the simple teachings of the mentioned teachers that will undo the followers of each religion. The Catholic Church is already seeing this with its present day sexual abuse crisis. The Nazarene stated, *"Heaven and earth shall pass away, but my words shall not pass away."* (Matthew 24:35) The simple, unadulterated teachings spoken by Jesus, like those of Moses, Buddha and Mohammed, will reverberate throughout time and space. Those simple and pure vibrations cannot be altered. Their softly spoken, simple words outweigh the misconstrued volumes attributed to their teachings. The compounded conflict upon the followers and leaders associated with corporate religions will one day implode, destroying those who continue to create conflict by espousing exclusive rights to a cult-created, "only," Lawgiver, Divine Prince, Messiah or Last Prophet of God Almighty.

Each time a Triad calls upon an enlightened Being, ascended Entity, ascended Triad Master, Celestial or Solar Deity, it is bound in a custodial relationship to respond. Our only obligation in this relationship is to attribute to them the aspects of our manifest form that are outside our known abilities. It is not necessary to directly attribute works to the lesser gods, those called into being by early humankind, such as the gods of early mythology. Instead, we openly attribute to the Earth Spirit and Logos. Knowing our relationship to the forces that work in cooperation with us to shape our thoughts into form is very important. Giving attribution, such as Jesus the Nazarene did when he stated, "It is not I, but my Father in heaven that does the work through me, as me." (from the Akashic Records), is posturing gratitude, not humility. Humility is of little importance in this work. Souls are intrinsically correct. As a knowing being, our consciousness should be forever focused on gratitude. Humility is not asked of us, nor is devotion. As a knowing being, we only use gratitude to express our relationship with the Divine. Humility breeds arrogance, just as Deity devotion breeds spiritual contempt. Gratitude and attribution are the only outward expressions of our relationship with the forces that shape life on Earth. Gratitude, above all other measures, is of the utmost importance in all spiritual work.

~ *Collective Manifestation* ~

In all group work, there must be a formalized consensus regarding the specific form to be called. The collective calling will fail if there is one individual in the group who does not share the vision or intention. The group should be without a "leader," and any member may initiate a gathering for the purpose of manifestation. Because your physical body amplifies both the reception and transmission of thought energy according to your biological rhythms, for three days before the group calling, each member of the calling will arise, eat and go to bed at exactly the same time. This is done to establish as nearly identical biological rhythms as is possible. In earlier times, group members would all live within the same compound and be on the exact same schedule. Maharishi Mahesh Yogi's advanced Siddhi meditation group demonstrated this rhythmic joining when they sat at the base of the Berlin wall for several years praying for an end to the Cold War. When prayer is offered up in this manner its effect is more immediate and lasting. In the example of the Berlin Wall, a great deal of Cold War energy had to be transmuted. In group manifestation, each member should enter the three days of preparation with complete knowledge of the purposeful need that is to be called from the ethers. This dispels any hesitation in the voice, and brings a full glamour to the gathering. All group work is done for a purposeful need outside the group's needs. If the calling is for a member of the group, it would be best if that member is absent from the gathering. This ensures no investment in the timing and finished form. In addition, if the calling were for a member, that member would unconsciously take on the mantle of "leader" for that particular calling by virtue of need. Group calling is not led, but is inspired by a greater purposeful need, one greater than the group itself.

As a group, you will find ways to ritualize your collective approach to calling. This could be done in a ceremony or celebration-type presentation through which all members are equal in contribution. Those who gathered to call long ago did so on the different phases of the moon because they had no calendars. It was agreed that the day following a certain phase would be a day of ceremony and group calling. They never called during darkness, as is described in Wicca texts. Those following The Knowing Way believed that each thought and the true intention behind each thought were amplified through the sun's radiance. During the Dark Ages in Europe, The Knowing Way was corrupted into witchcraft and sorcery, with some Knowing Way initiates using thought manifestation as a means of subjugating less knowing individuals. The Catholic Church had Knowing Way practitioners in its ranks who dominated the poor with their unseen influences, but it was the force of dark sorcery that subjugated the wealthy. The wealthy are easily seduced by the promise of multiplying their riches. It is true that Knowing Way followers "sourced" for others' greater outcome and revelation, and they did this freely without expectation or payment of any kind. One individual who mastered the use of the Akashic Records through The Knowing Way teachings was Leonardo da Vinci. He could easily look beyond his own time into future moments to gaze upon the achievements of human kind as the records incrementally unfolded a greater knowing of this world.

Practice:

Believe it or else: every word you speak is a sacred vow. It is very positive to say, "Be kind and generous with your thoughts and words." We live in a negatively motivated world. The following guidelines should be reviewed from time to time: Do not take any god's or goddess' name into battle, i.e., do not use any god or Avatar to seek reprisal or to carry out a vengeance against any person, place or thing. Do not curse in the name of a Deity or God. That any world leader would proclaim a war under the name of God Almighty, puts forces into motion that will one day wreak havoc upon those who are drawn to fight such a god-directed war. Pity the leader who is then responsible for those innocent lives taken under such a declaration.

The following account is taken from the Akashic Records as an example of how such vows and declarations to a higher Being can take epochs to work out. A very long time ago, a gathering of people who had been enslaved for countless generations, sought the help of a Deity in the hope that they would be released and allowed to return to their familial lands where they would be free to follow the tenets of their ancestors. The more able and learned of the captives were used in the temples and palaces as healers and scribes, assisting the elders of the household with illnesses and the priests in their daily rituals of prayer and sacrifice. They were excellent understudies and over time came to fully understand the metaphysical practices of those forces enslaving them. The prolonged duration and profound consistency of their daily prayers and ritualized lamentations finally attracted the attention of a composite Soul, or Celestial Being. As previously stated, Composite Souls are vast Beings with unlimited ability to influence all consciousness and energy. This type of intervention is extremely rare, with the Akashic Records indicating such occurrences only a few times throughout the entire history of human consciousness on Earth.

A sacred agreement was formed between the elders of the slaves, the Soul of a future deliverer and the Deity, that if It delivered them from bondage, they would forever empower the Deity through new customs of ritual remembrances and sacrifice. Deities exist beyond human ideas of good or bad, right or wrong and simply respond to those Souls who command the bands of thought energy attracting them. This particular Deity, through a series of lucid dreams, inspired the plan for deliverance that could be readily understood by those praying for Divine involvement. A child was chosen from a virtuous family, a family known for its profound compassion and devotion, to be placed at birth in the ruling family's household as a tribute to the King. This had become a custom amongst the slave population in the hope that the contributions of their adopted child would put them in favor with certain households. This child of deliverance was secretly tutored in ancient traditions and newly accepted metaphysical rituals of the slaves. Then, at a precisely determined time in the future, the grown child would denounce the ruling family in favor of his genetic roots and demand that he be rejoined with his rightful kin.

The slaves rejoiced at such a demonstration of loyalty and began to celebrate the grown child as their deliverer. This angered the King's household causing a curse[5] to be placed upon the child's household. To save his family, the chosen child took everyone and all of their possessions, escaping into neighboring lands to await the instructions of the Deity. It took several decades of intense devotional practice to completely balance the grown child's inner conflicts as a preparation for his eventual return to his former home and further use as a Divine vessel. The final act of the covenant was for the Chosen One to allow the Deity to fully overshadow his personality/ego, not only as a means of protecting the deliverer, but also as a means of empowering the Chosen One with the abilities of a Composite Soul. In this state, the Chosen One could match and surpass the combined abilities of the priests of Amun[6]. A gathering of twelve Amun priests, as counterbalance to the twelve Souls of the Composite Being, was assembled to meet the Chosen One, and the battle for the collective mind of the slaves began. Each calling and act of magic or manifestation was countered by the opposing side. Because of the Chosen One's lack of complete trust, or better said, full knowing, he was not able to go beyond the skills of his opponents. The war of abilities and wills went on for almost seven years. This trading back and forth of curses was dividing the peoples of the land into two separate gatherings: those wanting the separation into freedom and those wanting the familiar former system of enslavement. Most all of the slaves had known nothing other than this way of life, so the idea of moving into unknown areas caused them to side with the ruling classes. Also, many locals had fallen in love with and married slaves, had families together and wanted to join with them in their new freedom. This meant that they would have to leave their genetic gatherings, a very unusual decision for that time. In some parts of the realm it was impossible to know who was going or who was staying.

The callings and high magic elevated to such a point that each side was near exhaustion with the Chosen One showing signs of faltering. In desperation, the elders of the slaves decided to counter with an act that had effectively been used against several generations before: the King of that previous period, fearing an uprising, had ordered the killing of all the firstborn sons of all the indentured families as a way of instilling unquestionable rule over the hundreds of thousands of slaves inhabiting his realm. It had worked then; it would work again, the problem was that the slaves did not have the administrative abilities to carry the plan to completion.

During a collective celebration of devotional gratitude, the slaves enjoined the Composite Soul as it overshadowed the Chosen One, during the period of prayer and ritual calling, to carry out this deed as their sole force of deliverance. The Deity was compelled through its relationship to the Chosen One to oblige the calling, without regard for the outcome. The only thing standing in the way was the combined force of the priest of Amun that called (manifested) for the King. Thinking he would spare future generations from the karmic imbalance of this unnecessarily forceful deed, the Chosen One took it upon himself to systematically eliminate each of the priests. In this way, their rather potent blood was only on his hands. It was through their purity and clarity of knowing that together the priests could match the power of the Chosen One. One-on-one, he could easily take any of the priest's lives. Under the glamour of disguise, the Chosen One entered their chambers. The Soul of the first priest to die joined with the next priest's consciousness. They did this in an effort to allow the natural course of events to unfold through the collective will of all the people, by countering each of the Chosen One's callings. Each of their deaths was more horrific than the previous one. After killing the King's twelve priests of Amun, the Chosen One called upon the agencies of the Deity to quicken and move the etheric bodies of the firstborn of the King's generation of offspring in such a way as to cause their etheric and physical bodies to become separate, eventually resulting in their deaths. This type of death is more like a prolonged suffocation than a sudden attack. Great prosperity had been the mark of this King's rule, so these firstborn deaths were in the hundreds of thousands.

After a great and terrible mourning of the people, the King allowed an exodus of the slaves to begin that would span his life and the lifetimes of twelve future kings. Because of the deaths of the twelve innocent priests of Amun and those who were innocent among the dying firstborn, the Chosen One made a vow with the Deity that if future generations of his people could be spared from the conflict (karma) he and the elders had brought through the death callings, he would never entreat the collective will of the Deity again. Each time the Deity had overshadowed the Chosen One, the Chosen One's abilities and powers were broadly expanded even to the extent that he could part the seas with a gesture of his hand. After a long period of traveling, the people began to doubt the Chosen One's or Deity's ability to manifest the land of milk and honey envisioned by the elders of the people. The Chosen One broke his sacred vow when he called upon the Composite Soul to bring order to his people as they wandered in the desert toward the Promised Land. The Deity overshadowed the Chosen One a final time, presented unchangeable laws for the people to use as they unified their collective mind, and left his charge with the powers to perform all manner of feats and miracles necessary to guide the Chosen One's people to sanctuary. His second vow was to never enter the Promised Land. This he was able to keep. Unfortunately, by breaking the first vow, he released every curse uttered by every survivor of his and the elders of the slave's death callings.

The Chosen People of the Deity finally came to rest in their new homeland, but only after causing and experiencing great strife along their path. Later, as the story was altered, this land was called Canaan, as was promised by God to Abraham and his race.

Around the middle 1800s, the Composite Soul who had delivered the pleading Israelite slaves from the harsh hands of foreign kings once again answered the call of a metaphysically knowing gathering of Souls. Initiates of the ancient underworld orders of the Lord of the Khemenu and of the Re-Horakhty led this occult group as they gathered across Europe. This group spread the idea that the hard working people of Europe were being overrun and surreptitiously subjugated by another group, who thought themselves a Chosen People. It was felt that this Chosen People, living as an isolated gathering within each society, took for themselves first, and left little for anyone of differing customs and beliefs. It was eventually believed that they were drawing the very life out of the land itself. The Souls in Europe calling for Divine intervention were the very same Souls who had lost so much when the Chosen One called on the combined will of the Deity to deliver his people from captivity. Because of Its prior involvement, the Composite Deity, who had delivered the slaves from captivity into the Promised Land, was now compelled to honor the curses brought on the former slaves by the grieving survivors of the death calling made by the Chosen One and the elders of the Israelites. Had the Chosen One not broken his sacred vow by commanding the Deity to further aid his people by placing an unbreakable law into their hearts with himself as the Lawgiver, he, and only he, would have suffered the karma created by the conflict generated in the hearts of the Egyptian people. The curses raced forward in time and found the hearts of the people who had voiced them living in the circumstances necessary for retribution. In order to break the cycle of cause and effect, the Deity, instead of overshadowing other humans as it did with the Chosen One, took individual human forms to carry out the completion of this event. Each of the twelve Souls of the Composite Soul Deity manifested a separate body through impregnating a human. The inner core of Hitler's gathering was comprised of these humans. The profound dreadfulness and boundless horror of the Holocaust is the fruition of the ancient curses that were placed in the etheric body of the planet when the Chosen One, at the beseeching of his elders, continued to command the power of the Deity as a means of ensuring freedom for his people, even if it meant killing the innocent of a whole generation.

It is impossible to understand the full ramifications of the above story as it applies to humanity. What is important is knowing how our consistent and sincere pleas are oftentimes intercepted by beings capable of moving the very fabric of time and space. Being crystal clear in our intention, compassionately inspired in our actions and unlimited in our gratitude attunes us to the bands of thought energy significant to the highest forms of collaborators.

Most of us, through the course of our day use a form of cursing. Phrases such as, "Damn it all," or "Jesus Christ," when spoken in frustration are in fact curses. This is the intention of these phrases. Because these emotionally charged phrases have become a part of everyday language, we seldom are aware when making such statements. One such statement that can be the most damning is, "God damn it." The reason for this is that whatever is said after that statement becomes the subject of the curse. Even if nothing is said for a period of time, the focus of the curse is the subject of the next statement you make. For example, you have a less than perfect moment and in response emotionally state, "God damn it to hell!" and then a few minutes later state, "I wish my wife (or husband) would just listen to what I'm asking for in our relationship." In essence, you have just cursed the relationship and your wife (or husband). Each time you feel frustration with your spouse, this curse will come into play, especially if it is repeated. This seems extreme, and it is important to understand how your utterances influence everything. Everything. Make a list of all your favorite swear words and curses. Remember as far back as you can to the first time you heard use of such language, and who it was that was cursing. Be aware of any emotions that surface as you begin to change speech patterns. Once you have decided this belief is true, never again, under any circumstances, use curses. That is, unless you are fully prepared to live out the curse yourself. What we ask for others becomes our manifest destiny.

Invocation:

Follow the usage guidelines set up with the first invocation in chapter seven. Allow the cantor to find it own pace as you repeat the invocations. Different tones and patters produce varying results.

"I AM open and willing to allow my Soul consciousness to express in me, through me, as me, in my relationships. I AM open and willing to allow my Soul consciousness to express in me, through me, as me, in my relationships. I AM open and willing to allow my Soul consciousness to express in me, through me, as me, in my relationships."

"I AM complete and whole in every aspect of being. Physical matter and etheric substance radiate a complete vision of ALL THAT IS. I AM illumined and Divinely inspired to correctness and selflessness. All this I AM."

"I AM the personification of dignity and grace inspired compassion. Everyone I encounter experiences the presence of the Divine Holy Spirit expressing as the great works radiating through me into the world."

Thought:

The complexities of the past are released through the simplicity of gratitude.

Lifestyle Suggestions:

Meditation: The following is a continuation of the last chapter's meditation with a slight variation. Again, if you do not already have one, it will be important to purchase a pitch pipe. Very few people have the ability to hit a musical note on command. A pitch pipe will ensure the quality of your tones and allow you to feel the correct vibration in your chest, throat and face.

Each of the seven core chakras (energy centers) resounds with tone and color. It is easy to use your voice to activate the energy centers with the intention of bringing balance to your body, mind and Spirit. It is also easy to clear conflicted emotional energy by using certain thoughts while mentally focusing on the chakras.

Sit with your spine lifted by mentally putting a slight space between each vertebra. Take a moment to focus on your breath, watching the point between breaths. Begin this chant in a slow rhythm. The pace might want to change on its own after a few minutes. Let it.

The first sound, "LAH," is whispered in the key of "C" and is spoken with full attention on the base chakra. Feel it as heat at the base of the spine. See it as a deep red hue spreading around your hips. Remember the last incident in your life that seemed to generate a deep anger in your body. Bring the memory of that moment into the base chakra and watch as it dissolves into the hot red energy at the base of the abdominal wall and genitals. Feel the anger dissolve as the sound of your voice says in the key of "C:" "In gratitude I release anger. I Am demonstrating patience and tolerance." As the energy moves upward let it become a reddish orange.

The second sound, "BAH," is normally voiced with your attention moving upward into the spleen center just below and slightly left of your navel. Feel it as warmth and see it as a bright orange field of color, from the top of your pubis to your middle waist. Remember a moment in your life when you had more than your share of something: more meat at the dinner table, an extra piece of pie at desert, more beer than your guests. Remember all the secret feelings of having more than others, especially if you had to seduce someone to get more than others. Bring that memory into the second chakra and allow it to dissolve into the bright orange energy. Feel any shame fade as your voice says in the key of "D:" "Through grace I release gluttony and embrace abstinence of guilt and shame."

The third sound, "RAH," is growled in a low-pitched key of "E" emanating from the solar plexus. Say this sound from deep inside your body. See it as a bright yellow ball of light centered on your body and feel it as the radiant warmth of the sun on a bright, cool winter's day. Remember the last time you were obsessed by something you really wanted. This could be anything in the verb or noun categories. Bring as many details into your conscious mind as you can. Notice if you overly used your developed abilities to obtain that special something. Bring that memory into your solar plexus and allow it to dissolve into the bright yellow energy covering your mid-torso. Feel any tired feelings fade as your voice says in a low-pitched key of "E:" "In pure joy I release greed through charity." Allow that bright yellow energy to move upward into your heart.

The heart chakra is a happy sound of "YAM," (Yah-Aum) and spoken joyfully in the key of "F." Command this sound in a sincerely happy and firm tone. Imagine it as a deep green field of waving grass and feel it as a nuzzling sensation that chases away feelings of isolation and abandonment. Remember the last time you felt envy. Allow the envy to fill your chest. Recall as much about that particular memory as possible. Feel the envy enveloping your heart and overwhelming your mind. Feel secret feelings of being hurt at the success of others as you fully engage the envy of that moment. Feel a wave of wanton envy leave your body as you hear your voice say in the key of "F:" "Through knowing kindness I share success with others." Move the energy up into your throat.

In the key of "G," shout "HAH" as the life force moves through your heart up into your throat. Imagine waves of light blue energy swooshing over your body in a fresh wave of mint. Remember a moment out of your life when you told a lie to cover your laziness or blamed your apathy on someone else. Imagine how that lie affected that individual. Remember a time when you were falsely blamed for being lazy. Feel all of your secret feelings, then let them float away as your voice says in the key of "G:" "Through a greater knowing, I a diligent in all matters of my life." Move the energy upward into your third eye chakra.

In the key of "A," sigh the sound of discovery, "AHHA," as the energy continues upward toward your crown chakra and comes to rest in the third eye. It is midnight blue and feels indifferent to all sensations. Remember times when you allowed your focus to be distracted into mindless chatter. Bring those feelings of diversion into your brow chakra and watch them turn into clear images of concentration. Awaken all your knowing ability as your voice says in the key of "A:" "I am willing to fully utilize my mind's ability to concentrate on the most minute details while allowing the memories from other places and times in photographic detail." Move the energy upward into the crown chakra.

Alternating the keys of high "D" and "B," make the announcement, "AUM." Feel your whole body vibrate with a mighty (Au-Um) as a brilliant purple light surrounds your head. The feeling is complete contentment and the liberation of concern. Remember any moment when you were denied or rejected. Bring those feelings upward toward your crown chakra and allow them to dissolve immediately into the brilliant violet flame now surrounding your head. Listen to your voice say, "In all things I am grateful and joyful." Say this first in the key of "D," and then in the key of "B."

Repeat this once with the intention that, by dissolving past memory in each category, you have released untold numbers of similar incidences. The intention of this exercise is to immediately balance your energy centers, mind and Spirit.

Diet: Continue to eat in gratitude and joy. Infuse everything you touch with gratitude and joy as you prepare your meals. Drink water with the sure understanding that this fluid is life. Without the gift of water, you would quickly be miserable. Think thoughts of enlightened people, such as your teachers, or any avatars, such as Moses, Buddha, Jesus or Mohammad while you cook or clean. Whispering their names draws their energy close to us. They, through their individual demonstrations of life, are blessings to us.

Fasting: Take a break from fasting.

Exercise: Give every activity equal value, in that, be aware of all the muscles being used to complete an action.

During each day, take a moment to focus on your breath, allowing each breath to be fully felt in your body as in a complete yogic breath. Breathing in a deliberate, conscious fashion opens the heart chakra.

~ *Chapter IX Footnotes* ~

1 The Composite Souls that helped form our planet generated these beginning bands of thought energy. Later the Logos harmonically differentiated the interlacing bands of thought energy, and the Holy Spirit took form as the agency through which life took progressive meaning.

2 Those who forsake the flesh take themselves off the incarnational wheel of repeating birth and death.

3 In the Old Religion, the Wicca Way of Nature, such beings were called familiars or minions and were created by groups to carry out activities over distances, especially in areas where foot traffic was impractical or if the members of the gathering were aging and unable to physically carry out certain intentions.

4 Maitreya has been expected for generations by all of the major religions. Christians know him as the Christ, and expect his imminent return. Jews await him as the Messiah; Hindus look for him as the coming of Krishna; Buddhists expect him as Maitreya Buddha; and Muslims anticipate him as the Imam Mahdi or Messiah.

5 In the early Egyptian culture a curse was much like a current day Muslim fatwa, or call for death of the offending person or group. In this case it was the entire bloodline of the chosen child, which included several tribes.

6 Amun (Amen, Amon) a relatively modern god within the context of ancient Egyptian religion. His worship at Thebes is only documented from the 11th Dynasty.

"To handle yourself,
use your head;
to handle others,
use your
heart."

—. *Donald Laird*

Chapter X

~ *The Expansive Power of Joy as a Creative Force* ~

A balanced human lacks the notion that he or she is entitled to or deserves something because of an acquired ability, a natural talent, or a ranking in society attained through family or acquired through strategic actions. Good works or developed Spiritual abilities will not guarantee any special dispensation in the reality between incarnations, nor will they warrant an initiation into a higher order of knowing. Joy is the single purpose for all human enfleshment. Our life's work, be it a profession, calling, or mission, can be preordained or agreed upon before our birth, and our true purpose is to explore the boundaries of ecstasy, nirvana, rapture, bliss and pure joyful delight. The ability to allow joy to flow through you and out into the world as a creative manifest expression does open greater possibilities as you depart this realm after each life. Why then all the sorrow and misunderstanding? Simply, we have forgotten who we are and why we are here – nothing more, nothing less. Through religions, we have humbly accepted the concept of striving as the basic dynamic of the collective human experience. We accept the notion that life is our teacher, and that, to really make it, we must be good students and please the great teacher in heaven. In this dogmatically-driven system of beliefs, we allow ourselves to experience a very limited creation comprised of belief validation and the fulfillment of previous assumptions, some of which are hundreds of lifetimes old.

We all experience the expansive power of joy to the level at which we are currently awakened to the greater knowing of life. If our core beliefs and values, the definers of our inquiry and observation, are in alignment with the dynamics of that greater knowing, then we will emanate joy into the World in unlimited streams of life force energy. As such, we become a source for all people, not just those who are themselves embracing expansive joy as the foundation of their existence. We can be this source of boundless joy even if we are being nailed to a cross as a punishment for asking others to question the authority of those individuals who administer cruelly manipulated societal norms. Sorrow and joy are the two extremes of the same energy. Sorrow is born of a lack of knowing, while joy happens through us as we are liberated into knowing. In essence, this is the dynamic of humans as students – knowing as the path to joy. We are taught that to know we must learn. Remember how you felt as a young person when you connected the dots and suddenly understood the subtle inner workings of a subject – say, math. You struggled with the concept, then suddenly two plus two equaled four. You had two apples, you were given two more and you now had four. Those early discoveries were ripe with amazingly deep inner feelings of joy. Remember how happy everyone around you was at your discovery. You might even have been rewarded for your efforts with something sweet or with a little extra time to do a favorite activity. Pleasant, yes, but the joy related to this type of discovery is fleeting due to the socially validating aspects of the breakthrough.

If understanding of the scientific mechanisms that drive our dimensional World brought lasting joy, we would only have to study the many available scientific disciplines to be forever happy. If technological advancements ensured stability and balance, we would only need to ensure that everyone who wanted stability and balance had all the latest gadgets. If thoughtful prayer and profound meditation were all that was needed to brighten the lives of humanity, then all the past millenniums of spiritual devotion of thoughtful people would have the Earth's radiance rivaling that of the sun. Fully understanding who we are, why we are here and how we were derived is just the beginning of knowing. Allowing full knowing to permeate our molecules and thoughts relies on our ability to be grateful, to be gracious, to live life exclusively from the perpetual state of selfless-Self, the liberated Self. As the adage goes, "When in momentary doubt as to how to proceed, act as God would act – generously."

Without living demonstrations of joy, it almost impossible to truly know what it means to be without exception a selfless-Self, or realized, illumined human. The following elaboration of the exact moment when Giovanni Bernardone, son of Pietro and of his mother, Pica, awakened to the intimacy of knowing illustrates the moment of liberation we all must one day face. The god-intimate, selfless Giovanni has come to be known as Saint Francis of Assisi. In his youth he was anything but concerned with graciousness and joy, choosing instead to be seduced by every possible distraction life has to offer, and giving himself over to every indulgence. He was rather hedonistic, at least until the greater knowing began to reshape the template of his consciousness. Once the greater knowing had hinted at the possibility of its existence through a series of calamities, Giovanni threw himself at God with the same fervor as he had at his previous pursuit of worldly pleasures. The culture of Italy at the time dictated his approach to his moment of illumination – Christianity. Had he been born into a Buddhist household elsewhere in the world, he would have reached nirvana and stepped off the wheel of birth and death. A lot has been written about this lover of humanity and the natural order of Earth's many manifestations of life. The following story is a short glimpse into the moment of illumination that overtook his persona. He was the only one present in the rundown room of the abbey he had helped rebuild when this occurred, so nothing is written anywhere to lend historical fact to this account. The story is interpreted out of the Akashic Records:

As the morning sun topped the eastern mountains, the small ancient room filled to overflowing with shafts of fresh golden light. An animal-colored loosely woven rug, small wooden table and clay washbasin crowded against the austerity of the stonewalls and solitary kneeling figure. The plainly robed young man began his prayer aloud, saying in a barely audible morning voice, "Father, I have so longed to know your presence."

The raspy undertones of his whispered voice filled the cold shadows missed by the morning sun as his lament continued, "Help me see clearly what is needed in each moment to bring understanding to my journey here. In all earthly matters, make me an instrument of thy peace." The weight of his meager body shifted as he settled into prayerful repose. The sound of one lone bird played through the rowed olive trees slightly moving to a breeze in the garden beyond the wall. The morning arrived as it always had: calling his Soul on a single note's refrain.

Then, for an instant, everything, every molecule within and around, was deadly still exactly as it had been with each and every past pleading to his God. Yet something felt different, felt expansive. Unannounced, it came, shaking him, raising him from callused knees, pressing him back up against the lifeless wooden door that had led him to the moment's chamber. The voice came from on high, filling the chamber from the very center of his being. "Where there is hatred," it commanded with profound assurance, "sow love! Where there is injury, give pardon! Where there is doubt, restore faith! Where there is despair, impart hope! Where there is darkness, command light! Where there is sadness, radiate joy!"

He ran to the middle of the room, his arms outstretched in front, feeling the air as if he were suddenly struck blind. He shouted, thinking the voice might not hear him, "Divine Creation, grant that I may not so much seek to be consoled, as to console, to be understood as to understand, to be loved as to love."

Tears fell onto the forgotten garment as the warmth of understanding filled his expanding heart; his knees once again touched their familiar resting place as he lifted his Soul to embrace the coming response. Great feelings of renewal washed over his body causing the skin to quicken at the gathering rebirth.

The voice soothed this twice-born by announcing, "For it is in giving that you receive; it is in pardoning that you are pardoned and it is in knowing that you are born into eternal life."

The harmonics of the words danced along streams of consciousness as the twice-touched flesh radiated joy into the room. The silence that had been so constant following past pleadings gave way to the angelic sounds of the spheres and angels. He could not know his name for he was no longer, instead, in his place appeared the fresh face of Creation's generous compassion. Grace punctuated each move as he slowly raised his ascended form from its bent postulations. With upstretched arms he welcomed the radiance of all the Souls who had come to know this illumination; he received them as mighty companions.

His liberation had come in the least likely of moments, in the least likely of places. He was free to go; he was free to radiate joy. Austerity vanished as the magnificence of Earth's many forms vied for his brand new senses. His abundance immediately assured through the awakening of his Soul's conscious awareness, he made a place for joy's selfless god within the vastness of his twice-born state.

The stark austerity of his private room must have brought a vast beauty to his moment of self-realization. His etheric body and aura were ablaze with majesty as his Soul was allowed to radiate into the world. A king's coronation hall would have been more in keeping with the moment as a splendid Earthly balance to the otherworldly splendor being enacted in the moment. Anything and everything was his to command: ask at it would be his, and he chose to follow the expectations of those with whom he lived. He must have felt that this approach would allow the greater knowing to reach more hearts. As one who lived humbly, he taught of the abundance of life, not because the moment of his illumination demanded it, but because a humble life was what most people of his area fully understood. St. Francis demonstrated an abundance of God's Spirit and taught others to find peace within the assurance of God's great care, as opposed to attempting to find comfort through materialism. He knew that most of the people of his village would never be able to break free of the crippling superstitions and dogmatic beliefs that plagued their lives and kept them poor. It would have caused more conflict to reveal what he knew about life than to demonstrate pure joy. The people did not need another spiritual expert among them; they had the Catholic Church and its emissaries of God's only begotten son. They needed a demonstration of how to be joyful with what they had, as opposed to being sorrowful for what they did not have. The mission he chose, his purposeful need, was to bring joy to those who had very little except the possibility of joy. They had no real knowledge of life beyond their daily strivings; they would have no real opportunities to know more. He demonstrated the expansive nature of joy at their level of experience through miracles and wonderful conspiracies of coincidence. This afforded them joy. Through his selfless-Self, they were abundant. He helped them see where they were right in life. We humans allow joy when we think ourselves right. Joy is a self-reward.

~ *Joy – Exact Thought and Action* ~

It is impossible to impart the enormous importance of exact thought and action. When we connect exact thought and action in the moment, we obtain the abundance of our purposeful need. The greater the purposeful need, the greater the abundance. Through his family, St Francis had access to wealth and power. By the standards of the day, he was affluent. The Catholic Church's version of his life tells of a pauper who gave everything he had to the poor and downtrodden.

In our quest for knowing the greater truth within all things, we often forsake the social and monetary advantages given to us through birth and/or acquired abilities in favor of the liberation from material things. In the tradition of St. Francis, the crisis of renunciation and celibacy becomes the impetus to move inward toward greater knowing. We put the burden of insecurity and ambiguity into our lives to unconsciously and/or consciously "grow" from the experience. As children, we felt joy as we "grew" from each day's experiences to the extent that we began to equate learning with being happy. As adults, most of us look back on our high school or college days as periods of excitement and joy. Very few can say the same about their jobs or professional careers. The adversity felt with a life that was supposed to be better or somehow different closes an individual down. The inner conflict of wanting something that is believed to be outside the realm of possibilities is devastating to the adult ego and personality. Even a child in unfavorable circumstances gets joy from the discovery of how to avoid an abusive parent, how to overcome the empty feelings of poverty or neglect or the preoccupied indifference of the adults supervising his or her welfare. When the adult intellect believes it has experienced everything or decides, "What's the use of trying? Nothing ever changes," the individual has joined those who will create a sudden crisis to awaken. Usually this happens at midlife when the ego/personality decides it is now or never.

The primary difference between St. Francis and most who seek the greater knowing is in the approach. Giovanni had lived out all of his fantasies before he faced the crisis that opened his being to fully knowing creation. Being extremely popular with his peers, he not only felt the doting love of his family but also the inclusion of his community. This desirability gave him the opportunity to playfully explore his sexuality with both genders. The result for him was an early liberation from the tug of unquenched sexual desire and erotic distractions. In the time of Giovanni, the rivalries between towns were usually settled by battle. Because of this, he was able to experience himself as a warrior, a defender of his people at a very early age. He knew himself to be a hero. He traveled and explored regionally and felt the built-in freedoms of his native culture. He lived life on the edge: for the first twenty years in material intemperance and the last twenty-five in material dispossession. He attacked life from the moment he was a small child until he died an old man at the age of forty-five. Luckily for him, in the Umbrian countryside, there was only one version of god. The early pagan religions had all been incorporated into Christianity by the mid-first millennium, leaving one distilled approach to eternal life beyond the mundane happenings on Earth. There was no inner conflict over which religion to follow. There was only one path to liberation and Divine communion – accepting Jesus as Lord and Savior.

The approach today is to explore all the many varieties and flavors of god that have been created by humanity to explain the unexplainable. Most of the world lives in dire circumstances with very few having the luxury of fulfilling all their dreams within the span of one incarnation. The sorrow of not having what you dream as possible has become prevalent with the advent of global communication through various media. This inner conflict of knowing what is possible and not being able to fulfill those visions generates intolerance and isolation. The vulnerability and accompanying imagined threat brings acts of violence to numerous to imagine. Most individuals who hear the call to a greater knowing immediately want to forsake the greedy world with its inhumanity toward humanity and perverse priorities for all forms of life. This type of self-generated crisis is usually regretted later in life because it negates the foundation upon which that person's life was based. This type of starting over has little spiritual value and is more destructive to spiritual illumination than constructive. Natural calamities, such as the ones St. Francis faced, alter a life in such a manner as to build from the foundational experiences of the formative years. Instead of being disenchanted with life, St. Francis became awakened to the greater possibilities that include all of life's levels of expression. He chose to live in a manner that would affect the greatest number of people, that being a lifestyle of bare subsistence. He helped others with whatever means were necessary to help alleviate their afflicting circumstances, giving both wisely and prudently to all without prejudice. St. Francis was not against wealth and affluence. All knowing Beings understand the dynamic of power contained within the energy of wealth. They also understand the forces of manipulation most people believe to be power.

While it is entirely correct to help others find a greater sense of their journey toward the moment of rebirth through the mindful sharing of resources, it is also important to be prudent in matters of personal wherewithal. St. Francis, like Jesus and Buddha before him, seemed to have forsaken his earthly station in favor of dwelling among the indigent people who littered the Umbrian countryside. He had grown up with all of the indulgences of the day from parents who found joy in lavishing a very high lifestyle upon their son. He loved the good life. Through a series of events and health crisis epiphanies, St. Francis took up a spiritual mantel of selfless service. St. Francis' father was a wealthy merchant; Buddha's father was a king and Jesus' father was a successful builder and sole heir to the house of David. All three were raised in families of importance and social position within their communities. Each renounced wealth and took up poverty as a way of completely identifying with the masses, those who toiled with the adverse conditions of the times. Religions, with their Soulful call to the downtrodden to prepare for a better life in the hereafter, were built upon the backs of the poor and unknowing conquered tribes and peoples through the ages.

Most spiritual adepts usually allow others to manage their affairs, choosing instead to use their time and energy in matters of self-discovery. As example: Judas Iscariot managed the day-to-day financial affairs of the entourage that moved from town to town with Jesus the Nazarene as he taught the goods news of the Way to those who would hear and see. It is repeatedly stated that Judas betrayed Jesus for money. Money did exchange hands, as was the tradition for sealing a contract, and Judas wanted more for his efforts than money. Like any good Zealot, Judas wanted Jesus to act against the Roman occupation as a warrior leader. Judas wanted Jesus to be the promised "deliverer" the Zealots had expected would come based on popular interpretations of earlier prophecies. Judas thought that turning the Nazarene over to the local authorities for blasphemy would bring the necessary results. It did not. Jesus could have driven the Romans and their local Hebrew minions out of Judea with the utterance of one word – Go! His pure intention for their removal from power would have found the right ears, and they would have been compelled to leave at once. He did not utter one word. To do so under such dire circumstances would have obligated people to greater inner conflict than quiet liberation. He had to hold the power of his spoken word for the greatest moment – his ascension into that dimension of pure knowing joy that warmly wraps itself around the earthly realm. Money was never the motivation for the betrayal of Jesus as is reported by the Church in its marketing of Christianity. Simply, the Church needed money. By associating money with the betrayer, Judas, they could ask the unknowing to give whatever money they wanted purified to the Church, and in doing so, they would not only forever cleanse the betraying money but also their Souls. Portions of the purified money were then filtered into the monasteries and then into the surrounding communities through social services and community projects. Giving to the Church meant giving to all who needed help. The Church's renunciation of money as the source of all evil seems to run contrary to its hoarding of most tithing gifts. This was the basis for Martin Luther's movement to break away from the Church of Rome. While non-Catholic Christianity is somewhat less opulent and more altruistic, it still inflicts the inner conflict of guilt upon the faithful as a means of extracting money for the cost of celebrating the concept of God.

While the practice of personal renunciation is commonly reported as beneficial to meditation and prayer, it is also the base for the inner conflict of lack. Monetary wealth and abundance of possessions are only distractions if the individual overseeing such resources allows himself or herself to be preoccupied by the effects of wealth. Money is the most commonly accepted means of exchanging comparative energy between individuals and organizations. It only has the value given it by those wishing to exchange goods or services. This is important to reflect upon as you begin to manifest money to your purposeful need. Great wealth is as easy to manifest as any other level of wealth. It is simply a matter of releasing the inner conflict you carry about having great wealth and affluence. It was once stated, "Making a million dollars is comparatively easier than effectively giving a million dollars away." Money, as the root of all materialism, is without doubt blamed for most of the sorrows of the mechanized global community. Money is valued as power. It is believed that if you have enough money, you can accomplish anything. Usually, those individuals who have worked hard to gain wealth seldom ever do anything important or lasting with their resources. Their heirs usually are better at effectively disbursing the resources only because they are not invested in each and every dollar. This is important to understand: wealth for the sake of being wealthy is without conflict. Achieving wealth for the sake of wielding power is loaded with conflict. Where there is conflict, there is sorrow. Wealth and joy go hand in hand if the wealth is without conflict. Joy is simply the absence of conflict.

If an individual applies exact action and thought to all aspects of daily life, he or she can live without conflict even when going against social conventions. Because the world's human population places so much importance on wealth and its associative powers, those who manifest wealth effortlessly are always suspect as to their worthiness. Worth and wealth have little in common other than the fact that they are confused by the less knowing as being one and the same. Mother Theresa commanded millions through various sources. Personally, she was able to accomplish all she envisioned as her purposefulness. She was always direct and exact in her dealings with money. When she gave money to other organizations, she knew where every dollar was going to be spent. She gave value to money by being prudent with her means. There is no mystery to obtaining money: if you value money, you will manifest all the money you so command.

In the everyday mundane world it is said that when your thoughts and actions are one, you are operating from integrity. Material success comes quickly to those who are truly able to keep the vision of what they want by operating through exact action. Doing leads to more doing; effortlessness leads to effortlessness.

~ Joy – The Absence of Desire ~

Desire ceases to exist when thought and feeling are joined in the moment. Desire exists as a reflection of the inner conflict that arises when thought and feeling are separated. Most of us, male and female, are trained to keep our thoughts and feelings compartmentalized in an effort to hide our deep inner processes lest we be considered weak by our disclosure. In Far Eastern cultures, it is extremely important to maintain the proper countenance even in the direst of situations. To do less would bring disgrace upon family and close associates, and death upon self. Usually these patriarchal cultures are warrior based and place great value on hiding any weaknesses from their enemies. Unfortunately, over a few millenniums' generations of training, it becomes impossible to determine who is the real enemy, and everyone becomes suspect. Joy as the absence of desire happens when we join thoughts, with exactly corresponding feelings, as expressions of our most authentic selves. Most children are good at this, and those children, who are not naturally good at asking for what they want by joining thought with feeling, resort to throwing tantrums or otherwise acting out in an attempt to get what they want through extortion. In a world based on raw human force, extortion is effective for the most part.

Joy is experienced when thought and feeling are one. When the subconscious and conscious minds are one, thought is expressed through the will center (throat chakra) into the etheric body of the planet, on the excitation of the voice. The voice command is acted upon by the seen and unseen forces of this dimensional realm as an immediate call to formation of the energies contained within the realm of non-matter matter as a demonstration of creation within the moment. This union of thought and word becomes the nexus of the new forms called into existence. The more enthused the energy of the voice during the command, the more time collapses, allowing the form to manifest beyond consensual time. The matrix or medium of the called form is generated from within the intention of the individual calling thought into form. Even though there are very few original thoughts, every called form is original to the frame of reference of the individual who knows himself or herself as being in the moment. Each and every moment of each and every incarnation experienced by the individual calling the new form comes into play on the spoken word. If an individual calls a butterfly into existence, every encounter with every butterfly from every incarnation is expressed in the moment of the new butterfly. You only need to join conscious awareness with the subconscious mind within the intention of calling a specific form and all the details are filled in by your many life experiences on Earth. To do this, all desire for the new form to be a certain way is relinquished to the form becoming its own expression through the memories held within the etheric body of your Soul. In the above example of the butterfly, the surviving Dyadic awareness that formed your present human form also contributes its knowing from the many times it lived as a butterfly.

This is important: There can be no hesitation, uncertainty, indecision, vacillation, wavering or faltering when calling thought into direct existence. Your custodial relationship to called form is the same as that of Creator God's to us: you have brought into dimension that which is in your image.

Practice:

Notice when your thoughts and feelings are separate, especially during times when you feel vulnerable, such as in a work environment or social setting where your behavior is being watched by others. Be aware of inner conflicts that keep your thoughts and feelings from joining.

Example: You are at a business function and are surrounded by people who are very competitive. You are asked a direct personal question, one that does not related to work but is meant to expose an outside interest not shared by anyone else from your group. You feel exposed and instead of answering directly with confidence, you move the subject away from yourself by asking someone else a vague question about work, one that can be answered by anyone.

Example: You go home for the holidays and promise yourself this time it will be different, you will not let any relatives shut you down by not accepting the person you have allowed yourself to become. With that thought, you have already begun the process of separating thoughts and feelings. With each hello, you are retreating into the place where you learned to separate your memories from associative feelings.

Example: You are out with your significant other and she or he exposes to your mutual friends a personal issue that you had recently brought up in privacy but with which you were uncomfortable. So, it had been dropped before being resolved. You immediately feel angry, but, to put on a good face, you laugh it off.

We all carry around with us the unresolved moments from the recent (this life) and distant (past lives) past when we disempowered ourselves by separating our thoughts and feelings in a moment when it would have been more expansive and empowering to risk our authenticity scrutiny by others. If you risked your authentic self and were humiliated, the unresolved energy of that encounter will stay with you in the Soul's etheric body and be engaged by the ego/personality each time a similar event is reenacted.

Every day notice at least once when you have gone to extreme measures to separate your thoughts from your feelings. Keep a journal and remember as many similar situations as possible. Then imagine what it would be like to be able to live a deeply authentic life in which every thought and feeling was forever connected as a completed energy.

Your feelings will always seek liberation; your thoughts will always want to build a box around the slightest discomfort. Notice how thoughts fly across the mind and feelings continue to echo through the body. Thoughts are externally stimulated by the conscious mind while feelings are internally generated by the subconscious mind.

Invocation:

Follow the usage guidelines set up with the first invocation in chapter seven. Allow the cantor to find its own pace as you repeat the invocations. Different tones and rhythms produce varying results.

"I AM open and willing to allow my Soul consciousness to express in me, through me, as me, in all my relationships. I AM open and willing to allow my Soul consciousness to express in me, through me, as me, in all my relationships. I AM open and willing to allow my Soul consciousness to express in me, through me, as me, in all my relationships."

"I AM complete and whole in every aspect of being. My thoughts and feelings are one expression, joined in a radiance that flows outward into all my relationships as my authentic self. I am a self-validating Being and seek always to empower others toward illumination and liberation. All this I AM."

"I AM the personification of joy. Everyone I encounter experiences the presence of the Divine Holy Spirit expressing as my combined thoughts and feelings articulate my vision of possibilities for life."

Thoughts:

Affluence is a state of mind that is unlimited in every way.

Harmony and joy are my choice in each moment.

Lifestyle Suggestions:

Meditation: The following breathing pattern is extremely important to this work. Its form has been taught for thousands of generations and was the primary life force energy work adopted by the Atlatians as they ventured into this cycle of separation thirteen thousand years ago. The form is used to gain chi (prana) from the Earth, which in turn, brings balance and calm and helps ground the physical body's etheric field.

It is important to do this exercise exactly as it is given. Variations on the posture or process itself will produce less than stellar results. The intention of this breath is to bring chi (prana) into the body as a way of nourishing all the chakras.

General attitude: First, there is the scooping action of pulling energy up from the Earth as you begin your first inhalation. The attitude during this movement should be as though you were actually scooping up liquid energy from the Earth's etheric body. The downward movement of the first exhalation is meant to push the scooped chi energy down into the base chakra. The upward movement of the second inhalation is meant to evenly spread the energy just placed in the base chakra upward to all of the other chakras. The Atlatians believed that when you take energy from the Earth or Sun, you should first blend it with your core harmonics (base chakra) before using it to balance and energize the remaining chakras. The movement of the hands over the head is of an offering nature to the unseen forces that help with the details of your life. Imagine energy radiating outward through your finger tips as your hands separate and begin their movement back to the base chakra. The energy fills your Soul and physical and etheric bodies with radiant light. Imagine the energy growing more and more brilliant with each successive repetition of the pattern.

Begin the exercise by putting your feet at shoulder's width apart (see illustration 1 below). The concentration of weight should be on the inside ball of your feet on the inhalation and on the outside ball of your feet on the exhalation. Practice this yin (inside ball) and yang (outside ball) focus for a few moments before the first time you try the breathing pattern.

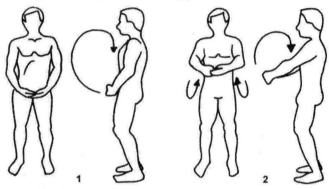

With feet positioned at shoulder's width apart, bend your knees slightly while keeping your back lifted (see illustration 1), giving you the feeling that you are riding horseback. You should feel comfortably grounded in this position.

Your hands should be resting together in front of your body at the base chakra (see illustration 1) with one hand resting in the palm of the other. As you breathe in you will move your hands outward and upward as though you were scooping up energy from the space in front of your body (see illustrations 2 and 3).

This scooping motion should last for the full duration of your inhalation. Make certain that the top arch of your upward motion does not move up above your chin line (see illustration 3).

Both hands should be turned with palms facing downward, with one set of fingers overlapping the others slightly in front of

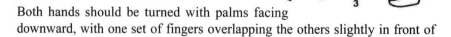

your chin (see illustration 4).

Without pausing between breaths, begin to exhale while slowly pushing your hands downward toward their beginning position. This downward motion should last for the full duration of your exhalation (see illustrations 5-8).

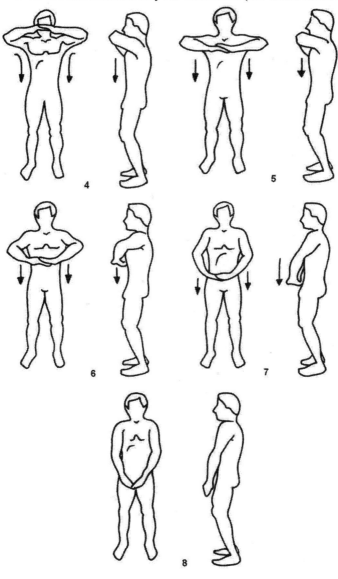

At the bottom of your exhalation immediately begin to move your hands upward (see illustration 9,) retracing the path of their downward motion.

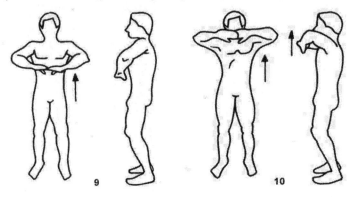

The palms must continue to face downward until the hands reach the throat chakra level (see illustration 10) where they naturally turn outward facing away from the body as they continue their journey upward. Your hands should be facing palms outward and upward as they pass your crown chakra (see illustration 11-12).

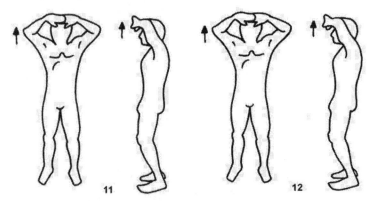

Reach up as high as you can with the fingers still overlapping (see illustration 13-14 on the next page).

Begin your exhalation as the fingers separate and move out, away from the center of the body in a downward swooping movement that ends with them coming to the position where they began (see illustrations 15-19). Your exha-

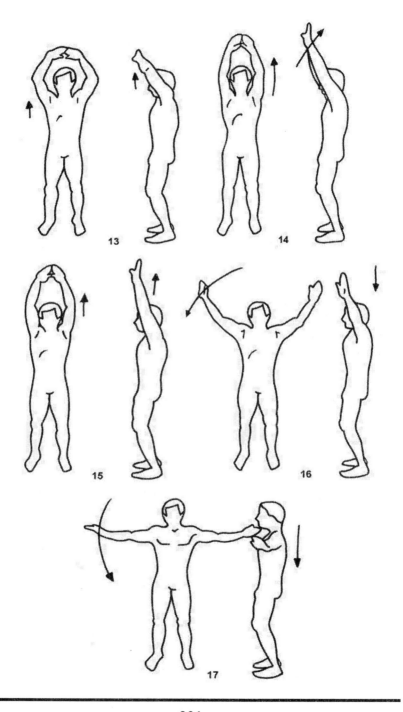

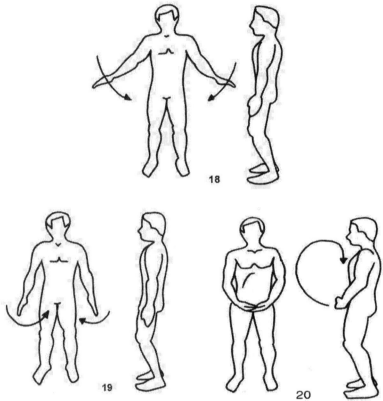

lation should be for the duration of the downward swooping motion.

Immediately repeat the pattern. Give a minimum of twenty minutes to this exercise. Stay focused on the movements of the body and the cyclical rhymthm of the breath.

Diet: Continue to eat in gratitude and joy. Infuse everything you touch with gratitude and joy as you prepare your meals. Drink water with the sure understanding that this fluid is life. Without the gift of water, you would quickly be miserable. Some need as much as three liters a day. Think generous thoughts of enlightened people such as your teachers, or any Avatars such as Moses, Buddha, Jesus or Mohammad while you cook or clean. Whispering their names draws their energy close to us. They, through their individual demonstrations of life, are blessings to us.

Fasting: Replace lunch with juicing between 8-12 ounces of fresh vegetable juice every day for two weeks. This will give your colon a much-needed rest and will make it unpleasant for any unwanted parasites that might have found a home in your crowded colon. To achieve best results, juice half an average sized beet along with two inches of ginger root into your concoction.

Fasting for another's health and joy is very powerful.

Exercise: Give every activity equal value. Be aware of all the muscles used to complete an action.

During your day, take a moment to focus on your breath, allowing each breath to be fully felt in your body as in a complete yogic breath.

THE *KNOWING*

*"Striving for
excellence
motivates you;
striving for
perfection
is demoralizing."*

—. *Harriet Braiker*

THE *KNOWING*

Chapter XI

~ *Traditions of the Way of Truth and Light* ~

Knowing who we are as First State Soul consciousness enfleshed in evolving Dyadic awareness is essential to our liberation from the harsh confinement of dimensional reality into the expanded expression of unlimited knowing and joy. This type of knowing is beyond the confines of self-importance and any Earthly idolatries; knowing brings a force into the world that melts away pride, envy, anger and the lust for power over others. In a fully knowing individual, one born into The Moment, a Twice-born, one who fully knows how he or she were derived and why they are here on Earth, there is inclusion and unity, honor and integrity. A knowing individual is unconcerned with the circumstances of his or her role in assisting others to find that greater sense of themselves; the individual is simply representing that First Moment (Creator God) without any hesitation whatsoever. From that individual's point of view, cultism or religion is impossible. A fully awakened Soul infectiously spreads the power of joy to all whom he or she encounters, not just through words but also through presence; there is no exclusivity as to who is entitled to receive the unlimited power of joy pouring through the awakened union of Triad and Dyad. Through the knowing person, joy is given without prejudice to the all of creation. In the mystical gnosis[1] traditions of the keepers of The Knowing Way, the grace of the master is transferred to the student over their life-oriented time together. The keepers of The Way believed that the written word of a teaching is little more than a textual map[2] of sorts, a device to point the student to greater knowing, not something to be worshiped as the only path to nirvana or eternal joy. For them it seemed wholly unfeasible that a book or scroll would be thought of as having been written by the hand of an almighty god. These joy-filled generous beings understood that a higher power of knowing is constantly moving out into the world in the words and deeds of those individuals who elect a balanced life in favor of an unfocused life of overindulgent distractions. This allows for an oral conveyance of the knowledge from each generation of way adepts to the next, and usually only through only a handful of individuals at any given time. To the keepers of The Way, gnosis is all that is needed to attain illumination. Corruption is possible when the greater knowing of Creation is written and represented by a group of interpreters who accept an elevated position as intermediaries to an almighty god or one of its prophets.

The exception to this rule of oral transference of the greater knowing is allowed at times of vast transition, and at immense intersections of human endeavor so influenced by the shifting of cosmic cycles such as the one presently shaping the collective consciousness of humankind. All Knowing Way documents, or textual maps, are copied into the words and cultural understanding of the initiate at the time he or she receives the grace of knowing, both physically and spiritually. In this way, the text is not venerated or elevated to importance as a spiritual artifact but instead is kept as a relevant living document. To further ensure this, each page of the previous adept transcriber's textual map translation is destroyed as the new translation is brought into present time. Those who know the way of truth and light live very proficient lives dedicated to bringing knowing into the world through every word and deed and have little regard for the cult practices of organized religions. Instead, they inform others of the necessity for balanced thought, balanced speech, balanced conduct, balanced persistence and balanced effort through balanced self-concentration that is practiced in every adjoining moment in all dimensions and all universes of expression.

The adepts of The Way condense The Knowing information into certain practices and rituals, that, when performed with gratitude and focused intention, liberate the seeker from the delusion of sorrow and misery. Once liberated, the mystic seeker becomes an emissary of the First Moment (Creator God) and are themselves a light unto the world. As such, they are perpetually inclined to offer all they know to all who seek after the greater truth. They are the messengers guided by the unseen watchers of the way.

~ *Messengers are never the Message* ~

As it has been stated in all the world's spiritual paths, from the Aboriginals of Australia to the Zoroastrians of the Middle East, we are not alone in our journey toward completion and liberation. Each of us is cosmically guided and Divinely cajoled into ever-expanding degrees of enlightenment as we move from incarnation to incarnation through the process of birth, death and rebirth. This is true of even the most enlightened of humans: Moses, Confucius, Socrates, Buddha, Jesus and Mohammed. They are messengers of greater knowing, keepers of the way of truth and light; they are not the greater knowing itself. Cultures, cults and religions establish themselves around such liberated Soul consciousnesses when misguided followers seek to establish their beloved teachers as more than just the messengers, but the grand message Itself. This tendency to exalt the teacher is more from the influence of teacher and student repeatedly incarnating together as a way of assuring liberation from the wheel of birth and death than blind worship. It is true that we are teachers, or better stated, awakeners for each other, and there are unique relationships of world teachers to a specific collective of seekers over several incarnational cycles. This type of relationship is powerful in that it continues uninterrupted even by the advent of death nd birth. Once a world teacher is finished, he or she becomes Avatar leaving the group to select for itself a new world mentor.

By way of example (as translated from The Knowing Way material and Akashic Records): EL Akhwahl of Lemuria/Mu incarnated into the Atlatian culture as Djwhal Orge, First Counsel of the Unity Cycle. After the deluge, he incarnated into Sumeria as the First Ningishzida[3] and then later as the fourth Myrdlwyn of the Druidae[4] until incarnating as the historical figure remembered as Confucius. This Soul had many less notable incarnations between those mentioned, some eight hundred and thirty-three that were spent in preparation for the role of world teacher. Confucius, more properly known as K'ung Ch'iu, was designated posthumously as The Grand Master of All Ages by emperor Ch'ing Hsi of the Ch'ing Dynasty in the year 5 CE. Not much can be added to better describe Confucius. His accomplishments influenced every living creature in China. While there is no real physical image of Confucius, he is described as having been of a supreme dignity of bearing, graceful of movement, formal in conduct, formidably eloquent and deeply compassionate in voice. His vast accomplishments penetrated every aspect of mundane and spiritual life. Confucius advocated legal justice for all as the foundation for human life in an ideal world where human principles, courtesy, filial piety and the virtues of benevolence, righteousness, loyalty and trustworthiness prevailed. He believed that every citizen should take an active contributive role in life with a well-defined responsibility within society. Leadership, in turn, should provide a high standard of living, moral education and the opportunity to ritualize eternal gratitude toward those influences that give life to all creation. His focus was on balance and harmony within the individual that would project into the world through empathic and intuitive streams of conscious discernment to all Dyadic and Triadic substance. This brilliant individual came from very humble origins and was elevated to the highest position in his culture, revered for thousands of years by the Chinese people who still follow the basic tenets of his teachings since he introduced them in his eighteenth year. Shortly after his death, Confucius incarnated as Socrates.

Socrates began life in humble circumstances as the son of a sculptor/stonecutter. In his early years, Socrates was a pupil of Archelaus studying the scientific theories of Anaxagoras. Later he shifted his inquiry of life to the development of the human psyche, but more chiefly, the development of moral character. The two notions that formed the foundation of his ideology were the beliefs that each individual should do what he or she thinks is right even in the face of universal opposition, and the need to pursue knowledge even when opposed.[5] After inheriting a modest fortune from his father, Sophroniscus, Socrates used his financial independence as an opportunity to give full attention to inventing the practice of philosophical dialogue.

For the balance of his life, Socrates devoted himself to engaging the aristocratic young citizens of Athens through in lengthy, unrestrained discussions with which he insistently questioned their unwarranted confidence in the truth of popular opinions. These students had been his devoted followers during his life as Confucius in China.Unlike most teachers of his day, Socrates deliberately declined payment for his work with students. His open disdain for the material success that was embraced by most of his Sophist contemporaries influenced many of his students to fanatical loyalty. His students' influential parents, however, were often displeased with his influence on their offspring which, when combined with his non-democratic political views, led to the charges held against him of "corrupting the youth and interfering with the religion of the city." After a short trial, he was sentenced to death in 399 BCE. He accepted this outcome with remarkable grace and equanimity, dying in the company of his friends and disciples.

Because of his argumentative inquiry, Socrates was viewed generally as a cynic. The one positive statement that he seems to have made was a definition of virtue (arête): "Virtue is knowledge." He argued that, "If one knows the good[6], one will always demonstrate the good. It follows, then, that anyone who does anything wrong does not really know the good." For Socrates, this argument justified the tearing down of people's moral positions, for if they had the wrong ideas about virtue, morality, love, or any other ethical idea, they could not be trusted to do the right thing.

Shortly after his death, the Soul who was known as Socrates incarnated in Tibet into the Che clan where he achieved complete illumination and enlightenment as a continuation of the lineage of the clear light gods. There he taught The Knowing through the ancient Lemurian rites that survived the shift into separation from duality thirteen thousand years ago. As an Avatar, he now moves freely between the veil separating our dimension from the next, continuing his guidance of humanity.

~ *Sananda of Lemuria* ~

This story interpreted from the Akashic Records further illustrates how the messenger over time becomes the message. This particular story takes us back forty-two thousand years ago when the human population of the planet was a little more than five hundred million and people lived in low valleys warmed by thermal springs in a global community called Lemuria. A great deal more ice existed on the continents than scientists presently suspect, making these valleys that dotted the globe much like the Garden of Eden described in Genesis. As has been the case for the last thirteen thousand years, the Lemurian culture existed during a cycle of separation, with the occasional birth of Souls who exhibited extraordinary knowing and resolve. A Soul came to this system from a similar world scientists would associate with Sothis (Sirius) in Canis Major and, as was the custom of the Lemurians, he was given the name of Sananda, which meant brightest star. This Soul had ascended through the separately layered dimensions of his home star, coming to Earth to experience the enormous joy of being both Soul and flesh within one-dimensional experience. From very early on Sananda excelled at allowing the full knowing of all his experiences to pour through him into this world, exhibiting superhuman abilities in all aspects of life. By the time he was three years of age he was given to the priestly class of his culture to be raised as a leader. With the exception of a few remote areas, most of the population of Lemuria knew of and marveled at the abilities Sananda exhibited. He was instantly proficient at every aspect of Lemurian life, excelling in the spiritual knowing of his time, which was a combination of ancient Earth lore and off-world sciences. By the time he was twelve, Sananda had both the power to kill with a word and the power to instantaneously heal by simple touch. He was both eloquent and formidable, compassionately wise and ferocious in battle. By twenty years of age, he was legendary, having demonstrated more of life than any human before him. As a result, people began to call on his name as both a curse and a blessing. Eventually his immense popularity demanded that he be made co-leader of the Lemurian culture alongside the genetic grandparents of his mother. Most of the surrounding less evolved groupings of humans that shared Earth with the Lemurians immediately paid homage to the enormous abilities and profound presence of Sananda. From that moment peace, harmony and balance prevailed around the globe with all of the valley communities joining under the guidance of this Soul. Sananda interacted with all the peoples of the Earth as he allowed more and more of his knowledge of creation to pour through him into this realm. In his two-hundredth year as co-regent, Sananda was to be elevated to global counsel. He rejected the unprecedented offer, choosing instead to lead a large group of Lemurians, about one third of the population, on a great migration through which Sananda intended to completely shift the collective consciousness of his followers toward self-generated unity, away from the law based culture of Lemuria. The best of all the people joined him in his pursuit, leaving the central cultural areas void of their greatest minds and artisans. This group moved from their home in a valley that is now covered by the Sea of Japan, across the land and ice bridge at the Bering Strait to finally settle in a large valley just off the coast of California, some of which is now covered by the waters of Santa Monica Bay. As they traveled through foreign lands, Sananda invited the best minds of those subcultures to join the Lemurians as they made their way to the place he had envisioned as home. Once there, the Lemurians used the less-evolved humans who had joined the march to create a vast temple complex unlike any that had previously been built and that, when finished, was dedicated to Sananda's brilliance. This complex also housed thousands of memory crystals containing the full history of human life on Earth and humanity's interaction with off-world beings from many different star systems. Sananda took up residence in the center pyramid where he directed the activities of Mu as this new gathering place was called.

Sananda had perfected the ideals of harmony and balance in body, mind and Spirit and truly personified the popular idea the Lemurians had of a faultless man. By his three hundred and eighty-third year, the Divine energy pouring through him was such that it would cause man and woman alike to experience supreme ecstasy should they come within a few meters of his physical form. This altered state of consciousness would last for several days, presenting itself as a fully aware but sensually disinterested state within the personality. Once recovered, the individual's consciousness was permanently expanded to include complete awareness of physical, etheric and the more subtle auric emanations of physical matter. One continuing side effect of this encounter was the recovered individual's disinterest in anything routinely human. In extreme cases those who had experienced ecstatic nirvana through Sananda's outpouring of joy stopped all sexual interaction – they actually transformed into genderless humans incapable of sexual activity. It was because of this that a certain class of people was chosen to represent him to the general populous. This group was made up of those males and females who had undergone the spontaneous transformation brought on by encounters with Sananda's presence. To further ensure the human reliability within the community, each household, usually consisting of twenty-three members, had one member whose sole function was to monitor the activities of its other members, keeping them within the ideals fostered by the new priestly class surrounding Sananda. Life progressed forward in time creating many different types of technologies and specialized groupings of peoples within the culture. Eventually it was believed that, if the priestly class and family intermediaries were to have power over the less knowing inhabitants, they would have to elevate Sananda to the highest possible godlike position to get him out of the way of their intentions. This was also good for the temple business because, as Divine Deity, Sananda could be fully worshiped, equally by anyone any time they chose, through etheric altars stationed in each families' compound. He was deified and at the time of his transition was given the title of Pure Divinity Sun. Sananda lived to be six hundred thirty-seven years old, a little more than twice the average lifetime for enfleshed Souls of his day. He was buried along with the memory crystals he had generated for a time in the very distant future when humanity would need to know of its origins. It was taught that, instead of dying, he had vanished in a flash of brilliant light and taken up residence within the sun to nourish his beloved people for all eternity. Many of those who as direct initiates of Sananda had come to know the way of truth and light, used its powerful manifest influence to hold the devotion of Sananda's followers after he relinquished his physical form. To further ensure the continuation of their daily idolatry, the priestly class set up elaborate laws reinforced by mandatory rituals, all designed to keep the faithful tithing and praying.

A few hundred years after Sananda, the unity cycle that fostered the Atlatian culture overtook humanity. At about the same time, the amount of sunlight penetrating through the Earth's atmosphere increased, raising the overall temperature of the planet by several degrees. As the seawaters rose inundating their wondrous valley, Sananda's immediate faithful, led by his chief companion, EL, left the temple complex with its niggling priests, took the most meaningful contents of the pyramids and made their way back to what is now China. There they buried most of their artifacts in what is now the Gobi Desert in an identical complex of seven pyramidal temples along the Hei He River, where the early inhabitants mimicked the Muians by continuing the worship of the sun as Divine Deity. The sacred artifacts included Sananda's mummified body.

The Muians then quietly melted into the surrounding mountains to take on life as unified humans or to incarnate into new bodies genetically free of the previous separation cycle's molecularly embedded conflicts. We know of their abilities through the remnant Sil Lum practitioners of ancient China. After the great ice flows melted, the sea level rose some four hundred fifty meters inundating most of the ancestral valleys, pushing the inhabitants to higher less-proven areas and creating a dramatic drop in the overall population of humanity.

Those priests who had created the laws to control the devoted citizens of Mu were not allowed to move back to their place of origin and remained with the temple complex they had created in Mu. Through the inner conflict generated by their spiritual arrogance, they perished as the temple complex submerged. Had they truly understood the coming cycle of unity during which all would equally know, they could have advanced great personal change. Instead of expanding their consciousness to the level Sananda had attained, they faltered in their continued glorification of Sananda as the only true divinity. Through his profound knowing, Sananda had loved them all with boundless, unlimited love. Sananda has incarnated once since Mu: 7,486 years ago as the Emperor Fu-His. Sananda's greatest student and most mighty companion, EL Akhwahl, continued the teachings of Sananda/Fu-Hsi as Confucius, then as Socrates and finally as the head of the Che clan of Tibet.

The stories of religion and the corruption of truth by fervent followers are much older than can be archeologically and anthropologically proven. The true origins of the familiar myths and epic stories told over and over again to countless generations will never be known to modern science. The moral of each story is always the same: "Arrogance chains its keeper to the wheel of life and death. Absolute power over life and death is the pinnacle for those wearing arrogance's liturgical headdress." You need only look to the Catholic Church of a few hundred years ago to know the full depth of this statement. Arrogance in any form will stop spiritual expansion and illumination in its tracks.

To ensure against this from ever happening again within the teachings of The Knowing or The Way, certain safeguards were included in the general text. Around 10 BCE, the elders of the Sons of Light movement first did this as a way of keeping any of The Knowing Way adepts from becoming the messiah in the eyes of their students. At that particular time in history, there was an outcry for a spiritual leader to organize an uprising against the occupying forces of Rome. Knowing adepts had all of the abilities the average person on the street might assign to a messiah: the ability to heal all manner of physical illness and mental affliction, and the ability to transmute plentiful forms of matter, such as water, into more needed forms, such as wine for sacramental offerings by just commanding it so. They also had the ability to overcome death by raising the dead. Jesus, as a knowing adept, was only one in a long line of individuals who were touted by fanatical followers as the messiah. John the Baptist's public endorsement of Jesus as a Way master sealed his fate with the extremist multitudes. John knew he was about to be killed. His zealous followers needed a cool head to lead them through the coming years. John knew Jesus to be a master teacher and revealer of The Knowing Way; John also knew Jesus would never proclaim anything but the greater knowing, even if faced with his own demise. All messianic contenders prior to Jesus had failed by recanting their beliefs as they were tortured. Some survived the torture; the luckier ones did not. Those who made it through the lashings and physical brutality were disfigured and handicapped for the balance of their continually ostracized lives.

An individual free of arrogance will naturally know to question certain ideations offered through the teachings. Those still struggling with greed and lust for power will not be able to see around certain corners within the teachings and will become frustrated by their lack of progress after a certain point. This is not meant to exclude anyone from knowing, rather it is meant to keep him or her from harm's way. You need only look to Adolph Hitler of Germany to fully appreciate the magnitude of the spoken word's influence when the speaker is an initiate of the greater knowing. Hitler had studied several spiritual disciplines while he was wandering around the German-Austrian countryside. If he had continued his Third Reich movement without experiencing conflict over the actions taken against the Jews, he would have been unstoppable. No power on Earth could have kept him from manifesting all he imagined. Only his inner conflict stopped the German Third Reich from conquering all of Europe. Through his knowledge of The Knowing Way, he was able to manifest for himself and others just as long as he was clear regarding intention and outcome as one expression. The moment he felt the inner conflict of the Final Solution, he was powerless to proceed.

~ *The Written Word* ~

It was believed by early mystics that, should the greater knowing be put into symbolic or textual form, those who wished to enslave humanity would manipulate the truth by interpreting the subtle meanings to suit their needs and using the manifest powers to create a domination of one more-knowing group over another less-knowing. The very simple laws of Moses, the Ten Commandments, which Jehovah chiseled onto stone tablets as he spiritually overshadowed his prophet, were expanded into the detail-strewn Talmud and Torah, which eventually formed the basis of Hebrew law and culture. The balanced message of Buddha's Eightfold Path has spawned thousands of fiercely competitive writings that evolved into as many different sects. The grace-filled teachings of Jesus the Nazarene have been interpreted in the New Testament by a few disciples and one Saul of Gischala in Galilee (Saint Paul) who claimed to have directly experienced Jesus after his crucifixion. Just like the followers of other world teachers, Saul envisioned a need for the textual presentation of Jesus the Nazarene's teaching, the teachings in a form that would enliven the faithful until his promised return at the end times.[7] Saul saw this textual form of Jesus' teachings as a means of spreading the good news to the all of humanity while humanity collectively waited for the cleansing final justice and assured deliverance.

If the above examples of knowledge fixed into text and altered by interpretation are any indication of the corruption of knowing, the mystics of old might well feel have felt justified in keeping the greater knowing truth as an oral tradition, well away from those personalities bent on personal gain through the exploitation of humanities' hopes of deliverance from sorrow. Authorities pushing their interpretations of textual knowing have destroyed countless individuals and cultures, bringing havoc upon humanity and the world. Being a messenger of truth can be very dangerous, especially during the collectively vulnerable periods at the end of great cycles such as the one approaching in 2011. The faithful proponents and followers of textual or scriptural knowledge often attack living messengers of the greater knowing. They do this to give life to the words written in their beloved books. By killing the living messenger, they keep their books alive. The living truth always threatens the scholarly and those who follow their interpretations of textualized truth. The messengers, however, keep coming, each with their own style and verve. It is important to remember that the messenger is always just the messenger, never the message itself: Siddhartha Buddha and Jesus the Nazarene were pure unadulterated messengers of knowing. Those who felt threatened by the purity and simplicity of The Knowing pouring out into the world through these personalities brought about the premature end of their lives – the one poisoned,[8] the other crucified. Yet, the corruption of their teachings was due to the few followers and devotees who needed them, for their own selfish reasons, to be the message – the one and only message. Jesus instructed, *"This is the knowing, the way of truth and light. Cause nothing of this to be written, instead keeping it alive through the voice of the messenger for those who have ears to hear. Be of good cheer for the kingdom is now at hand."* (as interpreted from the Akashic Records)

Again, the task of reducing the greater knowing into verbiage begins the corruption of the truth. Socrates was also of the opinion that nothing concerning the way of truth and light should be written but should instead be kept alive in voice. He believed that truth could only be passed on to a student through the subtle energies carried by the voice of a master and not through the exactness of each word within a phrase. Because of this belief, we only have accounts of his teachings, most notably through Plato. While it is true the Knowing is corrupted when written, it must also be stated that the written truth serves humanity by allowing a greater number of interested individuals to gain access to certain forms of knowing which might be otherwise unattainable with so few enlightened masters to serve all who would want to know. Be it greatly diminished through layers of interpretation, the written truth of who we are, how we were derived and why we are here opens as many doors as it closes.

~ *The Living Truth* ~

In the Akashic Records, there is a series of vaticinations concerning the present time period of humanity, especially the years between 2009 and 2011 and 2022 and 2026. These divinations run contrary to the apocalyptic prophesies pronounced by John in the Book of Revelations in the New Testament. The most intriguing of these promises is more a statement of assurance for those taking the spiritual knowing path. These promises were voiced by one of the elders of the Rose Monastery on his deathbed. The following is a loose translation of his exact words. *"Those initiates willing to forego their expectations with life, being joyfully present in all matters of life, who hold gratitude as their atonement thus willing to know their true magnificence, who are willing to live their truth, they will live as the greater knowing in the moment and will not hunger nor thirst but instead will be a quencher of those who do."* - The Akashic Records

Each of us is a living master of the greater knowing when we live life without conflict, giving gratitude in each new moment for all that is and will be. We can live as a true master of life from within the definition of a specific ethnic group, culture, political structure or organized religion without having to change those structures that serve the collective physical and emotional bodies of that gathering of Souls. If an individual lives within the geogenetic[9] influence of his or her ancestors, their ability to live without conflict will be greatly enhanced. If one lives outside his or her geogenetic influences but is surrounded by members of a community made up of a majority of individuals who are of the same heredity, that person is better off than if living in a gathering of people who are overly diverse. The harmonics of genetics is very real, just as is the harmonics of Soul groupings. Genetics determine certain behaviors that set into motion certain circumstances, which give us our gender, racial and ethnic stereotypes. While it is improper to hold an individual to stereotypical definitions of physical traits and behaviors, it is proper to state a natural comfort and alignment found within the boundaries of like-mindedness and genetic similarities. In a world concerned more with political correctness than enlightenment, this notion seems to work against the idea of forced diversity as a means of overcoming natural harmonic intolerances. This being stated, it will take a greater effort from those individuals living in North America and certain regions in Europe to achieve unity of body, mind and Spirit than from those living in less genetically diverse regions.

If an individual lacks a clearly defined geogenetic origin, he or she will be less harmonically influence a genetic grouping. In a balanced individual, this can be a blessing in that he or she will feel more like a citizen of the World. However, non-geogenetically centric individuals who are unaware of themselves as spiritual beings often find within themselves a sense of not belonging that is quickly filled with the dominant beliefs of their culture. This can lead to an over identification with a culture, religion or geopolitical system, making it extremely difficult to achieve a knowing state of Soul consciousness.

Those Souls who have incarnated in Japan and certain areas of China have a greater certainty of shifting their consciousness into unity, both because of their geogenetic centricity and certain genetic values inherited from the bloodlines originating in Lemuria. These genetic values, or life-enhancing behaviors that have been constant for tens of thousands of generations allow for a greater sense of ongoing Dyadic awareness through filial piety. In this regard, the Lemurian genetic value of harmony in all aspects of the human experience has developed into certain formulaic behaviors that are dominant to regional cultural beliefs and philosophy and are as precious as life itself. Throughout Asia, but less so today than a hundred years ago, harmony of surroundings and community was and is valued over individual life. It is because of this genetic value of harmony that it will be easier for those individuals in Japan and certain areas of China to intrinsically understand the core value of The Knowing Way. Souls who have previously incarnated into these older Lemurian and Atlatian bloodlines, but who in this current life reside in other geogenetic circumstances, will also have an intrinsic knowing of this core value of balance and harmony which will serve them as they shed the inner conflict of the current epoch. Because generations of Japanese have also understood the value of commitment to an ideal, they will be able to move into a more expanded state with less real effort.

Again, this does not mean that only those with the genetic values of balance and harmony will be able to release the inner conflict needed to consciously shift into the unity of body, mind and Spirit. There are gatherings of peoples all over the globe who embody the ideals of Lemurian and Atlatian knowing. These groups know the role of humanity on Earth and seek to gently move the collective in that direction. The Japanese culture will be able to collectively move toward The Knowing, and as such will be the single largest grouping of Souls to demonstrate the coming unity, living as Soul consciousness fully expressing through human form.

~ *In Conclusion* ~

Many factors have combined to create life on Earth: the sun's energy, the exact orbits of the inner four planets in direct relationship to the orbits of the larger outer planets, the gravitational fields of the larger outer planets protecting the inner planets from catastrophic impacts of space debris by pulling those objects into their surfaces, the quick rotations of the earth on its axis, the molten inner core of the Earth, the Earth's crust, water, molecular and cellular formations, our moon's influence on the surface fluids as the Earth rotates on its axis, Earth's electromagnetic fields, the right combination of layered atmospheric gases, the ozone layer, expanding bands of thought energy, the etheric envelope, the biological process of evolution, awareness, consciousness, etc. Several different global ecological systems emerged, flourished and died long before Souls took their first steps on Earth as humans. In the scale of time, we Souls are here now for a single heartbeat as compared to a long lifetime of cardiovascular rhythms. The point of our being here is not to become another biological experiment that vanishes into the organic mass of this realm. We are here to gain the greatest amount of joy from each moment of impartial observation and, through our observance, to bring to this world a knowing of itself through our direct experience of its manifestations. We are here to allow the awareness of matter a glimpse of the static completeness of the First Moment, just as we are here to lose sight of our eternal wholeness in favor of glimpsing the dynamic of unfolding perfection. We are here to radiate pure joy into inanimate and animate matter's awareness so that it becomes self-conscious. Through ascension, we are here to bring the opportunity of eternal rest found in completion to Dyadic awareness so that it may know itself as the beginning and the end. We are here to be in the mystery as it unfolds into solution. We are here to forget, then remember, our wholeness. This is our joy – to play a game of hide and seek amongst the molecules of Dyadic substance. We are here to serve each other's greater purpose of awakening to knowing. We are here to be joy expressed to each other as unlimited love. We are here to submerge our every fiber into the vastness of Souls as we collectively share our journey within the gracious offerings of the Earth Spirit and Logos. We are here to be here: to observe life in all its fullness. Everything else, every imagining, every hypothesis is simply an attempt to transmit the joy of our discoveries to each other. There is nothing here to overcome or to perfect or bring into balance save for our misunderstanding of our origin, our purpose and our release. Everything else is always as it is – nothing more, nothing less.

Practice:

At the mystical core of The Knowing teachings is the primary notion that each spoken word is a direct command of the Soul upon the natural energies of Earth and that this command must be obeyed and made manifest within the concepts of time in space. It is also believed that the sun gives off a harmonic resonance that enlivens the Soul. If the sun enlivens the Soul with its radiant energy, then the Soul enlivens the material world through the vibrations of its voice. Akhenaton (Amenhotep IV) of Egypt understood the dynamic of this mysterious notion. As Pharaoh, he commanded his subjects to raise their voices in songs dedicated to Ra, the hawk-headed sun god. Each day began and ended with a salutation and parting prayer to the sun as it broke the horizon in either direction. The Egyptian's abilities to manifest thought to matter were greatly increased through this knowledge of energy and vibration. A saying from the Vedas[10] claims, "Speech is the essence of humanity." It states that all of what humanity thinks and ultimately all that happens is determined by the expression of ideas and actions through speech. Everything, the Vedas maintain, comes into manifest being through speech. Ideas remain within the ethers until they are created through the power of speech. Without the utterance of the Soul through the body, the dream of life would remain unformed. Jesus spoke clearly about this when he cautioned his apostles about speaking one truth and living another, *"Hear, and understand: Not that which goeth into the mouth defileth a man; but that which cometh out of the mouth, this defileth a man."* Matthew 15:10-11

There are certain forms of words that when spoken can bring about miraculous change within the body, mind and Spirit of the one uttering such words. We have explored this through the invocations offered in previous chapters. In Vedic practices, mantras are described as energy-based sounds that are consciously combined with willful intention to bring about a desired outcome. The intention, when overlaid upon the wave form of the sound as the carrier wave, excites both the physical and etheric bodies at substantially higher harmonics. This higher resonance is in direct alignment with originating waves of thought energy coming from the Earth Spirit and Logos. Although there is a general spiritual meaning to most mantras, the only lasting definition is the result or effect of repetitively chanting the mantra. In this study, our release from conflict, no matter the form or manifest circumstance, is the intended outcome of the mantra.

Invocations are different from mantras in that an invocation is a command by the individual to the seen and unseen forces that bring thought into form. Mantras are more of a call for a specific divinity to intercede on our behalf. Invocations can be used for the same purpose but are not as effective when calling for assistance. The why of this phenomenon is not fully known.

This Mahamritunjaya mantra is from the Rig-Veda[11] and needs direct initiation from a teacher for attaining Siddhi.[12] Anybody can recite this mantra and attain permanent release from inner conflict. It should be recited preferably for forty days both in the morning and evening while sitting on a woolen blanket facing east. Recite the Maha-mantra 108 times (one rosary) or its multiples in each sitting. This is the greatest work of Maharishi Vashistha, a brilliant teacher whose life was dedicated to harmony and balance. Focus on your breath, taking several complete yogic breaths before beginning the Mahamritunjaya mantra. Consciously gather around you those divinities that guide your intentions to completion. Approach this mantra as a sacred gift given from the Divine Holy Spirit that comforts and guides us to completion. Ask Maharishi for his blessings and guidance as you begin this thoughtful prayer:

(As translated from Sanskrit)
OM (The omni present vibration of all creation)
TRYAMBAKKAM (The three eyes or sources of enlightenment. God as Omniscient - Brahma, Omnipresent - Vishnu and Omnipotent - Shiva)
YAJAMAHE (We sing Thy praise)
SUGANDHIM (The fragrance of Creation – knowledge, presence and strength – knowing, seeing and feeling)
PUSTIVARDHANAM (The Great Father of all - Brahma the Omniscient. The impeller of all knowledge)
URVAROOKAMEVA (Release from the powers of ignorance, falsehood and weakness)
BANDANAAN (Bound down)
MRITYORMOKSHEEYA (Release from cycle of death, rebirth and death through Mokshya)
MAAMRITAAT. (The gift of life rejuvenating nectar)

Again:
OM TRYAMBAKKAM YAJAMAHE SUGANDHIM
PUSTIVARDHANAM URVAROOKAMEVA BANDANAAN
MRITYORMOKSHEEYA MAAMRITAAT

There are several audio versions of this mantra available that can give you a better idea of the pronunciation and cadence. Ask at your bookstore for a cassette tape or CD of the Mahamritunjaya mantra.

Invocation:

"The pureness of my being is illumed in every detail of life. The substance of the World reflects a pure image of my Soul back to me. All this I AM."

Lifestyle Suggestions:

Meditation: During your day, take a moment to focus on your breath, allowing each breath to be fully felt in your body as in a complete yogic breath. Make your life a gift to creation and every moment will be a meditation.

Diet: Eat in gratitude and joy. Infuse everything you touch with gratitude and joy as you prepare your meals. Drink water with the sure understanding that this fluid is life. Eat that those who hunger may be fed and drink that those who are thirsty may drink.

Fasting: Fast one day each week taking only water as your nourishment As you fast, meditate by envisioning (imagining) the nourishment of others – family, friends, acquaintances – people nearby and in far away lands.

Exercise: In all ways, honor your body. Be as active as is possible for your body type, age and circumstances.

~ *Chapter XI Footnotes* ~

1 Intuitive knowledge of spiritual truths; said to have been an attribute of ancient Gnostics.

2 Each initiate copies the previous initiate's translation of The Way textual map in his or her own language and cultural syntax. These written reminders of the Way principles are never worshiped.

3 A title for the individual Soul who guarded the opening, or way between this dimension and the one most adjacent to us, thought of as the tree of life to the Atlatians.

4 Myrdlwyn was to the Druids as the Pope is to the Catholic religion.

5 Since he left no literary legacy of his own, we are dependent upon contemporary writers like Aristophanes, Xenophon and Plato for information about his life and work.

6 At the time of Socrates, "the good" was an adept's public phraseology for The Knowing Way.

7 The end times allege the return of Jesus the Nazarene as the Only Son of God Almighty when he will gather up his faithful to heaven and condemn the unbelievers to an eternal hell.

8 The Akashic Records show that Buddha died as a result of eating food tainted with mushrooms and that he did not die as a result of eating pork as is commonly believed by most devotees. It is not clear why he was deliberately poisoned and the Akasha shows that there were many different rival spiritual groups competing for the same populous' attention.

9 The term geogenetic is that geographical area through which your genetic ancestry was established.

10 The Hindu Vedas are the oldest known books and originate from the Lemurian period.

11 The Rig Veda is a collection of 1,017 hymns written by unknown poets over hundreds of years. The hymns seek the answers to philosophical questions and are the source of Indian practices and philosophies. Many scholars believe that the Rig Veda must be studied in order to understand Indian thought.

12 Siddhi is typically defined as "a magical or spiritual power for the control of self, others and the influencing forces of nature."

*"Words have the power to
both destroy and heal.
When words are both
true and kind,
they can change
our world. "*

—. *Siddhartha Buddha*

~ Glossary of Terms ~

Avatar – Any direct manifestation of an ascended Being, Soul Entity, Celestial Being or Logos.

Beginning Moment – The First Moment of all of Creation. Science refers to this as the Big Bang Theory of creation. This First Moment is the immediate beginning for all forms of energy and consciousness.

Bodhisattva – In this context, they are Dyadically derived Souls who govern all life relationships on Earth. They have evolved from particles of matter to single cells to complex animal forms then ascended out of matter to become Souls. Their ability to manipulate time and space comes from their having been born of the matter of Earth.

Calling – The use of the human voice to quicken the ethrioplasmic substance surrounding Earth for the express purpose of manifesting thought forms into three-dimensional material forms.

Creation – All non-matter matter and matter, i.e., all dimensional and parallel dimensional realities, all First State consciousness, energy and the urge and their ethrioplasmic emanations as well as all evolutionary awareness and energy that exists everywhere.

Creator or Co-creators – Enfleshed Triads are not creators. All that was created has existed from the First Moment. Dyadic substance seeks to complete all the probabilities and possibilities envisioned in the First Moment through the evolution of its various forms. In this sense, evolving matter is following a command from the First Moment (Creator God). Triads, formed in the image of Creator God, in turn area able to command the already existing substance to take desired forms based upon the natural laws that govern Dyadic structures within a given dimension.

Creator God – is the First Moment, the singular All That Is.

Dyad – Evolutionary matter that begins as a base particle and evolves into more complex form as a response to the First Moment's (Creator God's) vision of possibilities.

Dyad awareness – Awareness that evolves or develops in creation when matter particles become molecules, then a single cell and finally a grouping of specialized cells at which time a surviving awareness – Dyadic awareness – is formed within an etheric body that survives the death of that physical body which it created. This new awareness builds in scope and breadth as it explores the possibilities within its environment. In humans, this Dyadic awareness is multi-functional in that it helps to develop each subsequent body with retained information about how bodies are formed and function, as well as to carry forward the learned abilities of the most recent incarnation into the present form. Some adepts believe surviving Dyadic awareness to be the personality or ego. Personality and ego are an aspect of the Soul's etheric body and are developed over eons of repeated incarnations.

Ego – A survival awareness contained within the Soul's etheric body that is shared with the Dyadic awareness of the human form. In primitive humans, this dynamic was more of a cunning form of knowing needed for sheer survival. In our modern world this has evolved into the base dynamic driving the need to be right as a strategy for success. This awareness is an aspect of the Soul's radiant body or etheric from.

Enjoined Souls – In order for a Soul to incarnate into a physical dimension, such as Earth, it must first form a union with another Soul to balance the skew of their masculine or feminine orientation. Souls do not have a gender, per se, and they have a bias that drives their inquiry of Creation whether they are in a physical realm. This is due to the basic quality of their radiant or etheric body and by virtue of the given range of life force energy emanating from their core. The enjoining is for the expressed purpose of forming a balanced bias for sharing a complete view or observation of dimensional Creation. Each Soul of the enjoining retains its individuated frame of reference but shares every moment of its observation with the other Soul of the enjoining; so much so that the two seem as one. Because enjoined Souls are not fused together in a permanent state as one aspect of an eternal whole, but are merely partners, they may enjoin for one incarnation or three thousand incarnations. With that in mind, enjoined Souls can:
- incarnate at the same or different times
- incarnate while the other does not
- have one incarnation while the other has five hundred
- have no interest in the physical realms while the other seductively wallows in each now moment

- decide to experience all incarnations together, apart and every combination in between

Enjoined Souls are completely simpatico and empathic to each other even if one of the Souls is not in a physical form at the same time as the other. When enjoined Souls form a partnership on Earth, their complete unity of body, mind and Spirit is felt by other humans as an everlasting quality. In ancient times, only paired Souls were allowed to marry and have offspring. These Earthly marriages were virtually conceived in the "heavens," prompting the passage of the wedding ceremony from Matthew 19:6, *"Wherefore they are no more twain, but one flesh. What therefore God hath joined together, let not man put asunder."* Marriage vows were sacred oaths between enjoined Souls who transmigrated to this system within a Soul group from a previous system. Children were not allowed to choose their mates, but were joined with their pared Soul from early childhood, sometimes while still gestating. This began to change when marriages were arranged to squelch disputes between tribes or feuding families. Other names inspired through the experiences of enjoined Souls includes: Soul mates, twin flames, eternal twins, Bogart to my Bacall, Cream in my Coffee, Yin to my Yang, etc.

Etheric Body – The non-matter matter substance generated from within the First Moment to enclose the consciousness, energy and urge of a Triad. Etheric energy is also a non-matter matter envelope that contains the ongoing awareness of evolving matter. This ethrioplasmic substance exists in most worlds and is one of the most common forms of embodiment for consciousness and awareness.

Ethrioplasmic substance – A gelatin-like elastic non-matter matter of the Christ emanation created when two Souls enjoin for the expressed purpose of taking human form. The harmonic pulse of this thickened manifest emanation is equivalent to the tonal frequency of Earth matter without becoming matter. It would be the consistency of loosely congealed light particles.

Ether tide – The lowest point of density within the Earth's etheric body. This low point is experienced on the opposite side of the planet from the sun when the sun's gravity pulls on the etheric envelope surrounding Earth, stretching it against the lower atmosphere of the planet.

Earth Spirit – The Celestial Deity that formed the planet.

First Moment – See Creator God

First State Being – A completely formed Triadic Soul that is created in the image and likeness of Creator God, and imbued with its intrinsic nature.

Logos – On Earth, a composite Soul that opened the opportunity for Triad First State Beings to enflesh within the boundaries of Dyadic matter. Logos exists in all dimensional realities and parallel realms.

Personality – The "successful" mental and emotional memory behaviors carried over from all past incarnations.

Personality/Ego – The cooperative dynamics of survival mechanisms and success-oriented behaviors held within the etheric body of the Soul as memories associated with human enfleshment. This dynamic is stimulated as the Soul enters the physical form and remains the driving mechanism of the inquiry of a given incarnation.

Solar gatherings – Groupings of Solar Deities and First State Beings within the confines of a Solar Deity.

Second Moment – The harmonic response of First Moment's Creations (Triad and Dyad) to complete the visions of the First Moment.

Surviving Body Awareness – A continuing expression outside the boundaries of cellular mass. As cells join to build specialized forms, they develop awareness and intelligence. This intelligent awareness has a separate reality from the cellular mass and, as specialized forms become increasingly complex, the intelligent awareness becomes more conscious of its ongoing nature.

Third Eye – The brow chakra centered on the forehead slightly above the brow line. When fully opened by the upward movement of kundalini through the lower four chakras, an individual is said to possess clairvoyant sight.

Triad – A complete First State Being that is referred to as a Soul when relating to humanity. It contains consciousness, energy and the Divine Urge from its first moment of creation.

Triadic consciousness – Consciousness that is constantly aware of its origins as a First State Being.

Twelve Known Universes – The Akashic Records indicate twelve dimensional universes in which Triadic First State Beings enflesh within the boundaries of Dyadic matter and awareness.

Universal Law of Attraction – The harmonic resonance of matter attracts like matter within its given range of resonance. Dissimilar matter repels. The human experience is one exception to this Law in that Triadic Soul matter is dissimilar to Dyadic evolutionary matter, yet both share time within space.

World Consciousness – All intelligence whether animate or inanimate on Earth.

~ Suggested Reading ~

No Author. *A Course in Miracles*. Tiburon, California: Foundation for Inner Peace, 1985

No Author. *Holy Bible*. Revised Standard Version. New York: Thomas Nelson & Sons, 1953

No Author. *LIBER AL vel LEGIS SUB FIGURA CCXX AS DELIVERED BY XCIII = 418 TO DCLXVI An Ixii Sol in Aries - O. T. O. BGM/ANKH (The Book of the Law)*. Samuel Weiser, Inc. 1976

Abhishiktananda. *The Further Shore*. Delhi: ISPCK, 1975

Alexander, Thea. *2150 AD*. New York: Bantam Books, 1979

Allen, Richard. *The Annals of China*.

Arraj, James. *St. John of the Cross and C.G. Jung*. Chiloquin, Oregon: Tools for Inner Growth, 1986

Bachofen, J. J. *Myth, Religion & Mother Right*. Princeton: Bollingen Series/ Princeton University Press, 1967

Bacon, Sir Francis. *The History of Winds*. London, 1671

Baigent, Michael & Richard Leigh. *The Dead Sea Scrolls Deception*. New York: Simon & Schuster, 1991

Bailey, Alice. *Esoteric Psychology*. Lucis Publishing Company Out of print.

Baker, M. E. Penny. *Meditation – A Step Beyond With Edgar Cayce*. New York: Pinnacle Books, 1973

Bayley, Harold. *The Lost Language of Symbolism*. New York: Citadel Press, 1993

Becker, Robert and Selden, Gary. *The Body Electric*. New York: Quill - William Morrow, 1985

Besant, Mrs. Annie. *A Study in Consciounsess*. London, 1907

Brennan, Barbara Ann. *Hands of Light*. Bantam Books, 1988

Budge, E. A. Wallis. *The Egyptian Book of the Dead*. New York: Dover, 1967

Bulfinch, Thomas. *Myths of Greece and Rome*. New York: Penguin Books, 1981

Calvin, William H. *The Cerebral Symphony*. New York: Bantam Books, 1990

Campbell, Joseph (with Bill Moyers). *The Power of Myth*. New York: Doubleday, 1988

—. *The Mythic Image*. Princeton, NJ: Princeton University Press, 1981

Castenada, Carlos. *The Teachings of Don Juan, A Yaqui Way of Knowledge*. New York: Simon & Schuster, 1990

Cayce, Edgar. *Edgar Cayce on Atlantis.* New York: Warner Books, 1988

Chamberlin, E. R. *The Bad Popes.* Barnes & Noble, 1993

Cooper, J. C. *An Illustrated Encyclopedia of Traditional Symbols.* New York: Thames & Hudson, 1978

Cooper, Phillip. *The Magickian.* Samuel Weiser, 1993

Cottrell, Leonard. *The Lost Pharaohs.* New York: Grosset & Dunlap, 1961

Crookall, Robert. *Psychic Breathing.* England: The Aquarian Press, 1979

Crossan, John Dominic. *The Historical Jesus.* New York: Harper-Collins, 1991

Cruz, Joan Carroll. *Relics.* Our Sunday Visitor, 1984

Davis, Roy Eugene. *The Science of Kriya Yoga.* CSA, 1984

Dogen. (Translated by Thomas Cleary). *Shobogenzo – Zen Essays.* University of Hawaii Press, 1986

Drummond, Henry. *Natural Law in the Spiritual World.* New York, 1883

Duquette, Lon Milo. *The Magick of Thelema.* Samuel Weiser, 1993

Dyer, Dr. Wayne. *Real Magic.* New York: Happer-Collins, 1993

Eddy, Mary Baker. *Science and Health with Keys to the Scriptures.* Santa Clarita, CA: Pasadena Press, 1992

Einstein, Albert. *The World as I See It.* New York: Citadel Press, 1995

Eisenman, Robert & Michael Wise. *Dead Sea Scrolls Uncovered.* New York: Penquin Books, 1992

Fix, Wm. R. *Pyramid Odyssey.* Urbanna, VI: Mercury Media Books, 1984

Fontana, David. *The Secret Language of Symbols.* San Francisco: Chronicle Books, 1993

Fortune, Dion. *The Mystical Qabalah.* York Beach, Maine: Samuel Weiser, 1984

Gardner, Laurence. *Bloodline of the Holy Grail.* Barnes & Noble, 1997

Gelb, Michael J. *How to Think Like Leonardo da Vinci.* New York: Dell Publishing 1998

Goldsmith, Joel. *The Mystical I.* San Francisco: Harper, 1993

Grim, John A. *The Shaman.* 1983

Hall, Manly P. *The Secret Teachings of All Ages.* Los Angles: The Philosophical Research Society, Inc., 1989

Harricharan, John. *When You Can Walk on Water, Take the Boat.* Atlanta: New World Publishing, *1986*

Harris, Eleanor L. *Ancient Divination and Magic.* Samuel Weiser, 1998

Harvey, Andrew. *Hidden Journey.* Reed Business Information, Inc. 1992

Hawking, Stephen W. *A Brief History of Time.* Bantam Books, 1998

Head, Joseph and Cranston, S. L. *Reincarnation – An East West Anthology.*

New York: Aeon Publishing Company, 2000

Hills, Christopher. *The Christ Book.* University of the Trees Press, 1979

Hogue, John. *Nostradamus & The Millennium.* New York: Double Day - Dolphin, 1987

Holmes, Ernest. *The Science of Mind (Original 1926 manuscript).* H. I. Productions, 1987

Iyengar, B.K.S. *Light on Pranayama, The Yogic Art of Breathing.* New York: Crossroads, 1981

Joseph, Bar, Joseph. *The Nine Faces of Christ.* Great Western University Press, 1979

Jung, Carl Gustav. *Man and His Symbols.* New York: Doubleday, 1964

Kakar, Sudhir. *Shamans, Mystics & Doctors.* Delhi: Oxford University Press, 1986

Kempis, Thomas A. *Of the Imitation of Christ.* Baker Book House, 1973

Kraig, Donald Michael. *Modern Magic.* Llewellyn Publications, 1997

Krishna, Gopi. *Kundalini – The Evolutionary Energy in Man.* Boulder & London: Shambhala, 1971

Lacarriere, Jacques. *The Gnostics.* San Francisco: City Lights Books, 1989

Lavoie, Nicole. *Return to Harmony.* Sound Wave Energy Press, 1996

Le Goff, Jacques. *Medieval Civilization 400-1500.* Barnes & Nobel, 2000

Llewellyn Sion of Glamorgan. *The Bardic Triads*

Mathers, S. L. MacGregor. *The Book of the Sacred Magic of Abramelin the Mage.* New York: Dover Publications 1996

McCall, Andrew. *The Medieval Underworld.* Barnes & Noble, 1993

Monroe, Robert A. *Journeys Out of the Body.* Anchor Press, Doubleday, 1977

Moore, Thomas. *Care of The Soul.* New York: Harper Collins, 1992

Muktananda, Swami. *Kundalini The Secret of Life.* South Fallsburg, NY: SYDA Foundation, 1980

Nada-Yolanda. *Evolution of Man.* Miami: Mark Age Period & Programs, 1971

—. *Entrance to the Golden Age of Aquarius.* Miami: Mark Age Period & Programs, 1971

Newton, Michael. *Journey of Souls.* Saint Paul: Llewellyn Publications, 1994

Pagels, Elaine. *The Gnostic Gospels.* New York: Vintage Books, 1979

Prophet, Elizabeth Claire. *Forbidden Mysteries of Enoch.* Summit University Press, 1983

Prophet, Mark. *Dossier on the Ascension – Serapis Bey.* Summit University Press

—. *The Science of the Spoken Word.* Summit University Press

Rajneesh, Bhagwan Shree. *Beyond Psychology.* Cologne, West Germany: The Rebel Publishing House, 1986
—. *I AM THAT Discourses on the Isa Upanishad.* Rajneesh Foundation Int'l., 1984
—. *Discourse on the Desiderata.* Rajneesh Foundation Int'l., 1983
—. *I Say Unto You- The Sayings of Jesus.* Rajneesh Foundation Int'l., 1980
—. *Philosophia Perennis – The Golden Verses of Pythagoras.* Volumes I & II. Rajneesh Foundation Int'l., 1981
Ravenscroft, Trevor. *Spear of Destiny.* Red Wheel/Weiser, 1974
Rennolds, Joyce. *The Energy Connection.* Atlanta: Rencor Publishing Company, 1987
Restak, Richard. *The Brain.* New York: Bantam Books, 1984
Roberts, Jane. *The Seth Materials.*
—. *Seth Speaks.*
—. *The True Nature of Reality.*
Robinson, James M. *The Nag Hammadi Library.* San Francisco: Harper Collins, 1990
Rogo, D. Scott. *Leaving the Body. A Complete Guide to Astral Projection.* New York: Prentice Hall Press, 1983
Rosenfield, Israel. *The Strange, Familiar and Forgotten.* New York: Alfred A. Knopf, 1992
Rowe, Joseph; Leloup, Jean Yves. *The Gospel of Mary Magdalene.* Inner Traditions, 2002
Sannella, Dr. Lee. *Kundalini – Psychosis or Transcendence?* H.S. Dakin Company, 1978
Savedow, Steven. *Geotic Evocation – Volumes 1 & 2.* Eschaton, 1996
Sheldrake, Rupert. *The New Science of Life: The Hypothesis of Morphic Resonance.* Rochester, Vermont: Park Street Press, 1995
Shipman, Harry L. *Black Holes, Quasars & the Universe.* Boston: Houghton Mifflin Company, 1976
Sogyal Rinpoche. *The Tibetan Book of Living and Dying.* San Francisco: Harper/Collins, 1993
Starhawk. *The Spiral Dance, a Rebirth of the Ancient Religion of the Great Goddess.* New York: Harper & Row, 1979
Steiner, Rudolph. *How to Know Higher Worlds.* Hudson, NY: Anthroposophic Press, 1994
—. *Practical Advice to Teachers.* Rudolph Steiner Press, 1976
Swanson, Rueben (Editor). *New Testament Greek Manuscripts of Mark.*

Sheffield Academic Press, 1995

Swedenborg, Emanual. *View From Within: A Compendium of Swendenborg's Theological Thought.*

Talbot, Michael. *The Holographic Universe.* New York: Harper Perennial, 1991

Taylor, Terry Lynn. *Creating with the Angels: An Angel Guided Journal.*

Thomson, Arthur Dyott. *On Mankind Their Origin and Destiny.* London, 1872

Trungpa, Chogyam. *Meditation in Action.* Shambhala, 1969

Walker, Barbara G. *The Woman's Dictionary of Symbols & Sacred Objects.* New York: Harper & Row, 1988

Williams, Paul. *Das Energi.* Warner Books, 173

Williamson, George Hunt. *Other Tongues – Other Flesh.* Albuquerque: Be Books, 1954;

—. *Secret Places of the Lion.* Rochester, Vermont: Destiny Books, 1958

Wolf, Fred Alan. *Parallel Universes.* New York: Simon & Schuster, 1988

Yeats, W.B. *Fairy & Folk Tales of Ireland.* New York: Macmillan, 1983

Yogananda, Paramahansa. *Autobiography of a Yogi.* Los Angeles: Self-Realization Fellowship, Twelfth Edition, 1981

Yogi Ramacharaka. *Science of Breath.* Chicago: Yogi Publication Society, 1904

The Six Tibetan Rites

These traditional rites are used to enhance the flow of chi through the seven core chakra centers of the physical body's etheric body. Once you have achieved the optimum twenty-one repetitions for each of the rites, you will begin to be consciously aware of the chi force as it moves between your physical and etheric bodies. Once you are fully aware of chi movement, you can begin to direct the flow into concentrations of energy where ever that might be needed in your physical body. The overall affect of conscious chi movement and retention is the relaxing of energy contractions within the etheric body that often lead to disease in the physical body. With a consistent practice, within a short period, most practitioners report a revitalization of body, mind and Spirit.

The basic instructions for each of the rites are:

All body function and movement begins with the spine. Consciously placing space between each of the vertebrae allows the chi t flow more evenly along the nerve channels of the spine. Always begin each exercise by focusing on the spine.

Take your time in building to the full exercise of these rites. There is no hurry and forcing these exercises might slow down your progress toward illumination through this system. The proper mental approach is to allow the program to dictate your progress. Your commitment to doing these exercises each day is important. Only begin when you are fully ready.

Be physically reasonable with your approach to this program, especially if this is the first program you have ever done, or is the first program in a long while. Depending upon several factors, it may take six months before you can do each exercise the required twenty-one repetitions.

For an entire hour before beginning, slowly ingest a twelve once glass of water.

Before beginning for the first time, it is important to familiarize yourself with each of the rites by trying each one and making any adjustments needed, such as in clothing or surrounding space.

Follow the instruction and make any small changes that might be necessary to accommodate any physical limitations you might presently be experiencing. If you are only able to do one repetition of a certain rite, then only do one repetition for all the rites. The number of repetitions must be the exact same for all the rites. If on your very first pass through all the rites you discover that your current ability allows you to do twenty repetitions of the first rite and ten repetitions of rites two, three, five and six but only three of the fourth rite, then only do three repetitions for all the rites. This is important to generating a balance of chi in all the chakras.

Make your environment as relaxing as possible and if you choose an outdoor setting, make sure it is as free of harsh sounds as possible. If you want to use music, try Mozart or Brahms. Your sense of hearing, as well as the four other senses, will become very acute as the number of repetitions for each rite increases. Fast paced music or a constant rhythmic beat of drums will become a hindrance by overly distracting your attention away from the conscious process of balancing chi energy in the chakras. These rites have been practiced for untold generations in silent anticipation of the rising of the kundalini from the base chakra up through the spleen, solar plexus, heart, throat and brow chakras and finally into the crown chakra. The resulting cosmic awareness is the illumination of the Soul within the body.

~ Rite Number One ~

Remember to breath evenly as you do this rite. Consciously lift your spine by mentally and physically placing space between each of the vertebrae. Out stretch your arms at shoulder's level and as you exhale, begin to slowly spin from left to right. Inhale as you enter the second half of the spin. It is important to spin the entire body at the same time as a single unit. One repetition is a completed spin – returning to the exact direction as when you began the spin. Pick a point in front of you before you begin the first spin and come to that point to complete each turn. Do not stop at that point between repetitions. Just notice that point as a means of counting repetitions. Spin until you are slightly dizzy or you have reached twenty-one repetitions. For many, the first rite is the easiest to perform and allows for the greatest number of repetitions.

~ *Rite Number Two* ~

Remember to breath evenly as you do this rite. Consciously elongate your spine by mentally and physically placing space between each of the vertebrae. Lay face up on the floor with your hands flat, palms down, directly under each buttock. Your fingers should be kept together and hands should be turned slightly inward, toward each other while resting on the floor just under your sacrum. (Note: Due to differing body proportions your sacrum may be resting on the floor). Your legs should be straight and held together. Inhale as you lift your legs as far upward and over the body as is possible while keeping the sacrum resting on your hands or the floor. At the exact same time, lift your head toward your chest allowing the tip of your chin to touch your chest. Without pausing, exhale as you begin to lower both your legs and head at the exact same speed so that they come to rest on the floor in the exact same moment. This is one repetition.

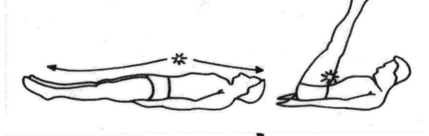

~ *Rite Number Three* ~

Remember to breath evenly as you do this rite. Consciously lift your spine by mentally and physically placing space between each of the vertebrae. Kneel on the floor with your toes touching the floor behind you, while placing your hands as far downward as possible on the backs of your thighs. Exhale as you lean forward, moving the tip of your chin toward your chest. Lean forward as far forward as you can without loosing your balance. Without pausing inhale as you come back to center and then immediately begin to move backward (exhale) as far as you can while supporting your weight on your thighs. Gently drop your head toward the floor as far as it will extend. Then inhaling, begin to bring your body back to center with the base of the spine reaching the center point first, then moving your head upward back to center. This is one repetition.

~ *Rite Number Four* ~

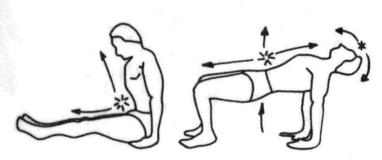

Remember to breath evenly as you do this rite. Consciously lift your spine by mentally and physically placing space between each of the vertebrae.

Sit on the floor with your legs and feet stretched out together in front of you. Place your hand palms downward next to your hips, thumbs touching your body. Inhale while bending at the knees raising your hips to shoulder's height as you bring your chin to your chest all in one movement.. Your legs and arms should be perpendicular to the floor and you should resemble a table. (Note: Due to differing body proportions your table might vary in exact horizontal attitude.) Exhale as you allow your head to gently drop downward toward the floor. Then inhale as you slowly bring your head upward and your body downward into the beginning position. Exhale and repeat.

~ *Rite Number Five* ~

Remember to breath evenly as you do this rite. Consciously lift your spine by mentally and physically placing space between each of the vertebrae.

Place your body in the "push-up" position with your hands shoulder's width apart, flat on the floor and your feet resting on the tips of your toes. Keeping your legs straight, exhale as you lift your hips as far upward as possible. As

you push inward and upward, bring your chin to your chest. Tense all your muscles, then keeping your arms and legs straight; inhale as you gently lower your hips to just above floor level. Exhale while lifting the head outward and upward as you open your chest. (Note: Push the chest forward by dropping the shoulder blades downward and inward.) Tense all your muscles and inhale as your return to the beginning position. This is one repetition.

~ *Rite Number Six* ~

(Please note: Only perform this rite if you are not in a committed sexual relationship. This rite will cause the sexual energy of the practitioner to become neutral by transmuting the base energies of the base and spleen chakras to match those energies of the third eye and crown chakras.)

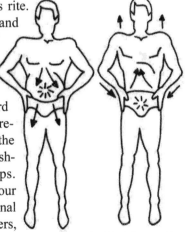

Remember to breath evenly as you do this rite. Consciously lift your spine by mentally and physically placing space between each of the vertebrae.

Stand with your hands on your hips and your feet shoulder's width apart. Exhale completely as you push the abdomen outward away from the spine. (Note: As you exhale create a deep sigh.) Vigorously inhale pulling the abdomen inward toward the spine while pushing your hands downward onto your hips. Slightly shrug your shoulders at the top of your inhalation while vigorously contracting the anal sphincter muscle. Keep lifting the shoulders, contracting the anal sphincter muscle and then contracting the facial muscles, creating an ugly expression while holding the breath for a count of three. Exhale with a sigh while pushing the abdomen outward. This is one repetition.

These rites are of greater significance when used in a conscientious program whose intention is to awaken the latent kundalini force dormant in the base chakra at the base of the spine. As in all such esoteric practice, it is important that all practitioners proceed with caution with ancient technologies. It is important to approach this activity with balanced intention and unhurried commitment. If you are already doing dynamic spiritual practices, check with your instructors as to whether or not these rites fit into the overall dynamics of your current program. Always refrain from these rites or other suggested spiritual activities if adverse conditions arise in your physical body. Adverse conditions such as, sudden and unexplained weight loss, heighten anxiety, irritability, and anti social behavior can result if the rites are not performed as described. Several unusual, but not life threatening, conditions can present when dormant kundalini energy begins to move upward from the base chakra toward the crown chakra. Heightened or overly exaggerated sensory awareness, sporadic clairvoyant imagery, spontaneous out-of-body episodes and auric sight are the most commonly reported experiences. These types of experience only happen when the practitioner hurries himself or herself through the process. Take your time with this and all other practices.

Food Combining

~ *General Guidelines for More Effective Digestion* ~

Before you move on to the chart, it is important to know that, if you are like most Americans, it will take a very conscious effort to overcome decades of bad eating habits. This information is public domain and freely disseminated through various means. By all means, experiment with this information and regularly fast as a means of bringing your body back to balance. In general, the following is true for most individuals:

Proteins
- Eat proteins and carbohydrates at separate meals
- Eat only one concentrated protein at each meal

Dairy
- Take milk alone (all cheeses can be eaten with non-starchy vegetables)

Juices
- Treat fresh juices (fruit or vegetable) as whole foods

Fruits
- Only eat fruit alone as a fruit meal
- Do not eat sweet fruits and acid fruits together
- Fruits should not be eaten between meals while other food is digesting in the stomach and small intestines
- Melons are best eaten alone, but can be mixed with acid and sub-acid fruits

Miscellaneous
- Irritants and bitter foods should be eaten sparingly or not at all
- Avoid desserts
- Cold and overly hot foods inhibit digestion

In using the chart on the next page, note that either proteins or starches combine well with green and non-starchy vegetables, but not at the same meal *(there is no direct line between starches and proteins); likewise, sweet and acid fruits do not combine well with each other (there is no direct line between sweet and acid fruits). Do not combine proteins with fats and oils.*

Food-Combining Chart

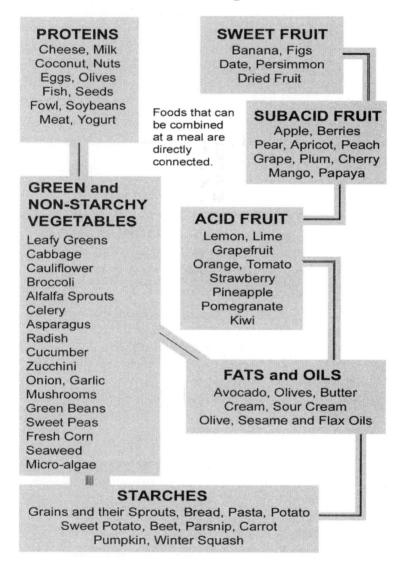

PROTEINS
Cheese, Milk
Coconut, Nuts
Eggs, Olives
Fish, Seeds
Fowl, Soybeans
Meat, Yogurt

SWEET FRUIT
Banana, Figs
Date, Persimmon
Dried Fruit

Foods that can be combined at a meal are directly connected.

SUBACID FRUIT
Apple, Berries
Pear, Apricot, Peach
Grape, Plum, Cherry
Mango, Papaya

GREEN and NON-STARCHY VEGETABLES

Leafy Greens
Cabbage
Cauliflower
Broccoli
Alfalfa Sprouts
Celery
Asparagus
Radish
Cucumber
Zucchini
Onion, Garlic
Mushrooms
Green Beans
Sweet Peas
Fresh Corn
Seaweed
Micro-algae

ACID FRUIT
Lemon, Lime
Grapefruit
Orange, Tomato
Strawberry
Pineapple
Pomegranate
Kiwi

FATS and OILS
Avocado, Olives, Butter
Cream, Sour Cream
Olive, Sesame and Flax Oils

STARCHES
Grains and their Sprouts, Bread, Pasta, Potato
Sweet Potato, Beet, Parsnip, Carrot
Pumpkin, Winter Squash

~ Order Form ~

Telephone Orders: 800-871-4996
Fax Orders: 239-774-1890 (copy this form)
e-Mail: llennob@comcast.net
Postal Orders: Richman Rose Publishing
Post Office Box 1889
Naples, Florida 34106

Please send the following books or products: (Specify audiotapes or CD)

***YOUR BOOK of LIFE** – Accessing the Akashic Records:* 192 pages paper-back, annotated, six meditation scripts, reading list, index.
$25 x ___ + $5.00 ea. S&H* = $ _____

Accessing the Akashic Records: 2 tape set/1 CD. Introduction on side A, three guided meditations. **$15 x ___ + $5.00 ea. S&H* = $ _____**

Accessing Your Book of Life: 2 tape set/1 CD. Introduction on side A, guided meditations. **$15 x ___ + $5.00 ea. S&H* = $ _____**

***THE TWELVE DAYS of LIGHT** – Prophecy Concerning the Millennium:*
112 pages paperback. **$12 x ___ + $5.00 ea. S&H* = $ _____**

The Twelve Days of Light – The Photon Field: 4 tape set/1CD. Over six hours of information from the Akashic Records concerning the coming photon field that is causing a collective shift in Consciousness.
$25 x ___ + $5.00 ea. S&H* = $ _____

Sub Total: $_____

Sales tax: Florida residents add applicable sales tax: $ _____

Total: $ _____

Shipping: *If ordering more than one item, only add $1.50 S&H for each additional item. Call for next day or second day delivery cost.

(See next page for shipping and payment form)

(Copy, then e-mail, mail or fax along with order form)

Payment: __Credit Card   __Check (payable to The Bonnell Group)

Name on card: _____

Card number: _____Exp: ___/___

Billing address:

Name: _____

Address: _____

City/State: _____Zip _____

If paying by credit card, cardholder agrees to pay the card issuer above the total amount of this sale, pursuant to cardholder agreement for the products and services requested. All merchandise is guaranteed for thirty days against any defect.

Signature: _____

Shipping address: (Only if different than billing address)

Name: _____

Address: _____

City/State: _____Zip _____

Order online at www.garybonnell.com

THE *KNOWING*

~ Gary Bonnell ~

Formally educated as a psychologist, he is currently enrolled in the Doctorate program at the American Institute of Hypnotherapy in Santa Ana, CA. A certified hypnotherapist, and psycho-intuitive counselor, he is also an ordained minister through The Church of Inner Light in Los Angeles, CA. A successful businessman, Bonnell has substitute taught business courses at the Master's level at CU–Denver on the subject, "The Structural Implementation of Change." A student of Metaphysics for over forty-five years, Gary has studied in Europe, India, Canada and the USA. His teachers have included some of the most renowned mystics of this age. He has lectured and facilitated seminars in North America, Europe and Japan. He has been a featured speaker with the Whole Life Expo organizations of Los Angeles and San Francisco, with Voice, Inc. of Japan for the past ten years and more currently with the Holistica Expos. Through these organizations he has conducted workshops in every major city in North America and Japan on subjects ranging from Conscious Out-of-Body Exploration, Ascension, Practical Mysticism, and Accessing the Akashic Records, to Reprogramming the Subconscious Mind.

Bonnell is the author of ten books: five for the English market and five for the Japanese market. Four of his English titles have also been translated into Japanese. His ability to articulate mystical concepts into day-to-day guides for living life through a more expanded conscious awareness is well honed.

As Vice President – Marketing/Advertising, Bonnell was instrumental in the development of Designhouse International, an import company of fine European furniture, from one store in 1974, to a chain of twenty stores in five states by 1985. As a furniture designer, Bonnell has sold products in North and South America, Europe and Japan. He and his partner were the most prolific furniture design team to invade the European furniture industry from the United

States. Designhouse's stock went public (IPO) in 1985 and was sold a year later. Since 1986, Gary has devoted his time to writing, lecturing, and consulting for corporations (Structural Implementation of Change) and individuals (Developing the Mystical Path).

Gary has served as a senior change management consultant and marketing expert for IMA of Colorado, a consulting group serving clients from the Fortune 500 list of companies.

The "Flo" comic strip, featuring a delightfully out-of-step administrative assistant who takes the intuitive hig- road to a rather not-so-understanding boss, was developed for a California based financial corporation's quarterly newsletter. The nationally published strip is written by actress, Claudia Gallion, and has been illustrated by Gary for the past sixteen years. He is an accomplished artist, with one work entitled "Ascension," in a permanent collection at the Franciscan Monastery in Conyers, GA.

During the last twelve years over sixty articles in magazines, newspapers and periodicals have described his work in the areas of business and mysticism. Reviews of his writings have appeared in hundreds of regional, national and international periodicals. He has been a guest on numerous regional, national cable and network television and radio shows.

His two accomplished daughters have both set aside professional pursuits and chosen to undertake the fulltime jobs of being wife and mother. The oldest daughter has two children and his youngest has three. Both daughters are married to wonderful and successful men who care greatly about this world in which we live. Their children are being raised in homes focused on Spiritual values and commitment to living life fully. Gary lives in North America with his incredible, widely talented and beautiful wife who owns the cosmetic manufacturing company, Vibrant Skin, Inc. Visit her all natural cosmetic website at www.vitasage.com.